THE
DEATH OF
AN AMERICAN GAME
The Crisis in Football

John Underwood

A *Sports Illustrated* Book
Little, Brown and Company
Boston–Toronto

First Edition

LIBRARY OF CONGRESS CATALOGING IN PUBLICATION DATA
Underwood, John, 1934–
    The death of an American game.
    "A Sports illustated book."
    1. Football.   I. Title.
GV951.U48   796.33'2   79–19354
ISBN 0–316–88735–8

Sports Illustrated Books
are published by
Little, Brown and Company
in association with
Sports Illustrated Magazine

The author is grateful to *The Columbus Dispatch*, the *Oklahoma City Times*, the *Maine Times*, and the *Milwaukee Sentinel* for permission to quote excerpts of their articles.

Quote from "Doonesbury" on page 88, 1972, G.B. Trudeau. Reprinted by permission of the Universal Press Syndicate.

Portions of this book have appeared in *Sports Illustrated*.

BP

Designed by Susan Windheim
Published simultaneously in Canada
by Little, Brown & Company (Canada) Limited

Printed in the United States of America

THE
DEATH OF
AN AMERICAN GAME

To set the cause above renown,
To love the game beyond the prize,
To honor, while you strike him down,
The foe that comes with fearless eyes

—SIR HENRY NEWBOLT

CONTENTS

THE
DEATH OF
AN AMERICAN GAME

PROLOGUE

In 1962, when Amos Alonzo Stagg was nearing his 100th year, I made a sentimental journey to California on behalf of *Sports Illustrated* to see him. Like me, *Sports Illustrated* is a sucker for sentimental journeys. The memory of the visit, like that of a lost love, has stayed with me since, but it is even more vivid now, when the sport that that noble man so greatly influenced and so tenderly chaperoned is showing the discolorations of a serious decay. When the leaves rot on a tree you look to the roots, perhaps to see if the tree is worth saving, perhaps to rediscover what made it grow so tall in the first place.

Stagg was living out his days in a rest home in Stockton. At that point, it was not so grand to be the Grand Old Man. Once he had heard the beseeching cry of the football multitude; now it was the muted prattle of old ladies, rocking in patches of shade on the yellow lawn. The jaw that jutted firm on the sidelines of Chicago Stadium was slack. The blue eyes were clouded by cataracts; the left one drooped. His hair was wispy and white as tissue. At ninety-six, he ran laps around the fig trees in his backyard. Now, as if prodded by the uncompromising voice within him that always demanded Spartan discipline, he insisted on frequent walks on the patio of the rest home, out in the sun. But he had to be led by the hand.

Stagg had coached for seventy years, until he was ninety eight (the Associated Press prepared his obituary thirty years before). But in the last few months he had drawn inward and become occupied with his infirmities. He had become, at last, an old man. Still, he seemed to brighten on my arrival, and there was a touch of the wryness that often characterized his vigorous life. "I may go on forever," he said, "because statistics show that few men die after the age of one hundred."

Preparations were under way for a series of birthday celebrations, none (thank God) at the rest home. Stagg, in absentia, was to receive coast-to-coast certification of his greatness. Speechmakers at extravagant banquets would review his achievements as player, coach, innovator, teacher, unstinting disciplinarian, humanitarian, father, Christian, citizen, and — at New Haven — Yale man. Typically unmoved by such effulgent displays, Stagg, in a plaid flannel bathrobe and plaid slippers, sat in the Stockton sun and, haltingly, expressed his own wish for the occasion. In a voice that seemed to come down a long corridor, reedy and ethereal, he said: "I would like to be remembered as an honest man."

Amos Alonzo Stagg was so honest he twice was asked to referee games his own teams played in. Football to Stagg was a means to an end: teaching young men to be honorable. The incorrigible Alfred Doolittle of *My Fair Lady* advises his contemporaries that the world "is always throwing goodness at you, but with a little bit of luck a man can duck." There was no ducking Stagg. He force-fed his own impeccable standards to his players and to his family, and though some eventually strayed, he was adored for what he believed and, rarer, practiced.

Pappy Waldorf, who coached against him, compared Stagg

to a "giant Sequoia that looms over the forest — hardy, sturdy, long-lived, an object of admiration and inspiration" (Stagg at his prime was 5 foot 6 and weighed 160 pounds). Years after he was an assistant to Stagg, Fritz Crisler, the nonpareil Michigan coach, snuffed out a cigarette in the palm of his hand when he saw the old man approaching. At Stagg's ninety-fourth birthday party, UCLA coach Red Sanders, who had just been nabbed in a recruiting violation, took his seat on the rostrum and said sheepishly, "Jesse James will now break bread with a saint."

The story of Stagg should not be compressed into a few lines, but for purposes of this message it is worth a try: born a cobbler's son in West Orange, New Jersey, at the time Stonewall Jackson was advancing on Manassas; the best college baseball pitcher of his age; an aspirant to the ministry who decided he couldn't preach ("I stammered terribly"). At Yale, where he lived on soda crackers in a garret, he contracted beriberi and still pitched his team to five straight championships, completing every game he started. He was on Walter Camp's first All-America football team, and became the University of Chicago's first head coach in 1892. He was there forty-one years, pioneering every aspect of the game, from such basics as the huddle and the center snap to the intricacies of the T formation.

In 1943, when he was eighty-one years old and coaching at the College of the Pacific, Stagg outpolled Notre Dame's Frank Leahy and was named Coach of the Year. His number-one aide at COP, anxious for advancement, feared Stagg would coach forever. Apparently Stagg planned to. At eighty-five, he went to Susquehanna to assist his son Alonzo Jr. — and signed a ten-year contract.

"Formally, he was my assistant; practically, he was in charge," Lonnie Stagg said when I went to see him later in

Chicago. Stagg, Jr., had quit coaching then to become a stockbroker. The firstborn son, he was given a letter that was supposed to go to him at his father's death. Lonnie got it when he was thirty-five, and his father still had a third of his career to go.

June 23, 1900

To My Son, Amos Alonzo Stagg, Jr.

You are only a little fellow now — a trifle over 14 months old; but I have loved you so dearly since you came that it has been on my mind to write you a letter in the event of my being taken away at any time before I have a chance to tell you many things which you need to know.

Your father wants his Boy first of all to love, protect and care for his Mother, giving to her the same kind of measure of love and devotion which she has given to you. Your father wants his Boy to be sincere, honest and upright. . . . Hate dishonesty and trickery no matter *how big* and *how great* the thing desired may be. . . . Treat everybody with courtesy and as your equal until he proves his unworthiness to be so treated. The man and the soul are what count — not wealth, not family, not appearance. . . .

Your father wants you to abhor evil. No curiosity, no imagination, no conversation, no story, no reading which suggests impurity of life is worthy of your thought or attention. . . . Train yourself to be *master of yourself*, of your thought and imagination and temper and passion and appetite and of your body. . . . Your father has never used intoxicating liquors, nor tobacco, nor profane language. He wants his Boy to be like him in this regard. . . .

Your father wants his Boy enthusiastic and earnest in all of his interests, his sports, his studies, his work; and he wants him always to keep an active participation in each as long as he lives.

[Lastly], your father wants his son to love God as He is revealed to him; which after all will be the revelation of all that I have said and left unsaid of good to you, my precious Boy.

Affectionately,
Your Father.

"To disagree with my father," Lonnie Stagg said, "was like breaking with God. His logic was unimpeachable."

A short, square man with grizzled hair and the old man's broad face, Stagg, Jr., recalled having bought a motorcycle once for fifteen dollars without his father's permission. "With great care, and without raising his voice, he explained why he preferred I not keep it. 'You're bigger in a car,' he said. I sold the motorcycle the same day. When I was just nine, lightning struck a tree within twenty feet of us. I fell to the ground in a fright. 'Why, Amos,' said my father, 'you mustn't let things like that disturb you.' He had not moved an inch. I was human, but he was different."

At the time of my visit, Stagg's wife, Stella, who caught his eye "playing men's basketball in her bloomers" as a Chicago coed, was still alive and living alone in the Staggs' modest, cream-colored frame house on West Euclid Avenue in Stockton. They had rented instead of purchasing it twenty-nine years before because Stagg didn't think he would live long enough to pay for it. Stella Stagg, at eighty-seven, was no longer able to attend to her husband, but she kept busy at home handling his correspondence and rummaging among the bookcases and orange crates that brimmed with his trophies, plaques, portraits, and old baseballs.

Originally jealous of his attention to football, Stella Stagg said she learned to diagram plays and to scout opponents, and to make his utilitarian meals palatable for the family. Once he showed her a new play he was going to spring on a COP opponent, diagramming it on a small blackboard. She quickly worked out a defense for it. "That'll stop your play," she said. Stagg scratched his white head, puzzling, and padded off to the kitchen for a glass of water. Finally he returned. "He had a gleam in his eye and an eraser in his hand," said Mrs. Stagg. " 'You can't stop it now,' he said with triumph, and erased one of my players. 'You were using twelve men.' "

There was no swimming pool in the Stagg backyard, no big car in front. For all his success, Stagg lived without frills. "Money," he said, "is damnation," and he never had much. The New York Giants offered him $4,200 to play baseball in 1889; he refused because there were saloons in big-league ball parks. He once passed up a $300 speaking engagement because it meant missing a practice. His salary never exceeded $8,500, yet he contributed annually to the Yale fund, made a $3,000 cash donation to the College of the Pacific to purchase a twenty-one-acre tract adjoining the stadium, and donated $1,000 for chimes to the University of Chicago, stipulating that the alma mater be played at 10:05 each night as a signal for football players to get to bed.

The only real money he ever made was by cashing in on a 100,000-to-3 long shot: two life-term insurance policies, for $6,090 and $10,000, that reached maturity in 1958. He was once offered $300,000 for the movie rights to his life story. It was to star Spencer Tracy and Katharine Hepburn, who bore marked resemblances to the Staggs. When he turned it down, his sons, Lonnie and Paul, were aghast. "It's my life," said Stagg, "and I don't expect my sons to tell me how to run it. I wouldn't give the money to you, anyway. I'd give it to the university."

The only tangible rewards Stagg gave his players were sweaters and letters. Stagg abhorred recruitment of any sort and was never told — or perhaps did not want to be told — that there were players on scholarship at Pacific. He said that recruiting breeds dishonesty and was not right for a coach whose profession should be "one of the noblest and most far-reaching in building manhood. No man is too good to be the athletic coach for youth."

Until he went to the rest home six months before to live out his days, Stagg mowed his lawn with a hand mower. "He mowed that lawn to death," said Stella Stagg. One day a neighbor advised him that kids had been playing on it daily, ripping up the turf. "You'll never raise grass that way," the neighbor said. "Sir," answered Stagg, "I'm not raising grass, I'm raising boys."

1.

THE CASE

B. is a college administrator, one I have come to appreciate over a long association as a man who knows the ins and outs of the game he had played and now helps administer. He is a devilish advocate of football reform. Some of his suggestions reflect infinite wisdom (reforms I agree with); some, like the jabs of a fighter, are meant only to draw attention and perhaps gum up the thinking process (the ones I do not). He was among the first to suggest that the extravagance of two-platoon football and 120-man-squad rosters robbed the players — those who got off the bench — of half the fun of the game. It reduced football to production line mentalities and would, in the end, create serious financial problems. This was long before the cost spiral had hit the colleges, and B. was considered a heretic by some head football coaches, including the one at his own college who was a bullnecked champion of the Whatever-It-Takes approach to budget planning.

We had developed, B. and I, a tacit working agreement over the years. In return for anonymity, he was my sounding board on issues that could put him in warm water with his various administrators, while I was his conduit — however sluggish — for ideas to improve the college game. We first met when he was still at M——, at a chancellor's cocktail party before a big intersectional match. To the despair of our hostess, we had argued far into the night (and by dint of her skillful maneuvering, into the chancellor's den, out of earshot) about what I considered the fallacy of calling college football players "student-athletes."

"It is the first lie," I had said, "and the beginning of your troubles. They are *athlete-students*, paid the best and only way a college can afford to pay them for their services — by scholarship — and if you'd relax and let that go down you wouldn't look pop-eyed every time the subject of scholarships and recruiting comes up."

"We have a pretense to uphold," he had said. It is an answer I cherish to this day.

B. smoked a pipe then, the only pipe-smoker I ever knew with a developed sense of humor. I told him my Uncle Kevin, who smoked cigars and had a virtuoso wit, had advised me never to trust a man who smoked a pipe. B. said *his* advice was not to trust Uncle Kevin. "I, for one, don't even believe you have an Uncle Kevin," he said.

If B. was in my vicinity I would ordinarily send a taxi for him if I thought the subject I was interested in was down his alley, but this time he anticipated me and came anyway, by air, under the guise of "passing through."

Actually, we had talked by phone earlier. I had been hiding out in the Florida Keys, gathering research around me like a pack rat after a series of trips across the country. I told him I was "putting some things together on football" — just the kind of ante he instinctively rises to, having developed an incurable itch for examining the game's problems. This is only partly due to his having played it so well. His love for football is total. Indeed, in our mutual maturity we shared a mutual conviction: that football is the best American team sport, with a rallying quality that gives it meaning far beyond the parameters of actual play. Both its rugged physical properties and its ability to attract large numbers of paying customers make it the definitive American game — highly competitive, and capitalistic.

What I said by phone did not sit well with him, but did not seem to surprise him, either. I said that the large fragments of evidence I had gathered in extended research indicated that football was in trouble, that there was a sickness in it. A sickness that smelled of more sickness. I said the surface activity alone made it appear that football was becoming too dangerous, too brutal, too insensitive to its own pain, and that, down the road, there were consequences barely imagined by the game's custodians.

He scolded me then for "sweeping generalities" and hauled out the standard rebuttal, one I thought unworthy of him: attendance was up (more than 40 million people had watched the pros and college teams play that year), meaning the paying customers were happy. Ratings were up, meaning the various paying sponsors, the pushers of low-calorie beer and pieces of the rock, were happy. Accordingly, any boob could see that the nest was warm and well feathered.

I retaliated that turnstile counts and TV ratings had nothing to do with it (I was wrong; they have everything to do with it). I asked if he had given the injury lists an objective consideration, and if he had examined the various acts of savagery that passed for "techniques" in the professional game and were being immortalized on instant replay every Sunday afternoon.

He agreed there had been some awful sights. At the time, the football community was still in agony over the Atkinson-Swann incident, in which Oakland defensive back George Atkinson had put Pittsburgh receiver Lynn Swann in the hospital with a breathtakingly effective tackling technique — a sweeping forearm blow to the head. There had been a number of subsequent on-field muggings, given equal play by the networks and in the public print.

Most civilized social orders, even including the National Football League, will, in time, come to grips with a continuum of mindless violence and deal with it, provided it is ugly enough and of no lasting financial value. Football's natural roughness naturally spawns some over-the-line bullying, and you can even excuse some of it. This, however, is the brute face of a spreading barbarism that would not have blended into the fabric of play were it not for the greater outrage: the game's insane tolerance for its growing injury rate.

"The fallout," I said, "could be lethal."

"What fallout?"

"The most noxious kind. The kind that is dragging football into the courts with increasing frequency. The sport is crawling with lawyers."

Coaches, players, owners, and officials were, in fact, going round and round in legal battles, contesting everything from breached contracts to slander. When Pittsburgh coach Chuck Noll said after Swann's injury that a "criminal element" was loose in the game, Atkinson sued him. One of Noll's own players threatened to do the same.

Players — teenagers and adults — were suing over their broken bodies. Some were doing it from wheelchairs. Entire programs were being threatened with litigation. Manufacturers of the game's equipment were learning the meaning of judgment day.

In Miami, a former high school player named Greg Stead won a record Dade County judgment of $5.3 million against Riddell, Inc., the nation's largest helmet manufacturer. A quadriplegic since the night in 1971 when the face guard of his helmet struck the knee of an opposing high school ballcarrier and sent the back edge of his helmet crashing down on his spine, Stead settled out of court in May 1977 for $3 million. According to the *Miami Herald*, Stead's lawyers got $1 million of that. (No wonder they were swarming.)

Two other cases stuck in my mind, and I recited them for B. on the phone.

A sixteen-year-old high school player named Robert Francis Mudd, Jr., had been paralyzed as the result of making a tackle in a scrimmage at Lincoln High in Stockton, California. The last time I had been in Stockton was to see Amos Stagg, who had since passed on. When I read the accounts of the Mudd case I could not but think how that gentleman would have been saddened.

Mudd was in a wheelchair. A three-million-dollar lawsuit, with twenty-one defendants, had been filed on his behalf by his attorneys, one of whom was a former San Diego Charger and All-Pro tackle named Ron Mix. It alleged that the tackling technique (face-to-numbers) taught at Lincoln High was inherently unsafe, and that schools were negligent in permitting it. Face-to-numbers (actually both a tackling *and* a blocking technique) requires the head of the tackler to make contact with the ballcarrier by striking face guard first into the numbers of the ballcarrier's jersey.

Defense attorneys argued that the technique represented the "greatest amount of safety." Mix countered that no matter how one defined using the head — spearing, butting, face-to-numbers—"it amounts to the same thing," and that the human brain and spinal column were not meant to serve as a battering ram.

The trial took four months and set a San Joaquin County record for civil cases. It was not the verdict that bothered me so much (Mudd lost)—I wasn't sure Mix's argument was on firm ground, anyway (even the most safety-conscious coaches are divided on the issue); furthermore, all that could be gained or lost in court was money. What *did* bother me was what the boy had lost in life. Said his mother: "You wonder what kind of life he's going to have. Will he meet someone? Will he be able to get married? It's just a catastrophe, there's no other way to put it." Said the boy, now in his twenties: "You get bored. You don't have any friends. There's really very little you can do."

The second case had broader and even more baleful overtones. A seventeen-year-old Agoura, California, high school football player named Gregory Cole had died of a subdural hematoma after being injured making a head-on tackle. The dead player's family sued (I have forgotten whom—the prospects, I have learned, are often numerous). Partly as a result of the case, the state of California had been pressured by schools and parents to make mandatory the attendance of a physician and an ambulance at every high school game.

On a typical California weekend, there are as many as fifteen hundred schoolboy football games. There are probably not that many private ambulances west of the Rocky Mountains. As for doctors, even if they were available, they might not show up. In many California school districts they are no longer covered by the schools' liability insurance. A bill to make them part-time "employees" was vetoed by the governor as prohibitively expensive. Because of the growing legal threat, insurance rates had soared — as much as 848 percent in some districts. And, haunted by the specter of malpractice suits, doctors have a tendency to run to the movies on game nights.

Later, the state's high school federation verified what had been rumored for months: that California's entire sports program, from kindergarten to the junior colleges, was in jeopardy. The insurance crunch atop other inflation-fed expenses was bankrupting the schools.

I had posed for B. the two questions raised in my mind by these events, beyond the sobering sight of football struggling for absolution in courts of law:

1. If the cost of indemnifying a high school sport against the threat of litigation eliminates that sport, what happens to college sport? And, down the line, to pro sport?

2. More ominously, if you have reached a point where an ambulance and a physician are needed at fieldside every time two teams go out to play, is it sport?

"I see what you're driving at," B. had said. He promised to get back to me after he "turned it over."

It was almost a month before I heard from him again and then he came, unannounced, to the Keys — on his way, he said, to arrange for an alumni weekender to Dry Tortugas. He had rented a car in Miami, and by the size of his soft leather bag (one that stores conveniently under an airliner seat) he was prepared for only a minimal stay.

The weather had been nasty, with bruising afternoon squalls, and the pattern was not improving. Each bulletin was filled with new omens. But when B. arrived the sun had spilled through the scudding metal-gray clouds, and when he insisted we take the boat out I objected only perfunctorily, as one might on being surprised by the accuracy of a called third strike. The urge to get out was on me, too; I had been holed up during the weather siege, just before which there had been a good run of kingfish. When I licked my lips I noted they were no longer the texture of dried snakeskin, a sure sign of a fisherman going soft.

Actually, the weather and a boat whose engines were sore and on borrowed time did not concern me as much as B. himself. It was a humane concern, not a full-fledged qualm. B. is a fine athlete but a pathetic sailor. When the sea reaches heights much above a flat calm he is likely to consign himself to what he calls "the porcelain prayer-basin." Furthermore, as only an occasional boater he refuses the logic of rubber-soled shoes. His concessions to footwear are all leather-bottomed. Thus, on deck he moves about on uncoordinated limbs, and has been known to make comic shrieking noises in averting a fall. He is, however, long-suffering.

"We have been having what the Conchs call a Norther," I said. "Seas have been up. Might get a little messy."

"I don't care," he said, patting his deceitful stomach. "I could lose the weight. I want to talk, and if we stick around here the natives will be on us and the phone will ring."

I quickly put beer and soft drinks and a package of bait into a small cooler (there was no time for serious food-gathering; the day was two-thirds gone) and led B. down to the boat. To my surprise, the suffering engines responded to the touch. With fresh confidence I eschewed the safer waters to the lee side of Ocean Reef and headed out Angelfish Creek to the sea, then north on a parallel with the brawling black waters of the Gulf Stream. Trolling the stream itself on such a day would have been carrying confidence too far.

At a spot off the Ragged Keys I clambered down off the flying bridge and dropped anchor in fifty feet of water. B. volunteered to do it, but I told him it was tricky business in leather shoes. "I know," he smiled. The wind was up, but steady, and the sea rhythmic. The old boat swung around dutifully on its tether and rode far more gently than I expected.

I rigged two light lines for bottom fish and presented one to B., ignoring his plea not to bait his hook. "I only want to fish," he said, "I don't want to catch any." He nevertheless made his customary stab at participation, making a cast (unnecessary under the circumstances) of the type Ted Williams calls "Chinese." We both watched, awed, as it spiraled like a winged bird to the surface and ducked under.

This done, B.'s interest in the gadget in his hands expired. He pulled his St. Louis Cardinal baseball cap — a gift from an old Gas Houser — down over his eyes so that the greater mass of his hawk nose was covered against what little sun there was, stretched his legs out, one leather sole propped over the other on the fish box, and stared resolutely at the sea, as if his thoughts could be refined there. It was a front, because he and the sea are not on speaking terms.

"What do you have?" he said without preamble.

"A bleak projection. One that makes me feel like a flaming alarmist."

"Don't let that stop you. One day the whole world woke up and the alarmists who said we were running out of gasoline had become prophets. So tell me."

I did.

I suddenly found myself, after so many months, hungry to talk it out.

I said that if it were not so tragic and ironic it would be laughable, but that football was committing suicide. At the peak of popularity (it would seem), at the extreme of empire (it would seem), it was constructing its own scaffold, right under its own nose. "That's important, because mostly it doesn't realize it, the business of being an unwitting suicide," I said. "The most stupid of crimes."

I said the leaders at the upper levels, the professional league and the major colleges, had been like a shuffling chain gang, blind to anything but their own dogged steps. Blind to twenty years of breathtaking neglect. To an unacceptable, epidemic, injury rate. To the ugly rise in brutal play. To all manner of cheating and rules bending, and to the enemies gearing up against the game.

"It's a depressing sight, like watching a favorite relative go mad. I could write a how-to book on it. How to discourage participants. How to intimidate coaches, tax administrators; how to confuse and alienate the fans. A pattern of abuse that is not only cynical but wanton."

"Is that your premise?" B. seemed unmoved, as though I had recited a lively but familiar recipe.

"Essentially. I don't like apocalyptic terms either, but there are voices out there weeping for football. I've heard them. It's an alarming cry. Teddy Roosevelt almost abolished football seventy years ago because it was too brutal. A killer sport. It is brutal again, but now, at a time when it is actually killing less, when death on the field is virtually no factor at all, it is killing itself. Ironic."

"Have you a common denominator?"

"Money. What Uncle Kevin calls The God Bucks."

"Not very original."

"Yes, but eternally effective."

I said I wasn't talking about just money, I was talking about money in stupefying amounts. Money so blinding that while the sport's public image grew more prosperous, its inner excesses were causing a frightful disfigurement. Money so blinding that it had allowed the game to create at its most influential level, the pro level, a blood lust that was just now being understood by the game's better thinkers as counterproductive.

"Who do you mean, 'better thinkers'?"

I recited for him the places I had been, the players and ex-players I had interrogated, the sources that the efficient arm of *Sports Illustrated*'s correspondents bureau had mined on my behalf, from one side of the country to the other, the influential coaches I had seen or conversed with — Bryant, Paterno, Royal, Parseghian, Majors, Devine, Corso, McKay.

I had watched film until my eyes ached, with coaches and referees. I had been instructed by experts — by Herman Rohrig and Gene Calhoun of the Big Ten, by Pete Williams of the Southeastern Conference, honored game officials. By Dave Nelson, head of the NCAA's rules committee and himself an honored ex-coach, and Art McNally of the NFL.

I had talked with trainers and team doctors, to orthopedic surgeons, and to helmet manufacturers plagued by lawsuits.

I had talked with college presidents and high school principals, and athletic directors at both levels, many of them scared stiff.

I had talked with lawyers who made no bones about their intentions to make the game pay for its mistakes. One called it "football's profligacy."

I said I had heard so much grim testimony that I felt like a drunk coming out of a long weekend, slow and reflective, and apprehensive, of both the future and the immediate past.

Just before he retired nine years ago, Dr. Eric Walker, the president of Pennsylvania State University, told Joe Paterno, "Joe, if you don't do something about the injuries, soccer will be our national sport in ten years."

"Joe says he thinks about that when he realizes not enough people see the problem," I said.

"Did all your witnesses agree that doomsday was at hand?"

"No, they don't *all* agree on anything, but they are all concerned, for one reason or another."

"What about Rozelle? Did you talk with Pete Rozelle?"

"No."

"How come?"

"Rozelle is a publicity agent. Only the National Football League would think to name a publicity agent as its president. I don't go to publicity agents when I think there's something rotten in the corporation."

"He will be the first to scream."

"Let him. The pros are the core of the game's worst behavior — the violence, the mindless savage acts, the unsportsmanlike conduct. The pros took over as the game's style-setter in the Fifties and Sixties, and it's been downhill ever since. Players desperate to succeed, doing whatever they have to do to stay where all that money is. You hint at something like that to the front office of the National Football League and they'll shovel a ton of television ratings at you."

I said I did not doubt Rozelle's brilliance at doing what he is paid to do: merchandise pro football; keep the competition keen and the wheels of profit churning. Rozelle grew up in the job after the late Bert Bell worked the kinks out, and he has become poised and polished and a graceful asset at all the fancy parties. Now when you deal with him you tend to imagine you have a superior to contend with. At maximizing the game's television profits, he *is* superior. A quarter-million-dollar salary seems little enough to pay for the 650-million-dollar deal he made with the networks.

"But Rozelle does not minister the same game I'm talking about. His NFL is the NFL of the Super Hype. Hotpants and bulging halter tops, and Monday night excitement with Howard Cosell and Dandy Don. A monstrous ratings game. If they dug trenches across the fifty-yard line and issued grenade launchers to the players and it caused a tremor in the Nielsen, the NFL front office would say it was terrific."

I said I thought Rozelle would be as appalled as the next guy if he had to hear the sound of a crunching kneecap at ground level, "but you don't hear those things too well in an air-conditioned VIP booth. My experience with the NFL is that it sucks up criticism on injuries like it was baby's milk. Unless you hit a nerve.

"I talked with a guy in California, a psychiatrist named Arnold Mandell. Doctor Mandell is also a research pharmacologist, with a pedigree a mile long. He made studies on the use of amphetamines in the NFL. For a year he was the resident shrink of the San Diego Chargers, and wrote a frightening book about their drug habits. His conclusions might have been overstated, but he had the advantage of a front-row seat. He said that huge doses of speed just before a game put some pro players in a state of terrifying rage, which was a principal cause of the unnecessary violence and injury.

"The NFL's conclusion was that Mandell was a quack. The league came down on him like a ton of bricks, and tried to get his license revoked. But Mandell was a tougher nut than they thought. Even now, four years later, he's still blasting away in medical journals, and the NFL is still trying to discredit him. It's a standoff. Mandell continues to grind his axe, and the NFL sneers at him and does nothing to clear up the doubts he raised."

A nudge on my line broke my concentration, but there was

no follow-up; whatever had passed below had kept going — a piscine snob. I went through the ritual of reeling in and changing bait, and complained that we might be better served with something fresher to present to the milling giants I knew were there. B. shifted in his chair, his first movement since we sat down, and with placid condescension agreed that the bait was not doing the job. He said he didn't mind so long as we didn't catch anything. The boat's restless pendulum had intensified, but he seemed to be holding up all right.

"You realize, of course, that we can't live without pro football," he said from the shadow of his cap, which was now of no service because the sun was under cover again. "Pro football has set in like hyacinths around a lake. It is now our Most Popular Spectator Sport, according to *TV Guide*. You might as well go up against the graduated income tax."

"I'm not against pro football," I said. "It made rich men out of some very worthwhile human beings I have known — Larry Csonka, Don Shula, John McKay. I don't even blame McKay for defecting from the colleges, all the money they threw at him in Tampa. I think it's great that the average Joe player makes — what, sixty thousand bucks a year? I think it's wonderful that O.J. is a movie star and the coaches get to make commercials for reclining chairs.

"But in the hands of the National Football League, progress winds up looking a lot like dissolution. I think justice is served when men like the Rooneys win a championship in Pittsburgh. They were pioneers in the game. They paid their dues. But mostly what you hear from the new breed of owners are threats to take their wonderful game the hell out of town if the community doesn't accept their inflated ticket prices and build 'em a new stadium.

"The pro game was a game for millhands and factory workers

when it started. Now millhands and factory workers can't get tickets anymore. Can't afford 'em, either. What do owners care about hometown fans? They've got television. Pro football sold its soul to television."

"They got a good price," B. said. "Besides, who hasn't? Give television long enough and it'll rid the entire world of good taste."

"That's not the point. The point is that somewhere along the line pro football suffered a terrible breakdown in judgment. Pro football embraced violence. Maybe it's a carry-over from the days it played second fiddle to the colleges and had trouble making the payroll. Maybe it's the fear that plain vanilla football wasn't enough. I don't know. I do know that the bigger it got, the more willing it became to accept brutality as entertainment.

"I don't mean the leadership sent out a bulletin encouraging it, but they didn't stop it, either. Vicious got to be fun. Everybody laughed when the highlight films made comedy out of the most brutal hits they could splice together. Television put it to ragtime."

Intimidation, I said, is now an art form in the NFL. The chickens have come home to roost. Pro players are glorified for the macho way they break the rules. "Cheap shot" got currency as a pro term; so did "clotheslining." Vicious acts meant to maim. "The hammer" is not only a pro term, but a nickname for a pro star. Forget sportsmanship. Batter the quarterback. Break his ribs.

"But you don't have to wait for venal demonstrations. Some of the worst examples of sportsmanship are now part of the show. The object isn't to play to win, the object is to humiliate. Taunt the other guy. Shake the ball in his nose. Wave your fingers as you cross the goal. And when you do, make a big display. Spike the ball. Do the funky chicken. End-zone discotheque is great for the ratings.

"The result, as any arm-chair psychologist knows, is that all of football suffers when its most prominent member sets a bad example. The influence filters down. You should hear the testimony I've heard. Colleges and high schools have to write new rules all the time to keep their players from imitating their elders."

B. sat up, bringing his leather shoes hard to the deck and leaning toward the fishbox. The motion startled me. I remembered his past performances and flinched, but it was a false alarm. Without looking at me he reached into the box and extracted a beer from the cooler. In the years I have known him, I had not experienced a time when he was such a compliant listener. I suspected he was biding time, waiting for an opening.

"So why not blame television?" he said, getting his lip over the foaming can in time to catch the first eruption of fluid.

"You don't blame a shark for doing what comes naturally," I said. "Give television something to chew on and it'll devour it."

It baffles me, I said, that we continue to doubt television's capacity to make waste. Television could care less. In its lust to sell razor blades and beer, it overwhelmed boxing — a televised fight almost every night of the week. The fight clubs that spawned boxers dried up like apples on a sidewalk. Only when a sport is comatose and can no longer shill for the important items of commerce does television let up. Pro football is now televised all day Sunday and every Monday night of the season, and sometimes on Saturdays and sometimes on Thursdays. If TV chews up pro football, it'll go on to something else. When we don't buy "Playhouse 90" anymore, television gives us "Laverne and Shirley."

"But even if pro football can withstand overexposure," I said, "has anybody stopped to ask what this has done to the colleges and the high schools? I don't mean Alabama and Oklahoma and USC, I mean the colleges that can't stand to lose a single paying customer. And entire high school programs where attendance has been on a chronic decline for the last three decades."

I felt a chill on my neck, followed by the sting of driven water. The wind was much stronger now, and gusting, but with our backs to the bulkhead we had not felt it build. The boat had lost its rhythmic roll and was tugging on its leash like a hound. The chairs made sliding noises where we sat. But as B. did not complain, I ignored it.

"Go back to the injuries," he said. "If you think there's an obvious correlation between all this money-grubbing and all the injuries, why do you think it hasn't been dealt with? There are a lot of good people out there who care more about injured players than they do about financial sheets — at least among the people I deal with."

"Tradition," I said. "But not so obvious. Football has always had to downplay its injuries. It's a hard-hitting game. Half the fun is the physical contact, being able to out-tough the other guy. Bones snap on occasion, and the game's more virile believers have traditionally been able to make nonbelievers look foolish. Critics, it was said, preferred effeminacy to manhood. Critics wore horn-rimmed glasses and panicked at the sight of a raincloud. That's traditional.

"But the injuries got out of hand. Nobody likes to talk about them, and while they were being overlooked — not by everybody, but by the majority — they got out of hand, and now they can't be swept under the rug anymore. One survey reported by the *New York Times* said that football injures a million high school players a year at more than thirty thousand schools and seventy thousand college players at more than nine hundred schools, and will inflict a hundred-percent casualty rate on the National Football League — at least one injury per player."

"I suspect those figures are high," B. said.

"They probably are, but that's the trouble. Everybody accepted injury too long, and now they 'suspect' without knowing. Everybody has a different survey to refer to, and not one of them is complete. Not one is computerized across every level of the game. Mostly the surveys are done by a few highly motivated people, with limited resources. Even the best ones get little or no national funding. The results are always 'suspect' because the survey methods are suspect. As Dave Nelson says, 'Garbage in, garbage out.' "

Even at that, I said, you have to wonder what football would do about it if the causes of injury were clear. I found out, to some degree, what the National Football League would do. The NFL commissioned the Stanford Research Institute to study its injuries over a three-year period. The report was supposed to be private, but it got around. It showed that the game's rules and some of its equipment needed to be over-hauled to keep pace with a hard reality: players were bigger, stronger, and faster than ever. The laws of physics are constant: force equals mass times acceleration. The players had reached an astonishing capacity to hurt each other — and were doing so.

I talked with Joe Grippo of Stanford, who headed up the project. Everything from the rules of blocking and tackling to the severity, time, and place of injuries was catalogued. The report concluded that "without radical rule changes, and an equally improbable altering of coach and player attitudes, football will continue to be the world's most injurious sport." The NFL treated the report like it was science fiction.

"Give me an example," B. said.

"Okay — a lulu. The study found that in seventeen out of seventeen categories, natural grass was safer to play on than the artificial surfaces then being produced for football. Safer for the head, the face, the teeth, the neck, the shoulders, the arms, the elbows, the wrists, the hands, the fingers, the thorax, the feet, the toes, the back, the hips."

"You're talking about AstroTurf."

"It's the only one left, now. But then there were three and on them head injuries doubled, according to the findings. And despite an early claim that AstroTurf would reduce knee injuries, the bane of football, *more* knees were injured on it. Grippo said his group's conclusion was that synthetic surfaces could not be justified, not on an injury-prevention basis, not on a relative-cost basis. He said the alleged advantage of better land economics was a poor tradeoff.

"Did the NFL tell everybody to roll up the rugs? Of course not. NFL cities have a lot of money invested in artificial fields. The NFL had pushed artificial fields. Since the survey, three more have been put down, and the only time they've gone back to natural grass is when the municipality decided grass was cheaper in the long run. At the Orange Bowl in Miami, for example.

"According to Grippo, the entire report cost the NFL thirty-five thousand dollars — about the price of hors d'oeuvres for the Super Bowl party. But Stanford Research was not commissioned to make any more studies. Joe Grippo wasn't upset. He said without 'dynamic rules changes' — his words — it would be a waste of money. He said he didn't like to do research for the sake of research. He said they needed a new hypothesis to work from, otherwise they'd get the same result. A new hypothesis meant changing a lot of things. The NFL didn't want to do that. Injuries were actually up the third year of the study — to a record number, about twelve injuries for every ten players.

"Thus you wind up with a highly provocative syllogism: you make a study and find that only change will curtail injuries. You don't make the changes, injuries increase. Therefore, the thing to do is to not make any more studies."

B. pushed the brim of his cap back on his head and drained his beer. "Why don't you blame the coaches?" he said. "You've always parroted what Bear Bryant says about its being a coach's game. Coaches develop the techniques, they allow the styles of play to get out of hand. They don't talk about injuries, either, only in terms of who's going to miss practice or the big game on Saturday. Only to excuse a defeat. Coaches object to injuries only in a pragmatic sense."

"I don't hold coaches blameless. They are conservatives, basically, and conservatives resist reform. Coaches say injuries are 'part of the game,' and 'the breaks,' even when they know better. They are reluctant to give up cherished and 'proven' coaching tenets, no matter how consequential. They fight rules changes. Clipping wasn't outlawed until the game had been played for almost half a century.

"But for the most part, coaches are special people, a caring bunch of guys. Especially at the lower levels, where remuneration is not a factor. They just want to teach young people. Some of them work incredibly long hours for incredibly low pay. I have a friend who figured it out after ten years as a head high school coach. He'd been coaching for thirty-two cents an hour.

"The problem with coaches at the upper levels is what we've made of them," I said. "Desperate to win. Desperate enough to do things they shouldn't, or allow things they shouldn't. They are pinched by an occupational reality: when they lose, they're out on their ear. They can't call a meeting of the board and throw it off on a junior executive.

"Any rational person would deplore Vince Lombardi's line about 'winning isn't everything, it's the only thing,' as simply not true. An unsound philosophy. Not realistic, not viable, not sporting. But it *is* the way coaches live.

"At the pro level, and at the major college level, it's the way players live, too. The result is as completely confused a set of ethics as you can imagine. In some respects, you in the colleges are more to blame because you should be above it. But you've developed the same profit-and-loss mentalities, the same dependance on television, the same need for financial deliverance.

"Deliverance for the coach is winning more games, and that's an awful pressure. Deliverance for the hotshot player is no longer the education his skills have made available, but the chance for a big pro contract. He couldn't care less about the education. That's pressure, too, because his chances to make the pros are one in a hundred.

"So what has happened? College football has become a ritual of bribery. Your recruiting costs are obscene. *Recruiting* is obscene. It's the rot at the center of all your problems. You try to keep it from eating you alive, but every time you slap on a patch it springs a leak somewhere else. The NCAA's recruiting rules are a morass, the work of scared parents afraid of their own children. They're like IRS guidelines, honeycombed with traps and loopholes. The players don't understand them, the coaches think they're crazy — many of them are. They don't make sense at all.

"Oklahoma boasted that it spent ten thousand dollars to recruit Elvis Peacock a few years ago. Peacock was a hotshot high school running back — in Miami, Florida. The Oklahoma coaches flew thousands of miles, back and forth across the country to recruit him. Oklahoma could afford it, and it was okay by the rules. Oklahoma could have spent *fifty* thousand to recruit the boy. But once he got to Norman, the rules prevented a coach from getting him a pair of pants at a discount, or driving him to the airport at Christmastime, or buying him a hot fudge sundae.

"No wonder some coaches came to the conclusion that it is sappy to go by the rules. The rules are made to be broken. Break them and win and you keep coaching. You've always had cheating coaches, and you always will because no sin is too great for absolution. If they win, they know everything will turn out okay. A coach gets caught cheating one year and is named 'Coach of the Year' in his conference the next. It happened.

"As a result the NCAA has a monstrous enforcement problem that grows thornier every year. Enforcement used to be a one-man operation. Now Walter Byers has fifteen or twenty on the job, roaming around, sniffing into things. It's like spitting in the ocean. They could add a thousand more men and not come close to solving the problem, because the cheating is the result, not the cause."

The root of it, I said, as any moralist or recently fired football coach knows, is money. The way money is spent, the way it is lost, the need to get in the black — or out of the red. To break even. Breaking even has become the clarion call of college football. After a hundred and ten years, the game has come to that. A dollars-and-cents, bottom-line existence. Just like the pros. College football has, at last, become like the pros. Complete with litigation.

B. cleared his throat. "The fact is, we aren't breaking even. The number of big schools who can't do it increases every year.

At the top level, the Division One schools, we're down to almost half — fifty-three percent breaking even. We hang on television money like it was the breath of life. At M—— one year if we hadn't gotten a regional telecast we'd have gone under, and I'm not sure it wouldn't have been for the third time."

"It's your own fault," I said. "I have no sympathy for you when you make football only worth something if it's making money. The schools in divisions Two and Three don't even make a pretense at balancing the budget. They still play the game."

"Yes, but a lot of them are wondering why."

The rain hit us like a club. The advance line of the storm whose signs I had ignored came suddenly from our backs, sweeping over the bow of the boat, picking up the sea and hurling it into us in stinging black slices.

Discussion was immediately suspended. We reeled in our lines frantically and scrambled for the cabin. But once there I decided it would be better to get back to Ocean Reef. Darkness was coming on; there was already precious little light. B. said he'd take care of the anchor, and was gone.

I climbed the ladder to the bridge, to the controls. A bimini top is a sun shield, not a true cover, and mine did nothing to interrupt the slanting, driving rain. Fearing the worst, I hit the starters of the two decrepit engines. Again they responded, perhaps as anxious as I to get out.

B., however, was in a desperate, comic wrestle on the foredeck. Tugging at the anchor line into the teeth of the storm, his leather shoes scraping for traction, he was like a cow on ice. Twice he lost his footing and sprawled to the deck, his legs sliding under the bowrail and over the edge.

I shouted for him to wait, and eased the throttle forward to give him slack. This time he got into a crouch and was hectically retrieving line when we got directly over the anchor. There it held, apparently hung up on the coral below. No amount of human crane work would budge it.

"Never mind," I yelled over the cry of the storm. "Cleat the line and I'll pull it up."

He was squatting over the cleated line like a freezing man over a fire when I throttled forward, again taking up the slack. The bow plunged with the tension from the line, allowing the next wave to catch B. full face. He cursed me loudly, but at the same instant the anchor freed and the bow lifted. He shouted his approval and waved before pulling up the last fifty feet of line. One flute of the grapple was bent grotesquely.

B. crawled on his knees and ducked inside the forward hatch. When he finally got up to the bridge I noticed he had his shoes tied together by the strings and slung around his neck. He grinned, but I am not sure if it was meant to be a concession or not.

Pushed by the wind and the heavy, following sea, we wallowed in our retreat, but it was only an awkwardness, not a peril. We were safely to the dock within an hour. By now it was totally dark, and the rain, no longer bullied by the wind, beat down steadily and even heavier than before.

We closed ourselves into the cabin, which took on the immediate glow that always comes to a warm, safe place after a brush with nature, however insignificant. I fished into the cooler and handed B. another beer, and looked him over for signs of disrepair. He was drenched, and his Cardinal cap, which had never come off, was a spongy red pancake on his head. The bill was bent to one side like the anchor.

"Nothing to it," I said.

"Beats fishing," B. said, and removed the shoes from his neck.

After that he said nothing until his beer was half gone. He sat hunched over, in a kind of sodden state of grace, listening to the rain, and I have never known him to take so long to gather his words.

Finally, he said he had a "few things to add" before we closed the subject, and since I had done the lion's share of the talking to that point, he would as soon proceed without accompaniment. I said by all means.

He said our first discussion by phone had caused him to take time to evaluate his own feelings. He is a college man, and a football man, and much of what he calls his "honest prejudices" have been crystallized over many years. The injury problem, the costs — about those he said he agreed with almost everything I had said. ("Found," I corrected him.) But that within the college community there was a growing anger, even a despair, over football, although he, personally, did not think the dice have been rolled, never to be picked up again.

"I want to build an argument for you, along lines familiar to me," he said. "Taking it one at a time.

"First, I agree that we at the top level of the college game long ago latched on to a cost spiral that could, in the end, ruin us. The more expensive football got, the more we spent, trying to recoup. It's an old economic trick: you spend more to make more.

"But now, really for the first time, I think, we're acting out of fear. We're scared of inflation, scared of litigation. We're scared of Title IX. Scared that the women, who are trying to get what a lot of us feel they deserve, will do it over football's dead body. A lot of the women say that, you know — that the only way they'll ever make it is if we deemphasize football and parcel the money around.

"When you act out of fear, you do selfish things. We're not

together. We're devouring each other with selfish financing. We're to the point where we don't give a damn if the other guy makes it or not. We used to, but not anymore. We say, 'Your program is hurting, you're not drawing any people at your place. We can't afford to honor the contract to play you there. Come to our place, where we draw seventy thousand a game, or we'll cancel.'

"Nebraska and Ohio State tried to pull that on Indiana. Alabama *did* pull it on Miami. It's happening more and more. It might be sound economics, but if college football becomes strictly a matter of who can make the most money, we'll wind up with thirty or forty schools playing at the top level. Maybe not that many.

"Our fears take on many forms. We do many desperate things. We've always had cheaters, and as long as we have scholarships we'll have recruiting problems. We can solve most of them, and live with the rest, if we keep up the pretense of being a group of colleges engaged in sport instead of a farm system for the professional leagues.

"And *that's* where we're failing. Every day, more and more. That's where we've sold ourselves down the river, and where I fall in line with what you say.

"We are, indeed, destroying our good name. We're engaging in the worst kind of cheating — academic cheating. Exploiting every well-intended loophole, every regulation that never got written. I think the majority of our coaches work very hard and want very badly to have their kids graduate with something to go through life with besides a football letter and a rejection slip from a pro camp. But not everybody has the integrity of a Joe Paterno, and not everybody has the clout of a Bear Bryant.

"Morons are getting into college today, just because they can throw something or hit something or get from here to there faster than the next guy. Not just underprivileged kids who need a chance, but uneducated kids who don't have a chance, not in the classroom. We've subverted the whole idea of the two-percent rules, and the affirmative action programs. I know of one school on the West Coast that has a two-percent rule and almost fifty percent of its football team is in as part of the 'two percent.'

"Education is not for everybody. Some guys might have made first-rate jugglers if they'd left school early, or become excellent plumbers. When a dumb kid is herded into college to play football, we say it's better that way. The rationale is that if you allow him a protracted exposure to the classroom, certain things might rub off. A little bit of learning.

"It's hogwash, and it's a sham. He's there because, one, we want him for our football team, and, two, he wants a chance to play pro football. We're the pros' farm club. Four years later he's the proud owner of enough credits to qualify for upper-freshman. The NCAA doesn't have a consistent rule for normal classroom progress. That's what happened to that kid in the Ivy League — four years of 'normal progress' was no progress at all. His mother sued the school."

B. looked up from his beer, hard-eyed. There was bite in his voice, and something else. A strangling kind of frustration.

"Why do we do it?" he said. "Because we're scared, and because we're stupid. Stupid enough to believe it's really okay for us to be farm teams for the pros. To fatten up the talent and run 'em through the process. We say, why not? A kid wants to make football his career, why not give him the credentials, the way we train a CPA? Sharpen his skills so he can go on to the Packers and make a zillion.

"That's a beautiful rationale until you see it for the pan of worms it is. Less than one percent of the college players playing right now at the top level will make a pro roster. Do we tell 'em that when we recruit 'em? Some of us do, but what difference does it make? Some of 'em have trouble reading a menu or a street sign, anyway. What do they know? And look what we've done to our own standards and our own self respect. We know better, but we do it anyway.

"And who pays for this farm system? Surely not the pros. All they do is reap the benefits. They rob us of our resources like they had a gun at our head. They wreck the programs of the big-city schools, and the schools near the big cities, and never bat an eye. They take everything, and nobody yells, Stop thief. Bear Bryant talks about it. He says it's nuthouse-dumb. We recruit, we feed, we train, we shape and mold the players for the pros, and even publicize 'em, and all we get is a pat on the back and a kick in the teeth.

"The pros are drying up football. They put nothing back into the game. Zilch. Their idea of a show of appreciation is to hold a punt, pass, and kick contest, and then make a big-deal TV production out of it. What pro team worries about the disastrous high school attendance figures or the spiraling costs to run the high school programs? What pro team worries about the negative influence of saturation television? What pro league makes injury surveys for the high schools that can't afford to? What pro team worries about the aberrational behavior that is picked up by impressionable high school minds?

"The only time pro owners are polite is when they've got empty seats. Any time you see a pro owner smiling it's a bad sign. The Dolphins quit drawing capacity crowds a couple years ago, so they offered to let the high school teams in Miami sell their unwanted tickets for them — on a fifty-fifty profit basis. The program didn't work. Maybe the high schools realized how self-serving it was.

"I can't say we weren't warned. Fritz Crisler banned pro scouts from the Michigan press box years ago. He saw a truth few of us have come to grips with: that as good as the college game is, it is threatened by the pros, not because the pro game is better, but because it's a bloodsucker. Instead of telling 'em to kiss off, we invite 'em in for tea. We advertise our willingness to cooperate in our own demise. Our coaches drink with their coaches, and compare notes. Pro scouts are invited around. College publicity directors make lists and devote pages to players who have 'graduated' into the pros.

"But the real plaintiffs at the bar are the high schools. For them it's murder in the first degree. All over the country it's the same — in Philadelphia, in New York, in Los Angeles, in Chicago. In states that used to be hotbeds of football — Ohio, Florida. They're wringing their hands over declining attendance and growing costs. They've got their kids out selling doughnuts and pretzels, and holding car washes to make ends meet.

"Talk to any high school athletic director, especially in the big cities. I talk to 'em almost every day. They all say the same thing. The fans have been expropriated by the pros. The pros, via television, have convinced everybody they're the *ne plus ultra*, and you're a radical if you don't agree. I say you can have just as much fun watching your high school team play, and that it's a helluva lot more meaningful. And cheaper. But the argument falls on increasingly deaf ears. Nobody wants to go to high school games anymore, except the fathers of the boys in backfield."

The storm B. had raised inside the cabin began to wane simultaneously with the one that had been swatting it from the outside. The heavy rain passed and the wind dropped as though a switch had been thrown. I opened the cabin to the cool, sweet after-rain, but the chilly night air against our wet clothes accented the need to get inside and change. B. agreed. While we were gathering up equipment he said he had a finishing remark to make.

"Football needs to be criticized," he said. "It needs to be taken by the scruff and shaken soundly. It can take it. It better, because it's too good a game to lose. But the solutions are there, too. Criticism without solutions is punishment, not rehabilitation.

"Don't be gulled by those of us who believe football will survive no matter what. Football people have a colossal mental block on that point. Some of us don't even understand soccer, and what we see of it we can't imagine anybody preferring it to American football. But Paterno's friend, the ex-president, may be right. There's a whole generation of kids out there who see things we don't see. Eight-, ten-, and twelve-year-olds, flocking to the soccer fields. Kids who found organized football at that level a drag, and soccer fast and fun and skillful — and physical, too, without being brutal.

"I've got one myself who's into it now, and I go and watch and I'm bewildered. But he's not. He's having fun. He loves it. And he can play it without having to listen to some knee-jerk facsimile of a Lombardi tell him to bury his tiny little helmeted head in somebody's groin so we can all get a trophy and be number one.

"Suburban kids are fleeing organized football. Check it out, you'll see. If we don't curb the injuries, do something about the trend, it may be irreversible. Football may well become a game for the lower classes. A ghetto game for young gladiators desperate to get a leg up and willing to sacrifice their bodies to do it. It would be a terrible tragedy, but it would be our own doing. Our legacy."

B. paused. In the diffused shore light, I could see only his outline. I imagined that his face was as somber as his voice, which was grim as mourning weeds.

"The injuries, the brutality, the dubious pro influence, the swarming lawyers — and soccer, too. Do you know the statistics on the growth of soccer in this country?" he said with sudden intensity. "Ten years ago, this guy, a founder of the American Youth Soccer League, walks into a sporting goods store in Inglewood, California, to buy a soccer ball. The owner tries to sell him a volleyball. He didn't know the difference. Do you know that last year that same store sold a million dollars' worth of soccer equipment? It's time we got to know our enemies."

"You forgot one," I said.

"Who's that?"

"The toughest of them all. Your most implacable foe."

"Who?"

"Mom. Every kid football player's mother. She has always fought the game, always distrusted it. She never understood football in the first place. She doesn't know a first down from a first inning. But it always scared hell out of her, the prospect of baby boy getting his head cracked. Now when she reads the casualty lists, and remembers the sad examples on television and at the little-league park, she is liable to become relentless. Soccer gave her an alternative, clean and practically injury free. It's her kind of alternative."

"The hand that rocks the cradle," B. said.

"Something like that. Don't underestimate the power of maternal enmity."

B. promised he wouldn't.

2.

THE BRUTALITY

I don't know John Cole. He is a name on a masthead. He was identified as the editor and part owner of the *Maine Times* when, in October 1977, he wrote the following explanation of why he was surrendering his place in front of the television set after a forty-year love affair with pro football:

Buried under the avalanche of the billions of dollars the game has generated for television and its advertisers, [pro] football's order has collapsed and chaos reigns. The only constant in today's game is brutality, and it is being fostered, not quelled.

With the lure of football money as their way out of the ghettos, the biggest, fiercest, strongest, meanest players are sacrificing their bodies and their humanity to get in on the dough. They pop opponents, break legs, heads and noses in a kind of relentless determination to succeed.

The game has reached the point where only violence holds, and only the most violent and most ruthless can survive on the Astroturf long enough to collect their outsize paychecks. These days, [brutality] is the strategy. . . . With the best players gone, the game is no contest. I'm giving it up, after 40 years.

Ideally, you should be able to play any game without referees or umpires. Men of sport should also be sportsmen. Ideally, officials of sport should be necessary only to distinguish between the fine lines of what is in or out, ball or strike, legal or illegal. Officials of sport are not supposed to be cops on the beat, hired to keep athletes from maiming one another.

But that is exactly what the officials are now acting as in football. It is naive and dangerous to think otherwise. Certain rituals of coaching and play, and the frantic drive to succeed, have made the participants responsive to base instincts, and therefore more likely to injure and be injured. The higher up the ladder they go, the worse they are. Violent play reaches its sophisticated peak in the National Football League.

Jon Morris, a center for the Chicago Bears and the New England Patriots, retired last year after fifteen seasons in the NFL. His valedictory included some remarkable admissions about the game he loved.

"Violence," said Morris, "is going to kill the game." Big money, he said, is responsible.

"The competition for jobs and big money is making the game immensely more violent," he said. "You see it especially among the younger players. They'll do anything to get into the NFL. That's why you see headhunters like Doug Plank. I think the league is in serious trouble unless something is done. But I realize violence is what the NFL sells. They say they don't, but they do."

Doug Plank is a free safety for the Bears. Plank thinks of himself as "an excellent example of a player who plays within the rules . . . the way I'm taught to play." And how does the player play? Plank gave *Sports Illustrated* this definition: "A player will do everything on the field he can get away with. If he couldn't get away with it, he wouldn't do it."

Football is not Rollerball; it is not even ice hockey. In the twisted belief that the game alone was not enough to pack them in, ice hockey opted for a blood-image at the professional level years ago. (I once heard the intellectual giant who presides over the National Hockey League brag to a television audience: "We *are* violent; we *start off* violent.") And although hockey is now having its own Armageddon in lawsuits, its fans can count on an evening of savagery whenever two NHL teams skate out to play.

Football, of course, is too good a game to pander to the blood lust of fans. Its primary attraction, despite everything, is still skill, not ferocity. But when a mentality is allowed to fester that debases the qualities of skill and technique and teamwork — when it is, in fact, not discouraged — the sport suffers. Brutality is its own fertilizer. From "get away with what you can," it is a short hop to the deviations that poison a sport.

Some of the more recent cases are familiar to the followers of professional football:

— The Cardinals' Tim Kearney clotheslines the Eagles' running back Dave Hampton, crashing a forearm into the side of Hampton's neck. Hampton is unconscious for seven minutes before being carried off the field on a stretcher. Kearney defends the blow as "perfectly legal." From his hospital bed, Hampton says, "That's football."

— On Monday night television, Mel Morgan of Cincinnati throws a forearm into the face of Pittsburgh receiver John Stallworth, who has just caught a pass. Morgan gets a penalty and a suspension, Stallworth a concussion. Moments later, Mel Blount of the Steelers kayoes Cincinnati tight end Bob Trumpy to even the score.

— In retaliation for his late hit on Oakland's quarterback Ken Stabler, Cleveland's Joe ("Turkey") Jones is speared in the back by Oakland's guard Gene Upshaw.

— Pittsburgh tackle Joe Greene pummels Denver's center

Mike Montler after he has already punched out center Paul Howard. Greene says it is "under the heading of taking care of yourself." He says he was "being held illegally" and thus "had to go outside the rules."

— The Redskins' Mike Curtis chases Baltimore quarterback Bert Jones. Jones falls down and, just as Curtis starts to pounce, kicks out at him. Curtis kicks back. Both benches empty to join the fight.

— On Thanksgiving Day, the Cardinals' Conrad Dobler, self-styled "meanest man in pro football," hits Dolphin linebacker Bob Matheson in the head and draws a penalty. Later, he and Tom Banks go after the Dolphins' A. J. Duhe. When Matheson and Dobler lock horns again, a bench-clearing brawl erupts.

— The Los Angeles Rams' linebacker Jim Youngblood crashes helmet first into the face of Tampa Bay's quarterback Doug Williams, breaking his jaw. No penalty is called. Tampa coach John McKay is livid. "The rules state that when a player is hit above the shoulders, there's supposed to be a penalty," McKay rages in the Tampa dressing room. "Hell, there's Williams, sitting there with blood pouring out of his mouth. Did they think he bit himself?"

— Dallas linebacker D.D. Lewis complains that his team has been "intimidated" by the Rams. "People were taking advantage of us. Like Isaiah Robertson spitting on players, and us not doing anything about it." Against New Orleans an opposing player pushes Dallas running back Tony Dorsett out of bounds. The Cowboys on the sidelines "do something." They jump the New Orleans player.

— In a game against Denver, the Bears' free safety Plank, his momentum carrying him ten yards after the play, rams his headgear into the chest of Denver's Howard. Howard leaves the field; X-rays show a fractured sternum. Plank says later, "So many times I come in with my head down and I'm not always aware of who I'm hitting."

At the time some of these inspiring episodes were being reviewed as part of a series of articles I had done for *Sports Illustrated* in the fall of 1978 — a series whose working title, incidentally, was "Brutality: The Crisis in Football" — the New England Patriots flew to Oakland to play the Raiders in an exhibition game. The star wide receiver of the Patriots was a Chicago ghetto kid named Darryl Stingley. Stingley's specialty was circus catches. Many of his catches were made "in traffic," as admiring coaches say when a player is not intimidated by crowds of defensive backs out to rearrange his necktie.

Oakland's star safety was a former Ohio State All-America named Jack Tatum. Tatum's specialty is making receivers pay for catching — or trying to catch — the ball. Tatum is a very hard hitter. In the lexicon of coaches, Tatum "can stick you." His nickname is "Black Death."

On a pass play late in the second quarter, Stingley lined up right and ran a short crossing pattern, cutting over the middle. The pass was intended for him, but it was poorly thrown — a floater Stingley had no chance to catch. The ball sailed over his head. But for a defensive back in pro football it is not enough to let a receiver get off with just an incompleted pass. A receiver who violates a defensive back's territory has to be reminded of the peril he has put himself in.

Tatum "stuck" Stingley, almost head-on. He didn't have to worry about the ball; he could and did devote his full attention to the receiver. It was, by dismal pro standards, a "clean hit." Not illegal, not inordinately vicious. Just "part of the game."

Stingley experienced a "flash of light" as the nerves which control his body movement snapped. He crumpled. At an

Alemeda County hospital, doctors trying to prevent a permanent paralysis performed a spinal fusion on the athlete. Stingley was still paralyzed. The prognosis was guarded.

By November, Stingley was "medically stable," and in residence at the rehabilitation center at Northwestern University in Chicago. He was "improving, slowly." He could sit in a chair at an eighty-degree angle for two or three hours a day. His right arm could function at the shoulder and at the elbow, and his left arm was "progressing." His legs were "aware of some spasms." He was able to listen to the Patriots' games by a speaker-telephone at bedside. His teammates sent him tape-recorded messages.

Meanwhile, Oakland's Tatum, not penalized on the play, was punished in another way. He found as the months went by that the memory of the hit on Stingley, and the consequences, affected his reputation as a hitter. He said he found himself "easing up on tackles a few times." Patriot tight end Russ Francis, a close friend of Stingley's, said it was "about time."

The play that put Stingley into the jaws of the Oakland defensive backfield, and at the mercy of Tatum, was subsequently taken from the Patriots' playbook. Francis said that what Tatum did was not intentional, "not a cheap shot, but it was unnecessary. The ball already was by Darryl's hands."

In Chicago, Harold Stingley, the player's father, was embittered by the tragedy. He said he wonders about a game "that did this to my baby," one that "causes one young man to go through life brutally hurt because of something that another boy has been taught" all along to do. He said he wonders if it is still "the same game" he played as a young man. He said he sees "a lot of wrongs out there now and I attribute it all to business."

By late January 1979, the *New York Times* reported that the

NFL Players Association had received contributions to a scholarship fund for the two Stingley children in the amount of $27,788. The Patriots themselves contributed $5,140. The Cleveland Browns, at that point, had donated $60. Three teams were unheard from — Los Angeles, Dallas, and Miami.

By the estimate of most football people, including the commissioner of the National Football League, the Stingley tragedy was a fluke. Not a venal act, just an unfortunate one. Pro football people point out that they have always done pretty well in the condemnation business when they have something really corrupt to rake over the coals (Paul Hornung's gambling habits, Joe Namath's business partners). Bulletins are sent out when the on-field activity becomes unusually deplorable. Administrators demand answers. Suspensions and fines are levied.

George Atkinson's forearm blow to Lynn Swann's head prompted Pittsburgh's coach Chuck Noll to charge that a "criminal element" was loose in the game. The incident still draws bitter references. Two years later, I sat at lunch with a college coach, Darrell Royal of Texas, and when discussion happened onto Atkinson-Swann, Royal's face flushed and his lips spread across his teeth in hard thin lines. "It was lethal," he said. "There was nothing brave or daring about it. A tough guy looks you in the eye, plays you jaw to jaw. It's a tough game. But that wasn't tough, and it wasn't football."

Royal had only seen the play on television.

It is a much more frightening matter, however, and an infinitely more dangerous one, when ruthless, intimidating play is allowed to spread *within the rules*. It is not so much the lawless acts but the unconscionable ones that contribute to the injury rate that is now epidemic in football — and to the ominous potential for litigation. When players grow cynical of even the most elemental forms of sportsmanlike behavior, excess begets excess.

Players are not blind to this license. What Tatum did to Stingley was not illegal (though it should have been). It was excessive.

As fate would have it, I had just come off a road trip and was settling down to a stack of mail and a Sunday afternoon football game. This was later in the 1978 season, and much of what I had plowed through was in response to or in some way related to the brutality series. Included were some clippings from newspapers in which Commissioner Rozelle had attacked the series' justification. He called it "irresponsible" and made a number of convincing remarks that exonerated the NFL of any wrongdoing.

Rozelle said that, after all, "thirty percent of the rule changes in the last ten years had been keyed to safety." Given the NFL's shameful record of being forever last in safety measures (behind the colleges and high schools — and a distant last at that), I was curious to see what kind of rules he was talking about. One was a rule put in in 1977 that made it illegal to strike an opponent above the shoulders during the initial charge of a defensive lineman — the infamous "head slap." The colleges had had such a rule since 1931.

Another rule "keyed to safety," the NFL said, was the moving of the goalposts to the end line in 1974 — something the colleges did in 1927. But when they got around to it in 1974, the pros didn't make a big deal "safety" claim, for that would have been admitting how long they had been *un*safe. They said it was because too many cheap field goals were ruining the game.

Once you start trafficking in hypocrisy, it is difficult to break the habit. When the NFL put in the 1978 rule that restricts contact on receivers to one hit beyond the line of scrimmage (a noninjury factor in the first place), Rozelle did not make claims about it being a bold strike for safety. He said they were doing it to "put some offense" back in the game. Scoring averages were down; passing yardage was down. The rule, of course, did nothing to outlaw the kind of hit Tatum made on Stingley.

As for the bad luck that was putting one battered, crippled quarterback after another in casts and traction, Rozelle said that the new liberalized blocking rules might help, but that the NFL "didn't feel there was anything that could be done without changing the basic character of the game."

The irony of what happened next chills me. I was halfway through reading still another exhaustive defense of the status quo, this one a vindication of the college rules-making body by Dave Nelson of the NCAA, when I looked up to see on television the Minnesota quarterback, attempting to pass, being manhandled by a Los Angeles player. The Los Angeles player was not content just to tackle the quarterback, almost a hundred pounds lighter and otherwise helpless in his grasp. He swung the quarterback around and, a good five yards down field, executed an emphatic earthshaking body slam. It was a specimen of viciousness.

The quarterback, Tommy Kramer, did not get up. As he lay there, the camera zoomed in to pick up the grotesque twitching of his limbs. He appeared to be having what medical men call a clonic convulsion. My wife, watching in horror (I assume along with millions of other sickened patrons, the pro game's popularity being what it is), uttered a kind of stricken feline groan. "They've killed him," she said flatly.

A stretcher was hurried out and Kramer was wheeled to a waiting ambulance, oblivious to the cheers of the Minnesota crowd. He was not moving. The sportscasters, Pat Summeral and Tom Brookshire, themselves former players, were properly subdued. The telecast went off the air, Kramer's fate unknown.

It was not until the next day that we were assured he would be all right, that there was no paralysis, that the injury was "only" a concussion. There were no recriminations. No rule had been broken on the play. No penalty was called. Business as usual.

Brutal play is not an exclusive diversion of the pros, of course. College and high school players have their moments, too, albeit with less frequency and with considerably less flair. It would not be cynical to say, however, that the brutality trade flourishes in direct proportion to the amount of "pressure" on the participants — i.e., the finances riding on the game, budgets, payrolls, etc.

The vast majority of players at all levels are law-abiding. So, I am convinced, are coaches. To be otherwise is to be counter-productive. As Dave Nelson reasonably asserts: "Players do not *want* to be injured. Coaches do not *want* players to be injured. [Certainly not their own.] Neither do administrators. It costs them money, team efficiency, maybe even legal suits."

Furthermore, says Bear Bryant, that practical man, "A fifteen-yard penalty will get you beat in a close game."

But those are merely the voices of reason and practicality. When a war ethic — what one team doctor calls "the coaches' concept of punishment" — is allowed to grow in football, reason doesn't always get the vote. Nelson: "The basic problem today is not to see if you can win within the rules, but to see how much you can get away with to help win."

The war ethic translates to the field as license to "do your thing," and reaches its refinement at the pro level. At the pro level, the aberrations have become, in the words of an interested trial lawyer, "insane — a coliseum in every city."

Insane?

Here is John ("Deac") Sanders, a young pro safetyman for the Eagles, describing for the *Philadelphia News* the "techniques" he learned watching the artists in the defensive backfields of the NFL: "First there's the George Atkinson Special. That's where you stiffen the forearm and cock it back and hit the guy upside the head. Atkinson got through the bar [face mask] and broke Russ Francis' nose that way, and gave Lynn Swann a brain concussion. Then there's the spear, where the guy's ready to go down and you come in and nail him with your helmet. Another one is where the guy's tackled but he's still moving and you want to polish it off. That's when some guys throw the forearm to the throat. . . ."

A coliseum in every city?

Here is the Eagles' linebacker Frank LeMaster explaining why he doesn't want to see "any more rules" messing up the Sunday forum: "Football is a brutal game, a vicious game. That's the way you're taught. You're taught to strip the ball from a guy and if that includes his head that's the nature of the game. The Stingley thing upsets me. Some day it may happen to me. But that's why you get paid good money. We're risking our lives, our careers. You see things like this and you realize people shouldn't be complaining about our salaries."

The process by which permissible legal aggression becomes mayhem is not difficult to trace. Sometimes it can be followed simply by opening your ears to the young men who play the game. Consistent in most of their testimony is the influence of "coaching" on the way they conduct themselves. It is, in their words, a learning process.

College player Dean Payne, a linebacker at Northwestern: "All the coaches stress gang tackling. You're taught to get to the ball — and once you're there, you're not supposed to stare at it. You're supposed to pile on. It becomes a really violent state of mind — you really get fired up and motivated to get someone. Everyone accepts things like late hits as part of the game. There is no being nice — the nice guys get hurt."

The college player advances into the pros, where his aggression is marketable and becomes a springboard to affluence. The pro is Jean Fugett, a tight end for the Washington Redskins. Fugett, talking to Charley McKenna of the *Milwaukee Sentinel*:

"I never understood the real violence of the game until I played pro ball. [At Amherst] I had to work very hard to be aggressive. I had to think stuff like, 'This guy raped my mother' to get psyched and mad at the guy opposite. Intimidation is the biggest part of the game. You can't let anyone get away with anything because everything you do is on film. If you let yourself be intimidated, the team you play next will see it and may try the same things. . . .

"On the street a rational person wouldn't conduct himself this way. He might just walk away and most people would consider him the better man for it. But in football you're forced into it. It's unfortunate, but it's the nature of the game."

Fugett said that when he was with Dallas he tried to avoid brute force, to make blocks with finesse. He said his style did not sit well with end coach Mike Ditka, a former All-Pro.

"Ditka was always saying I wasn't aggressive enough. Do you want to know how Ditka taught us how to block in Dallas? He told us to fire out and hit [the opponent] in the chest with our helmets, then bring both arms up like this and hit with both fists in the [groin]. Now I just couldn't do that, and I didn't. But if a guy does that to me, it's different. . . . This is one job where you can come to work every day and really take out your frustrations."

Ultimately, when he gets really good at it, the pro player becomes the consummate aggressor. He becomes Doug Plank, free safety of the Bears. Plank admits he is "not very well liked around the league," but as an example of a player "who plays within the rules . . . the way I'm taught to play," he thinks he is only doing his job. A good soldier. Not everybody agrees with this evaluation.

As a rookie, Plank knocked himself out — literally — making punishing tackles. His "reputation got to be a problem," he said, and his coaches eventually agreed to take him off some of the specialty teams because opposing players were "screaming wild" over his hard-hitting ways. "The coaches joked about it," he said. " 'Yeah, if we put you out there, they'll stick all eleven guys on you.' "

An ex-roommate describes the off-field Plank as the "complete opposite" of the character he assumes on the field. Plank is "not a maniac," says the ex-roommate. Plank's wife says, "You have to know him." Plank credits the system for allowing him to achieve his notoriety.

"Opposing players complain about my [borderline late] hits. They complain to me. I don't really feel I'm at fault if there's no penalty called. In other words, if I can go out there and possibly force a fumble even if it is very very close to the whistle, or make players on the offense aware that I'm always around the football or around them . . ."

Control of the game, therefore, "is really in the hands of the officials," says Plank, but "it's difficult for an official to see what all twenty-two players are doing every play. If somebody wants to get away with a dirty play, he can do it. If you did it every single play, you'd eventually get caught, but when there's tackles being made and there's a pile of people, there's certain things that can be done.

"[One] year there was a wide receiver who'd been trying to come down on me all day, throwing around my legs. It was difficult to give him a good shot because he was always down on the ground. On a kickoff return, I realized that once I had my man blocked, I was pretty much free to do whatever I wanted . . . so I found out where the wide receiver was [and] came running up behind him. He was the contain man. He didn't see me coming. Just as he was turning inside to face the ballcarrier — it was completely legal — I blindsided him and knocked him on the ground. He got up and said, 'Before the game's over I'm going to knock out one of your knees.' What can you say to that? I ran over to our bench and made sure I kept my eyes on him the rest of the game.

"What I did to the wide receiver is what the coaches might even call second effort. He was the second guy I took out on that play. The coaches like to see that.

"One year — 1975 — we played [the Lions] up in Detroit. Besides beating us on the scoreboard, they embarrassed us; they completely manhandled us. The second game was at Soldiers Field in Chicago. That game was filled with penalties. It was almost out of hand. Penalties meant almost nothing to the players. There was swinging across the line, cussing, out-and-out fighting. The rules were stretched, calling personal fouls only on the very extreme fights. Brawls between players were just broken up. The only people fined or thrown out of the game were the ones who were outright laying on the AstroTurf pounding each other."

The real issue at the heart of such misbehavior is sportsmanship. Bad sportsmanship is always shameful. In a sport where physical damage can result, it is intolerable. Football becomes what it does. When questionable — even venal — acts are excused long enough, they blend into the whole and become acceptable within the whole. A way of life. Men who tolerate them — coaches, players, administrators — when called to account are often dumbfounded by the charge — they had gotten "used to it." They say, "That's football."

You cannot peal away the acts of unsportsmanlike conduct like leaves on an artichoke, hoping to find a pure heart. Bad sportsmanship is a malignancy, spreading from within. Whether it is manifest in a gesture or a blow, it amounts to "getting away" with something and "taking advantage" — what one college coach calls "making up your mind to be uglier in order to win."

In that posture, you don't just put the guy on the ground, you shove him around. Rough him up. Intimidate him. Verbally abuse him. Before the rules-makers finally woke up, it was common practice in the NFL to see a defensive player take a free shot at an offensive lineman who missed the count and moved prematurely. However slight the move, it "legally" drew the defensive player offside, and gave him carte blanche to rip the unsuspecting lineman. Put him on his pants. Embarrass him.

Such studied disregard for the other fellow is only a half step away from the blatant acts of malice that everyone deplores. It also helps create an atmosphere that becomes so negatively charged that a player can remark, "If I ever get a chance, I'm gonna end his [Bear Walter Payton's] career," and not be called on it.

The logical place to dump the blame for such madness is, of course, on coaches. Players blame coaches. Administrators blame coaches. Coaches blame coaches. It is a coaches' game. Coaches say so. Nobody else really understands it. So, why not?

Team doctors blame coaches. Doctor Donald Cooper, the team physician at Oklahoma State, is a veteran coach-critic. "The whole concept of coaching today is 'punish the opposition. Punish 'em.' That's what they all talk about. A kid becomes a good college player and the pros want to know, 'Will he run through a brick wall?' Sportscasters talk about playing with 'complete abandon,' doing things with no regard for what might happen. The coach says, 'Wipe out the quarterback.' The crowd yells, 'Defense! Defense!' Everybody goes bananas. Then when they wind up with injured players all over the field they say, 'Too bad.'"

Players-turned-novelists blame coaches. Peter Gent, ex–Dallas Cowboy and author of *North Dallas Forty*, sees it in "their icy eyes." Gent says what you see on television may look like an art form, but at ground level it's violence, "the sound of helmet hitting helmet." He says most people don't see this "horrible debacle," but that the coaches do. A pro coach, says Gent, "can't compete with other pro coaches if [he's] moral about injuries. You survive by tuning out."

Gent says he never saw a happy NFL head coach. They were all too busy being grim reapers. "Coaches see helmets and shoulder pads," says Gent. "The bodies are just stuffing. And they can fill in more stuffing whenever they need it."

Even cartoon characters blame coaches. In a debate moderated by Tank McNamara, the facsimile ex-pro who leaps on anything that moves (a dropped cabbage, a tumbling doughnut) on the chance it might be a fumbled football, a hot-eyed cartoon coach yells at a sports doctor, "It's a game for *men*, Ace, not for girls."

The sports doctor suggests that "tackling and blocking with

the helmet must be banned." The coach responds: "Best way to stop a man is to hit him with that helmet. Second best, actually. Best way is with a .38, but they'd penalize you for sure. . . ."

In the next panel, the coach says, "Sure, football is a violent game, but putting on those pads and going out there knowing you're going to get hit builds men with the character this country needs." And in the last, he adds, "A little paralysis seems like a small price to pay for America's future."

The characterization is extreme.

Or is it?

Pettis Norman played twelve years as a tight end for the Cowboys and the San Diego Chargers. A bad knee forced him out of football and into the fast-food business after the 1973 season. The knee is now mostly steel and plastic. Norman is mostly regrets. Norman told Jack Murphy of the *San Diego Union* that pro football was "scary" to him now, that he would not want to play it, that too low a premium had been placed "on a man's flesh and blood."

"The violence in football the last three or four years is especially bad, and I know why," said Norman. "It's taught by the coaches. The players don't protest because all they see is the money and the glamour. Later, they'll learn what it will cost them in pain."

It is a rule of thumb that pro players do not complain about coaches until they can do so in retrospect, until they are ex-players. Two ex-players sat for an interview in Oregon — Bobby Grim, an ex–wide receiver (Giants, Vikings), and Bill Enyart, an ex-fullback (Raiders, Bills). They agreed that coaches teaching "devious means" are a problem. Said Enyart, there "tends to be a lot of dirtiness in the game — late hits, kneeing, jabbing, grabbing." Said Grim: "It's up to the coaches to stop it."

Can coaches stop it? Yes, all else being equal. Almost with a wave of the hand coaches could put a stop to brutal play — provided it was a unanimous wave. They do not have to teach the tactics that lead to it. They do not have to condone it. They can fire players who deviate, and lobby for action against coaches who persist. So in that sense, coaches are correctly blamed for their dereliction.

But coaches are not monsters, and all else is not equal.

As a group, coaches are probably more honorable than most. "Going by the rules" is not a luxury they can adjust on their tax returns. Breaking rules can get them beat, or fired. Or both. The great majority think of their calling as a high one, entrusted as they are in the development of young men.

The majority, too, are fair and sportsmanlike and would undoubtedly subscribe to the overview of the Cleveland Browns' coach, Forrest Gregg. Gregg played for Lombardi. He says: "You play aggressively . . . but within the rules. I want opponents [of the Browns] to know . . . they're in for a . . . physical game. That doesn't mean to go out and try to hurt people. I was fortunate to have a long career in football. I don't want to see anyone's ended prematurely."

But coaches at every level are under intense pressure to win. Their margin for error is painfully thin. "Winning is the only thing" puts a terrible strain on sportsmanship when for every winner there has to be a loser (an uncompromising equation lost on most fans and alumni), and it is a dreadful philosophy to boot. But it is the accepted battle cry of coaches. Thus, they become ever alert for a leg up. For the "competitive edge." For what is known in the business as the "fair advantage."

That pressure is exacerbated at the pro level by an even crueler pressure on the players, one that forever alters the coach–player relationship. The process should be familiar to the most casual follower of the pro game. Through a medieval and monopolistic ritual known as "the player draft," the players are graded and divided up like crates of eggs, garlanded with greenbacks and shipped into the pro camps for their big chance. If they make it, they go into the finishing stages of their dehumanization.

They discover that pro careers *aren't* long. That only a handful last more than ten years. That from day one it is dog eat dog.

They discover that it is nerve-wracking to live on the edge of a precipice, never sure if the next $100,000 check will be their last. (That is not meant to be funny. An abrupt comedown from a glamorous six-figure life-style to a job selling tennis shoes can be very traumatic for a thirty-one-year-old has-been.)

Perhaps most traumatically, they discover that the coach is no longer their father-protector, seeing to their comfort, helping them pass biology. If they don't fit into his plans, they are gone. If they outlive their usefulness, they are traded or "released" (a professional euphemism for fired). If they are permanently damaged — a slipped disc, a chronic sick knee — they're on the next plane out.

The coach *has* to have "icy eyes" to exist in such a system. He *has* to be immune. He is left to handle alone a grim, distasteful duty: when it is time to shove the player over the edge, he's the one to do it. If he hesitates, he is liable to go himself. He must not let stupid empathy stand in the way of building a juggernaut.

Not long ago I flew cross-country with Jim Lynch, the former Notre Dame and Kansas City linebacker. It was a chance meeting. I had not seen Lynch in years, since the "longest game" with Miami in the 1972 playoffs. But I had known him since college — a bright, handsome young man with a lantern jaw and an easy, asymmetrical grin that always made you think he was glad to have you drop into his conversation.

Because he had been one of John Ray's favorites, and because Ray, the Notre Dame line coach under Ara Parseghian, was one of mine, I had made it a point to get to know Lynch. Like most ex–Notre Dame footballers, he is articulate and candid. As Ray used to say, Notre Dame breeds well.

Lynch gave me his card. There was a "vice president" under the engraved name, although he had retired from football only the year before. I recalled that he had graduated on schedule in 1967, with a bachelor of arts in sociology. It is a dismal reality of pro football that the majority of its players never got their degrees. Or, for that matter, a decent education. That when they go over the precipice into the nine-to-five world, they are often ill-prepared.

We discussed Lynch's Notre Dame days; he obviously relished the recollections. Coach Ray had been an inspiring figure: a mountain of a man who never aged — never grayed, never wrinkled, never ran down — and had a hoarse bellowing voice that seemed always on the verge of a power failure. Lynch heard it often. Ray's teaching approach was frontal. His one failing, Ray said himself, was that he probably liked his players too much. Lynch remembered the throaty tongue-lashings as though they were papal blessings.

We moved on in our discussion, into less amiable territory. Lynch had lasted ten years in the pros, all with the Chiefs. I had been curious to know about amphetamine use among pro players, and he said, yes, by all means they were used, but he didn't think unanimously and he didn't know the dosages. He said he could understand players using pep pills, however. They helped the bruised and battered get "up" even when the flesh was unwilling. "You don't ever think about not playing," he said. "If you're hurt, and you sit down, you're an outcast. You might as well be in Siberia."

Yet he said he was grateful for his pro experience. That it had been profitable, that he had met "some fine people," in and out of the game. "But it was nothing like Notre Dame. The pressure to win was there, too, but it wasn't the same. There was more fun in it. More things to enjoy. The game itself was more fun. The pro game is a business. A very cold business. You can't blame the coaches for that."

When a business ethic takes over a sport, the sport adapts. It is not the other way around. Coaches do not own football teams. A few own *pieces* of teams, but the great majority are as helpless in the system as their players. Blaming coaches and players alone for the jungle warfare in professional football is not enough. When it comes time to cut the cake and pass around the indictment, there is reason to believe that our sights should be higher, toward those who profit most by the game.

Randy Vataha, the wide receiver of the Patriots, is not far wrong when he says that owners "are afraid of taking the fighting out of hockey, and they're afraid of taking the violence out of pro football" — both for the same reason: "It's a business, and when you're in business your priorities aren't always what they should be." Jon Morris, after fifteen years in the game, concluded that as "long as attendance and TV revenue keep the money pouring in, owners will say, 'Why make changes? If players get hurt, so what? We'll get somebody else to play.'" Morris says in such a vacuum of humanity he's amazed there haven't been more Darryl Stingleys.

The owners of professional football have massive investments to protect. Theirs is also a high-pressure world — the world of finance. They are mostly practical men, not disposed to liberal policies. When players' salaries go up, they complain like hell—and pass the cost on to the fans by raising ticket prices. They are used to being listened to, and catered to. In return for rewarding an area with their team's presence, they get special rental deals, tax write-offs and multimillion-dollar subsidies in the form of municipal stadiums. It is a system that spoils them rotten.

Some are notorious money-grubbers. One pro owner's initial investment in his club was less than ten thousand dollars. He now controls millions, and bullies the metropolitan area he is in, trying to get it to build him a new stadium. The old one was built and sustained for the colleges and high schools in the area. The pros are interlopers. They contributed nothing. The pros don't want to contribute anything to the new stadium, either. They want the taxpayers to build it for them.

Enlightenment in areas other than profit and loss comes slowly to the custodians of the National Football League. They are the last to change rules for the safety of their players. They resist change that might project a failing image, or a concession. They have been shamefully negligent in their handling of the drug problem, which may be one of the more serious charges against the game. (Blizzards of press releases do not explain it, a Los Angeles editorialist recently said. "They are no more than legal snow jobs.")

Their disregard of their own survey (by the Stanford Research Institute) on the relative peril of artificial turf is scandalous. Ed Garvey, executive secretary of the NFL Players Association, quoted one owner: "If we told them to play on blacktop, the players would, because it's our game." Garvey said he knew of a coach who had nine of his players injured the first time they played on artificial turf. "You know what he said? He said, 'Even if they played on top of marshamllows, players would get hurt.' "

Transferred to the field, the conservative business ethic of a corporate leadership combines with the desperate war ethic of coaches and players to produce a bastard offspring: a climate of permissiveness that results in the brutal transactions in dementia that are ruining football. Once a player performs a brutal act without being condemned for it, he will surely do it again. Soon he might even get a taste for it. He will surely get a reputation for it, one that is marketable.

George Atkinson, Freddie ("The Hammer") Williamson, and Conrad Dobler are three of the more recent examples of players who have profited by notoriety. Another who has been working on it, mainly with his mouth, is Dallas linebacker Thomas Henderson. Jack Faulkner, a coach and scout for the Los Angeles Rams, said he watched the films of the 1978 Dallas–Rams game six times. He said every time he saw Henderson shaking his fist over the fallen, bloodied Rams quarterback, Pat Haden, "I wanted to put my fist through the projector."

Notorious players are not drummed out of the business. More often than not, they wind up on the covers of magazines. "We glamorize hoodlums," says Darryl Royal. "The guys who foul and hold. The worst examples of sportsmanship become our heroes. The way Conrad Dobler plays is nothing to emulate."

In a glowing reminiscence for the *San Francisco Chronicle*, Don Paul, once called "the dirtiest player in NFL history" and "the prototype of today's dirty players," told of putting a hit on the Bears' Jim Keane that "ripped his mouth open. It took 14 stitches to mend the wound." Read the story, however, and you get the impression Paul was a folk hero.

It is not surprising, therefore, that the businessman–football player begins to see life quite differently from the average working stiff. He begins to see brutal play as a kind of specialty item demanded of him. Dennis Franks, captain of the Eagles' special teams, says writers should not criticize pro football players for being brutal because the writers don't have to lie in the hospital. He says players — presumably even those who lie in hospitals — don't ask for change. He says he "loves to hit people . . . I don't like to take it, I love to give it out."

Franks believes "a lot of fans come out to the games to see violence. . . .You take violence out of the game, you'll lose a lot of fans. They can go to a baseball game if they don't want to see violence. I go for three innings, then I can't stand it and I'm out."

Eventually, it is not just their actions but their words that mark these men. Pro players say things that, in almost any other context, would sound subhuman. Not even boxers say some of the things pro football players say, with or without impunity.

Pittsburgh's Mean Joe Greene, a mild-mannered sort of fellow off the field, did not care for some "calls" made against him in a game with the Colts three years ago. Speaking of the officials, Mean Joe said: "Given half the chance I'll punch one of them out, and it'd give me a whole lot of satisfaction." He said that if they got in his way he'd "cleat 'em in the spine. I won't go around them."

Before the 1979 Super Bowl game in Miami, nasty intimidating remarks tumbled from the lips of the contestants like jellybeans out of an Easter basket. Cowboy Henderson bad-mouthed Pittsburgh's Randy Grossman. Cowboy Cliff Harris warned Pittsburgh's Swann that he was in for some bad trouble. "I want to make him wonder if it's worth all that pain just to catch a football," said Harris.

Charlie Watters said the Cowboys would "have to mess up" Pittsburgh's quarterback Terry Bradshaw. He said Randy White would have to "smack him in the face when he throws. That'll mess him up." It was Watters who once told a national television audience, "If you're a pro, if it takes being a little brutal or a little overaggressive to get your job done and you make sure you get your paycheck the next week because you went for a guy's throat, that's what you're thinking about. That's what your job is."

How do the leaders of professional football excuse such behavior? Commissioner Rozelle, who has had to fine Greene for both his intemperate remarks and his on-field deportment, says he really likes Greene and has "mixed feelings" about his behavior. It was Rozelle who also said, "Injuries seldom involve a so-called 'illegal act.' " Dallas's general manager Tex Schramm says, "It's a rough game."

Schramm was interviewed by the *Boston Globe* after the Stingley tragedy. At the time, he was chairman of the NFL competition committee, a key man in the rules-making body. What, he was asked, does that injury to Stingley hold for the NFL?

"No one liked the assassination of President Kennedy, but the world had to go on," the *Globe* quoted Schramm.

What about violence in the NFL? he was asked.

"[Violence] is related to things like murders on TV, and guns," he said.

What about linemen swathing their forearms and hands in "bandages" to deliver blows?

"A definite misconception," said Schramm. "The wrapping is there as a protection, not as a weapon."

What about hard helmets? What about spearing?

"Spearing is your word, not mine. No one teaches spearing."

Finally, Schramm was asked about the danger of artificial turf.

The players, said Schramm, preferred artificial turf to dirt.

It is small wonder that college people tend to blame the pros for the spread of violence in their own game. They think it a virulent disease, highly contagious. They are probably self-serving in this — but not far wrong. Pete Williams, a former Navy halfback and now the top referee in the Southeastern Conference, says he is appalled by what he sees passing for sportsmanship in the NFL. Says Williams:

"Everybody says football is a violent game. It wasn't meant to be. It was meant to be a game of skill and speed and physical prowess. It has *become* a violent game. A game of intimidation. I watch the pros and it makes me sick. A guy is going down, a 260-pounder hits him anyway. Receivers are clobbered to 'make 'em think.' The Hayhook, The Hammer, The Clothesline — those things were coined by the pros, and they get copied."

Stanford coach Bill Walsh calls these the lethal "theatrics of the game," designed to diminish and to injure. Fifteen or twenty years ago, said Walsh, "you could name one or two dirty players on a team. Now there's continuous talking, insults, and before you know it, a clothesline from behind. Or a tackle on a player who is helpless, or when he doesn't expect to be hit without the ball."

In the Southwest Conference, Texas coach Fred Akers cites as one of the perversions of helmet use a practice known as "ear-holing," where a player aims the top of his helmet at another player's ear, with predictable results.

The "rake block" is an attention-getting device in which the blocker rams the chest of his opponent and comes up violently, raking his face mask into the opposing players' chin. The rake block is popular on the West Coast.

"Clubbing" takes on a variety of interesting forms, including the forearm against the neck, which has been outlawed by both the colleges and the pros. Vestiges of it are still around. ("People forget," says pro tackle Steve Preece, "you can put a forearm inside a face mask.") When I asked Art McNally of the NFL about clubbing he said it had been "cracked down on," but Dallas coach Tom Landry said it was still happening. Landry's assistant, Ermal Allen, said if McNally's officials didn't stop it, "someday some ballcarrier or receiver is going to lose his life."

It is stretching the indictment to blame all the aberrations of football on the misconduct of the pros, of course, but one sobering analysis is clear: the cancer spreads. Gene Calhoun, a Big Ten referee and former coach, sees the "influences" filtering down rapidly.

"We had to start calling penalties against guys showing up other guys, causing bad feelings. We had to stop the spiking and the end zone dances. The head slap was never used in the colleges that I can recall, but the pros did it and we had guys doing it and had to send out a bulletin to get it stopped. You allow a guy to do that and what happens? On the next play you're having to call something worse — a personal foul, a late hit.

"But don't think it stops at the college level. It filters all the way down. There's a high school coach in our area [Wisconsin] who has a 'Hit of the Week.' He isolates on the most vicious hit he can find in his game films. The hitter gets an award."

A high school coach named Herman Boone, at T. C. Williams High in Washington, D.C., told the *Post* that late hits and intimidating tackles and the "bull" of showing up the other guy with talk and finger-pointing were directly traceable to the "ignorant box. The kids watch the pros on TV and try to emulate everything they see, good and bad. But that's not football, that's war. It's like gladiators in the arena." Boone said he lost a game because one of his players sacked a quarterback on a third-down play and stood over him, "running his mouth. The official threw a flag — fifteen yards. They got the first down, and went on to score, and we lost."

A high school coach in Pleasant Valley, Pennsylvania, said the unsportsmanlike conduct and the dangerous blocking and tackling techniques he saw in increasing numbers were driving him toward an early retirement. "We're out there five days a week trying to teach high school kids to be good sports," said Gary Bruch, "working on the right ways to tackle and block. Then they go home and watch television, and what do they see? Pro players dancing in the end zone and spiking the ball to humiliate opponents. Spearing, taking cheap shots."

The executive vice president of the Pop Warner League, the largest of the little-league football programs, said that his game is "in the fourth quarter, possibly facing sudden death," because of such influences. "The great problem today," said David G. Tomlin, "lies in kids coming into football and having to be deprogrammed by coaches who try to undo the kid's perceived correct methods à la his favorite football TV hero."

Apparently the little-league coaches also need deprogramming.

Several weeks after I had completed the series on brutality for *Sports Illustrated*, I received a letter from a woman who identified herself as a "Little League Mom" in Santa Ana, California. Enclosed was a copy of an instructions list given her eight-year-old boy for participation on a team called the "Packers," evidently a miniature offshoot of the Green Bay arm of the family. Little League Mom said, "This may give you some idea as to why football has gotten so brutal."

Mimeographed under the title, "Rules for a Successful Packer Back to Live By," the following stirring advice was given her son:

Become an all-out runner: dig for more yards!

Punish the tackler! Put fear in his eyes! Bruise his body! Break his spirit! Bust his butt! Make him pay a price for tackling you! Dig for more yards!

Become a competitor! A competitor never quits. Be hostile! Be angry! Be violent! Be mean! Be aggressive! Be physical! Remember always — loosing [sic] is nothing! Winning is everything!

I am only guessing, but I doubt the coach of this particular branch of the Packers ever played pro football. I do not doubt that he has been influenced by it.

Not long after that, the magazine received, and ran among a heavy complement of Letters to the Editor on the subject, a somewhat mind-expanding letter from a high school player named David Deaton, living in Chocktaw, Oklahoma.

Young Deaton described himself as a sophomore linebacker who had played for six years, and although he had "suffered no serious injuries on the field . . . I've seen and given out a few." He said it was his job to protect the quarterback, and he would do it any way he could. "If that means I've got to crab block him or throw a forearm to his windpipe, I'm going to do just that. If I get a chance to tackle a fleet back, I'm going to put my face mask in his numbers so hard that I hope he never gets up. Someday I hope to teach the way I play. Stick him before he sticks you."

Deaton's prose style caught the eye of the *Oklahoma City Times*. The *Times* sent a staffer named David Ley to see Deaton. Deaton told him the rules changes I had recommended — actually a distillation of suggestions from coaches, doctors, administraters, et al., that I will cover later — were "dumb." That football is "just right like it is."

Deaton told the *Times* writer, "Even if I broke my neck, I'd love football. If a guy breaks his neck, it's either his own fault or some freak accident. . . . Like that guy Stingley who got hurt so bad . . . I don't think the guy who hit him meant to hurt him. . . . I like to hit people just like that, but I don't mean to hurt them."

He said he would coach kids to play the way he does, that his methods "weren't violent, just part of football." He said, "If I'm pass blocking and a guy on defense has ahold of my shirt, I'm going to pop him in the throat. It's a way of making things even. Conrad Dobler is written up to be the dirtiest player in pro football. I don't think he's dirty. I bet if you asked the linemen who play against him they'd say he's just a great blocker. You might say he's my idol."

This kind of reflection on their own grisly influence is not lost on all the players of the professional game. Not by any means. The Steelers' Jack Lambert, a notably hard-hitting linebacker, says he gets letters from kids at the stadium in Pittsburgh, "letters that say, 'I hit some kid the other day and broke his arm, and when I did I thought of you.'" Lambert is not flattered by the imitation. He says, "It's very disheartening."

Mike Barnes of Baltimore sees the pro influence as a horror unfolding. He says he wonders about "that ten-year-old watching TV, patterning himself after Lyle Blackwood. . . . That's frightening, because I wouldn't want to meet the guy who can hit better than Lyle Blackwood. He would not be putting these guys in the hospital the way Lyle does, he'd be putting 'em in the morgue, on a cold slab of concrete."

Wally Chambers, a former Bears' defensive lineman, says "it starts from the peewee leagues and crazy coaches, and people trying to prove something, and it gets worse." Chambers says his body will be bothering him the rest of his life, that he traded his health for ten years of football. He says, "If I had known the

NFL the way it is, I never would have played. If I ever have a son, he'll never play football."

In discussing his own influential notoriety, Doug Plank of the Bears blamed the permissiveness of play that he found in the pros.

"The professional game is less controlled," said Plank. "I don't think I could have gotten away with the kind of hits I make now in college. The thing that really shocked me [in the NFL] was the way players talk to officials. The language. That just wasn't tolerated in college football. Officials were held in much higher respect. I think that would be one good thing to reinstate back into the game: respect for officials."

But if rules are not enforced, if malicious mischief becomes a way of life that filters down, if respect for the game and for one's opponent does not endure past the first blow at the scrimmage line, what good is a little more respect for officials? About as much good, it would seem, as the directive Commissioner Rozelle sent out a couple years ago saying that playing-field viciousness and misconduct "do not belong in professional football" and would result in "disciplinary action." The "disciplinary action" meted out since then has reddened a few wrists and put a small dent in few pocketbooks, but has done little to stem the brute tide.

Nor, for that matter, have the custodians of the game done much to allay the fear that when facing this issue, in whatever form it takes, they will opt for the expedient answer every time. And then send out a press release lauding their efforts. Or one that condemns the poor fool who tried to make them look bad.

In 1976, a forty-two-year-old professor of psychiatry at the University of California at San Diego wrote a book about his experience as an unpaid locker-room analyst for the San Diego

Chargers. In *The Nightmare Season*, Dr. Arnold Mandell detailed the shocking use of amphetamines by professional football players desperate to get an edge in the battle for dominance and dollars.

The season was 1973; for a while, the nightmare was mainly Dr. Mandell's. His attempts to alert the National Football League to this monstrous situation, and to wean the players under his care from dangerous street "speed" by giving them prescription drugs, backfired. In April 1974, the NFL made (in Mandell's words) "sacrificial lambs" of the Chargers. The league announced that it had fined and placed on probation the owner of the team (Eugene V. Klein), its general manager and coach (Harland Svare), and eight players, and had banned Mandell from further contact with players.

No other NFL team has been so disciplined since, no other "drug abuse" uncovered, despite a common knowledge that amphetamines are a harsh reality in pro football.

Unfortunately for the NFL, however, Mandell did not then shut up. Writing in *Psychology Today* in 1975, he said a "drug agony rages, silently as a plague, through the body of professional football," and that "a clumsy ham-handed press conference at the end of the season would not solve a problem" that is an occupational disease in pro football "as surely as silocosis is in mining."

With his book due in the fall of 1976, Mandell says, he was warned by Svare that " 'they,' he didn't say who 'they' were, would sue me or try to get my license."

The book came out.

And in September 1977, the *Los Angeles Times* reported that Mandell said "the football industry persuaded the state of California" to take action against him for prescribing drugs illegally for unmedicinal purposes. After a fifteen-day hearing that included the appearance of Dr. Jonas Salk as a character witness for the defendant, Mandell was found guilty of "overprescribing" drugs by an administrative officer. He received a five-year probation but did not lose his license. His right to prescribe drugs was, however, suspended. An appeal is still pending.

The decision drew a remarkable medical rally around Mandell. Psychiatrists and physicians across the country launched "Concerned Health Professionals for Mandell": a committee to fund his defense and overturn the ruling. The *Clinical Psychiatry News* called the court action "retribution for his fight against drug abuse in professional football."

In a letter to the *Times*, Dr. Emery Zimmerman, a physician and narcotics expert at UCLA, said the NFL's "attempt to divert attention by promoting a courtroom dissection of Mandell destroys my confidence in their ability to deal with this difficult problem. The issue may be too important to be left in their hands. If drugs increase gate receipts, then the owners, as indirect pushers, are curiously close to the position they have placed Mandell. . . . I have no further interest to watch drug-crazed men bloody each other on Sunday afternoon."

Despite his probation, Mandell continued his crusade. "I haven't done what I set out to do," he said, "which is to get amphetamines out of football." He said amphetamines were "the single factor that causes unnecessary violence in pro football today" — not in low doses for fatigue, or as appetite depressants, "but enormous doses, as high as 150 milligrams. Higher than ever.

"People ask Pete Rozelle why so many quarterbacks went down last season from late and nasty hits. The answer can be found in the nearest pillbox. I'd be interested to see what would happen to the incidence of orthopedic surgery in the NFL if amphetamines were banned and everybody had to take a urine test before games."

The normal "diet" pill or capsule — Benzedrine, Dexedrine, Eskatrol — contains five to fifteen milligrams of amphetamine. The prolonged "high" from one is familiar not only to dieters but to long-haul truckers and students on preexamination study binges. Imagine, said Dr. Mandell, the effect of gulping thirty of those pills at one time.

"The result is a pre-psychotic paranoid rage state. A five-hour temper tantrum that produces the late hits, the fights, the unconscionable assaults on quarterbacks that are ruining pro football. They're at war out there, and the coaches, even if they're not aware [of the drug potential], are the generals. Coaches know the game is ideally played in controlled anger. They hang up clippings, and talk vendettas — 'So-and-So says you're a pussy.' Players get half crazy anyway, and if 60 percent of them have their heads filled with amphetamines, the injury projection is enormous.

"For the player in this state the negotiation of rules becomes highly complicated, and easily broken if the referee isn't looking. That's when you get the elbows, the hands being stepped on, the knees in the face, the kicking."

Mandell's expertise is in biomedical and pharmacological psychiatry, with twenty-two years in research, eighteen thousand hours treating patients. He has written six books and more than two hundred and thirty articles in his field. He serves on the editorial board of eleven scientific journals, is past president of the Society of Biological Psychiatry, and has received several federal grants for his work, including $500,000 over a six-year period for a study of amphetamine effects on the brain.

In short, Mandell is no quack, nor is he the irresponsible drug dispenser the NFL sought to have him appear. A wiry

5-foot-6, fourteen-mile-a-day jogger with a Phi Beta Kappa key and a sunburst of curly hair, he has an easy manner that ingratiated him with the Chargers. They called him "Arnie" and entrusted to him their deepest secrets. He became a close friend of Coach Svare.

Mandell says it took him almost a year to "realize what was going on." What he now calls "The Sunday Syndrome."

"Ordinarily, football players are warm, loving, decent human beings. They aren't drug addicts. They have to convert themselves to attain a state of hair-trigger readiness. For a while, I thought it was pure physiology, a group of men who somehow had this capacity.

"They'd come in on Sunday morning, light-hearted, well-dressed, no signs. Gradually they'd begin to change. About eleven o'clock, the tension would start to rise. Some would get loud and boisterous, and become more obscene. Others would withdraw, staring. Some would pace in repetitive turns. Those are all signs, together with a wider-based gait, an added clumsiness.

"The second time I went through the tunnel to the field, an offensive tackle I knew pretty well — a bright guy, a nice guy — I accidentally hit his elbow. He *banged* me into the wall. Really unloaded on me. Later, he apologized. That year we played at Houston, one of the sweetest guys on the defensive teams — I'll never forget — was literally drooling. It was quarterback Dan Pastorini's first year with the Oilers. The guy said, 'A rookie quarterback! It's like letting me into a candy store!'

"Amphetamines in large doses produce a paranoid psychosis. That means the guy doing the damage actually thinks the other guy is out to get him. It's Good Guys versus Bad Guys. The quarterback, as the figurehead of the opposition, is the number-one Bad Guy. It's open season on him. I laugh when

NFL players talk about the dangers of synthetic turf and helmets, and all the while they're permitting amphetamine-crazed athletes to go on the field and assault their quarterbacks. You *expect* to see the kind of thing that happened to Bradshaw, when he got speared in the back. It almost gave him whiplash."

Analgesics as well as stimulants, amphetamines mask pain — pain Mandell says would act at least as a partial deterrent to such mayhem.

"An enraged person who does not feel pain is a dangerous human being," he says, "not only to others, but to himself. Early on I had one player who lost twenty pounds over a weekend. He was coughing up blood before games. I asked him how he could play in such a condition. He reached in his pocket and pulled out a handful of 'Black Beauties' — street speed you buy in Tijuana. The next day he played super.

"This is not called stupid in the pros, it's called heroic. Amphetamines are controlled substances and therefore subject to stringent FDA regulations regarding their prescription, and their use without proper prescription is absolutely prohibited by the NFL. But even Fran Tarkenton has defended their use. In small doses, they give you the kind of work-drug high you might want to increase efficiency. But in large doses that nervous alert becomes something else, a rage players feel they must have in a game that requires violent aggression at a precise point in time.

"Amphetamines are certainly psychologically, and possibly physically, addictive. The post-use depression is severe. Sexual appetite diminishes. Some suffer temporary impotence. But you can't tell a veteran player that there is another way. He says, 'Doc, I'm not about to go out there one-on-one against a guy who's grunting and drooling and coming at me with big dilated pupils unless I'm in the same condition.'

"Harland Svare told me amphetamines weren't new at all in the NFL. The Giants (for whom he played during 1955–1957) 'used 'em, like baseball players use 'em today — in moderate doses, when we were tired or hung over.' I can see that. I'm not a prohibitionist. But along about the mid-Sixties the doses began to increase, and kept going up. I won't tell you who said it, but one Charger told me, 'The difference between a star and superstar is sometimes the difference between a dose and a superdose.'

"The older the player, the more likely his dependence. He gets desperate. I was trying to get one guy to lower his dosage. He told me, 'It's easy for you to talk, Doc, but I'm making $65,000 a year. If I lose this job, tomorrow I'm a bartender. I've got three kids, a home . . .' "

Mandell's evaluations coincided with studies made by Dr. L. Alan Johnson of San Diego in his doctoral thesis. Doctor Johnson's research dates back to 1970 when he questioned ninety-three players from thirteen NFL teams and found fifty-six (60 percent) admitted using amphetamines, the majority getting them from trainers, doctors, or teammates, but some from the street ("Black Beauties," "Purple Turnarounds"). Johnson said he had abandoned the study when the NFL allegedly instructed players not to cooperate.

Mandell and Johnson found that only about 30 percent started using speed in college, and then only in small doses. The use progressed along definite positional lines. Of the fifty-six who admitted their use to Johnson, more than 75 percent were defensive players.

"Quarterbacks don't take them at all," says Mandell, who has examined "more than one hundred" players. "Amphetamines restrain adaptive capacity. You don't think or reason as well. A quarterback needs mini-second adaptiveness. Runningbacks and wide receivers might take only small doses for the same reason. But in the trenches, it doesn't matter. They don't need that kind of coordination. The big users are the defensive linemen."

Mandell said when he realized people were "buying tickets to have speed freaks try to kill each other," the "ugliness really upset me. I think if the average fan could spend a game on the sidelines, he wouldn't go anymore. Svare told me once, 'This isn't the game I grew up with on the Giants. This is a cruel, win-at-any-price thing, without fellowship.'

"I tried to alert the league in 1973. I proposed urine tests. They told me it was an invasion of privacy. The players wouldn't stand for it. But in California, when you sign your driver's license you agree to take a blood test if the police stop you. They could write the same in a player's contract — not to say it's unlawful, but against NFL rules. Why not? They do it in European soccer. They've got rules against amphetamines in the Olympics. You could do it with a simple saliva test. You wouldn't have to test everybody, just two or three on each team. A spot check. If a test is positive, you go further, maybe take the game from the team.

"The NFL won't get involved because it has to protect its image. I offered to conduct a workshop on amphetamines at an NFL team physicians meeting in 1973. I got an invitation. A week before I was to go, Harland called and said Rozelle didn't want me there. That it was 'bad public relations.' Congress was going to have hearings in 1974. They got quashed."

The drug subculture that exists in sports has been examined many times, with expert testimony from men like Dr. Robert Kerlan, medical director of the California Angels. The use of drugs is undeniable. Professional athletes, reflecting the society as a whole, are well tuned to the proposition they might need help to face extreme pain, or to mask it. Team physicians, employed by the club owners, stuff them with codeine, drug their knees with Zyolocain, shoot their inflamed joints with cortisone. Playing hurt, or in pain, is a badge of courage in football, at almost every level. At the pro level, it is a way of life — "peer pressure," says Jim Lynch. "And it's not always courageous. It can be stupid. It's done because you don't want to sit down and be an outcast."

Don Meredith once went into combat for the Dallas Cowboys with a ruptured abdominal muscle, a knee that needed surgery, an arm so sore he could barely throw, and a broken nose. The Cowboy trainer said it was the key to Dallas's first league championship: "The other players looked at Meredith and said, 'Well, if he can do that, we'll play our asses off.'"

Los Angeles Rams' safety Dave Elmendorf took shots in 1978 so he could play with a broken rib. Trainer Gary Tuthill said: "The doctor told him, 'Dave, that's a broken rib.' And he said, 'Pad the damn thing, I'm playing.'" Tuthill said players like Elmendorf and the Rams' Merlin Olsen were "admired and respected" for playing in great pain.

Miami running back Delvin Williams was the Dolphins' Most Valuable Player in 1978. He may have been their sorest as well. Williams played with an injured left knee, a twisted neck, bruised ribs, and a body so aching that he needed a cane to go to the bathroom on Monday morning. With all that, he carried the ball twenty-one times in a game against the Redskins.

The 1978 Washington Redskins cultivated a reputation for playing hurt. One Redskin played two days after being released from the hospital where he had been treated for a severe intestinal disorder. Another played an entire game with a hand ripped wide open. Another broke his leg on a play and gained five more yards before collapsing. And still another played all year with a broken wrist.

Statistics do not show, however, how many ex-pros can no longer tie their shoelaces, or curl their fingers around a golf club. Statistics do not show how many can't sleep without narcotics and have to call their wives for help to get out of bed. When Mike Bass of the Redskins quit at age thirty-one, he blamed his intense headaches on having been kneed in the head in a game against the New York Giants. Coach George Allen said Bass was "too young to retire. I know he's got two good years left." Bass retired anyway. "I'm not going to comment on George's reaction," he said. "That's just the way people in pro football think."

With their hurting, aging bodies so willing for sacrifice, it is ludicrous to contend that pro football players would draw the line for a minute at something so obviously "life"-giving as amphetamines. Ken Gray, an assistant Denver coach and former All-Pro guard, said that drug use during his playing days with St. Louis and Houston (1958–1970) was "as routine as smoking a cigarette." After I had recited Mandell's experiences in *Sports Illustrated*, and in response to his remarks, Fred Cox of the Vikings told Jim Klobuchar of the *Minneapolis Star* that "using uppers was so common on some teams that the physicians or trainers actually passed them out." Cox said he knew "some of the guys I played with . . . took speed regularly, because they'd mentioned it."

John Crittenden of the *Miami News* recalled a time at the Super Bowl a few years ago in Miami when he waited to talk with a defensive tackle on the losing team. "He had been handled rather badly that day, but he was a salty old cuss and I knew he'd have some interesting things to say.

"Thirty minutes after the game ended, he came to the locker. He'd been hiding in the showers, trying to avoid newspapermen. He didn't look much like the guy I had interviewed a few days before the game. Twitches crossed his face in waves. His hands jerked so badly that he spilled a half-dozen cigarettes on the wet locker-room floor. Finally he asked me to light a cigarette and hand it to him. 'It takes me a while to calm down after one of these things,' he said. There were no salty quotes that day. He never played another game."

Quite by accident, Crittenden came upon another NFL player "just as he was about to pop a handful of pills into his mouth. His back was to the door. He had a half-dozen pills lined up in front of him, all different colors, as I walked by. 'Vitamins,' he said, raising his hand to his mouth.

"It was bitterly cold that day, near freezing, and the team practiced on one of those fields where the wind never stops blowing. Near the end of practice, the man who had taken all the vitamins made a wondrous catch, falling hard on the frozen ground and bouncing up as if he had felt no pain.

"Afterward, I asked the head coach about it. 'I certainly hope he wasn't taking anything,' the coach replied. 'That would be pretty far gone — taking pills for practice. That kid has less talent than any player on this squad, but he throws his body. That was some catch you just saw out there. He had never started a game in this league, and he may never start another one, but I'm going to start him Sunday because that was some catch.' "

But it is not the incidence of drug use that is the question here. The only people who remain skeptical about that are in the front office of the National Football League. The real issue is the injuries it causes. In his book *Broken Patterns*, no less a figure than Fran Tarkenton argued that despite the widespread use of "all sorts" of uppers in the NFL — not by him, by other players, "especially . . . defensive linemen [seeking] a final plateau of endurance and competitive zeal" — society is wrong to find fault, especially because society "turns around and accepts the fact that most great pop musicians are stoned out of their minds when they perform."

That argument frays at the edges when it is realized that very few 275-pound pop musicians try to sit on 175-pound quarterbacks. Where it unravels completely for the NFL is when one realizes that if the problem is one-tenth as bad as Mandell makes it, the league is shockingly remiss in dealing with it. In view of the injury rate, it is a delinquency the NFL can ill afford.

Other doctors besides Mandell have spoken out. Doctor Donald Cooper of Oklahoma State has written in medical journals about his concern over the "agitated, aggressive, sometimes paranoid behavior" of players high on amphetamines. "I've been on the sidelines in pro games where the physician watched a guy on his team jump offsides two or three times and said to me, 'I know that guy's problem — he's so high on amphetamines he can't see straight.' Sam Huff told me the two times he tried them he got thrown out of the game for hitting late. He thought he was playing great."

The recent literature of pro football is laced with drug confessions. Chip Oliver (Raiders), Dave Meggysey (Cardinals), and Bernie Parrish (Browns) gave graphic accounts of amphetamine use. Johnny Sample (Colts and Jets) said, "Most pro football players eat [them] like candy." A touching poem by Tom Bass depicted dependence on "the man" (speed, "bennies"), "a crutch I depended on more than my playbook." Meggysey wrote that NFL trainers and doctors "do more dealing in [amphetamines and barbiturates] than the average junky." He said that the "violent and brutal player that television viewers marvel over on Saturdays and Sundays is often a synthetic product."

In *They Call It a Game*, Parrish said that after he and a teammate got onto amphetamines at the University of Florida, "We put some licks on people they won't ever forget. . . . Both the players and coaches were wondering what in the hell had got into us. . . . I never played another game in my college or professional career without taking either Dexedrine or Benzedrine." He said at the end he was up to fifteen five-milligram tablets before each game "in the never-ending search for the magic elixir."

Doctor Cooper says there is no telling how much speed is used by college players. Amphetamines are prohibited by the NCAA. But he knows it is around because "every exam week we get kids brought in who are zingy on them." There are indications of an expanded use. The *Fayetteville Times* reported that North Carolina players had a "tradition" of using amphetamines. A former UNC player thrown off the team in 1974 for marijuana possession said getting amphetamines at seventy-five cents a pop was "no big thing."

The *Chicago Sun-Times* said the more affluent pro players now opt for cocaine, calling it "the biggest drug problem facing sports today." Part of the problem with coke is what happens when police catch you with it. Miami Dolphins' Randy Crowder and Donald Reese were nailed trying to sell a pound of cocaine in 1977 and served time in the Dade County Stockade. Pittsburgh tackle Ernie Holmes was found not guilty by a jury that believed him when he said he didn't know a souvenir silver bullet purchased "from a stranger in a restroom of a motel" contained cocaine. Although cocaine is generally used as an afterhours mellower, the *Sun-Times* said that players under its influence are known to "rip apart their lockers while working themselves into an aggressive mental state for a game." The newspaper said that among its other wondrous attributes, coke leaves no chemical traces, has a less profound downer effect than amphetamines, and causes no sex-drive loss — but it does cost two thousand dollars an ounce.

There is a greater cost players might consider when they start filling their bodies with exotic chemicals — the cost of their careers. So far, the users have also been the victims. Houston Ridge, a former San Diego defensive lineman, collected $302,000 settling a suit against the Chargers in which he contended, although it was never directly ruled upon, that he had "been so high on amphetamines" in 1969 he didn't even know it when he broke his hip. The pain didn't start until three days later. In 1971 Ken Gray filed two lawsuits charging that his former employers, the St. Louis Cardinals, and team trainers and physicians caused him to take "potent, harmful, illegal and dangerous drugs . . . so that he could perform more violently as a player." The cases were settled out of court for an undisclosed amount of money.

But what happens, says Dr. Cooper, when the users make someone else the victim? What happens when a defensive lineman high on speed clubs a quarterback into a coma? What happens then?

When drugs are used to gain an advantage, sport is corrupted.

When they are used in such a way that they inflict injury, the matter has ghastly legal overtones, not only for players but for coaches, teams, and entire leagues.

The NFL maintained a stiff upper lip through all this, and eyes one would have to picture as tightly closed. There *is* no "drug crisis" in the NFL. According to Jack Danahy, director of security for the NFL, "Alleged drug use in the league has been overstated." NFL director of information Joe Browne cited the league's "strong drug preventative program which has been educating players since 1971, as well as weekly counts of pills distributed by team physicians and trainers." Amphetamines? "As far as we can tell," said Browne, "they are not taking amphetamines."

He said that even as Danahy allowed that he doesn't believe the pros are into cocaine "in the same way they used to be into amphetamines" — that is, not as a stimulant before a game. Danahy said the NFL had found "no need for urine tests. It's demeaning to our players and unnecessary in the absence of a drug crisis."

Commissioner Rozelle entered the fray when the series in *Sports Illustrated* was concluded, the last part dealing primarily with Mandell's vivid recall of his experiences.

Rozelle said the drug problem was "not of epidemic proportions." (Which, of course, was not exactly saying one does not exist.)

He objected, he said, to Mandell's being portrayed as a kind of "Father Flanagan." He said Mandell's studies were "dated." (True. Mandell has not made any NFL studies since the league banned him from the locker rooms.)

He said Mandell should be remembered more for the indiscretion of distributing 750 pep pills to the Chargers

(Mandell never denied it), which got him in dutch with the medical profession, and not be exalted as a crusader.

He said the league had hired a pharmacologist to "audit the drug records of every club" and make "spot checks." (What did they expect to find—"Prescription for Crashly: 100 milligrams of amphetamines, so that he will be able to attack the quarterback with greater ferocity"?)

He said that he, Commissioner Rozelle himself, in "informal talks" with players, coaches, and managers, found it "quite clear the use of pills is greatly reduced from what it was in the Sixties and early Seventies." (What did he expect them to say in these "informal talks" — "Mr. Commissioner, I've been hoping you'd drop by so I can confess: I've been high as a kite on Black Beauties every game since 1973"?)

He said the league could not stop players from getting pills from their wives, but he was "confident they are not getting them from the ball clubs." (And neither are marijuana smokers buying reefers at the 87th Precinct.)

He said urinalysis was "a subject of collective bargaining, and Ed Garvey [of the NFL Players Association] has never agreed to it." Garvey had, after all, said such tests were an invasion of privacy. (Of course. And so are bed checks.)

Once more the NFL had investigated itself and found it was without sin.

The unfortunate Coach Svare once said this of the drug issue in the NFL: "The league's attitude about dealing with the problem reminds me how my father dealt with sex. Mean looks and lots of no talk about it." Talking about it resulted in the chain of events that cost Svare his job as coach of the Chargers, and led Mandell to the brink of professional disaster. The scars are deep. Svare and Mandell are no longer close. The last time they met was in a courtroom, where Svare was a witness for Mandell (a reluctant one, Mandell says).

There is no doubt that Mandell was more than just an irritant to the NFL hierarchy. He was an embarrassment. He opened a wound and kept it open — keeps it open still. His has been an abrasive voice, and like most crusaders he tends to overstate his case. As a result, he comes off sounding a trifle self-indulgent. To blame drugs alone for the brutality in football is just not reasonable.

But there is a greater harm in reacting the way the NFL has.

There is nothing starry-eyed in believing that the men who manage a commercial sport and the men who take part should combine with their business ambition a dedication to, and a real respect for, the things that the sport stands for. When profit becomes an objective that overrides elemental human concerns, sport dies. The name is retained, but it is a mockery. In death, it kills more important things than itself.

The money drive by the pro league has created a battle line between management and labor. There have been frequent lawsuits; there was a player strike. Owners complain they are at the mercy of exorbitant demands — escalating contracts, unremitting pressure on collective bargaining issues. Players counter that they make these demands because theirs is a high-risk occupation, and the risk gets higher all the time.

A career in professional football can be ruined in a split second. Growing old on the job is not a luxury a football player can count on. He will never — at least by natural causes — get to the point where age and an addled brain force him out. He will be gone long before that — the victim of that little death that comes to every pro athlete, always at a relatively young age.

To fail to give him every chance to last as long as he can — to

insist that he get that chance — is an insensitivity that management cannot throw off with a press release. Nor, for that matter,
palm off on the labor rep. It is stupid to ignore even the slightest
hint of a reason for the brutal play that now mars the game. The
drug influence is just one, but who is to say how far such an
influence will reach? Not long after the series ran in *Sports
Illustrated*, I read where a high school coach and two of his
assistants had resigned in West Florence, South Carolina. They
cited as their reason that the team was "so muddled by drugs it
couldn't play."

No one had said, and I am certainly not suggesting, that what
happened to Darryl Stingley had anything to do with amphetamines. It did, however, have a lot to do with the unnecessarily
violent play in the National Football League, and the insensitivity that breeds it. Insensitivity is the ultimate weapon.

Yielding to no man in the conviction that life imitates art, I
was interested to see that, subsequent to the above, Garry
Trudeau, the voice of "Doonesbury," covered this point in his
strip. A "Doonesbury" protagonist named B.D. is shown
slumped in front of the television set, from which emanate the
words of two sportscasters covering the big game.

"McAfee is down! He was hit very hard! Time out on the
field! The doctors are rushing out on the field. . . . They're
checking him out. . . . McAfee's being put on a stretcher."

"Rog, we just got a report from our man on the field. It seems
that McAfee is . . . uh . . . dead."

"Yes, but what a hand he's getting, Jack!"

"Right! I'll tell you, Roger — these are some kinda football
fans."

3.

THE LAME AND THE HALT

Traditionally I stay away from Super Bowl games, believing with Fran Tarkenton that they are "a crass example of money ruining the purity of sport." When the mountain comes to me, which is to say to the town I live in, I am, however, tempted. (Maybe it will be better this year. Can it possibly get worse? Maybe I should go see.) Before the last one I kept my option open almost to the final hour, waiting for the itch to pass. It did, as I knew it would, and I gave my 49-yard-line seats to a friend with a teenage boy who, my friend assured me, would "flip" over the experience.

He told me later that they had both "flipped." The seats were right near those of Teddy Kennedy, Don Shula, Jimmy Brown, and Jack Nicklaus. I was struck only a passing blow by this loss, however, because the last time I sat in the stands at a Super Bowl I was close enough to Raquel Welch to smell her eau de cologne and it did not save me from a stupefying boredom.

In lieu of joining the shuffling crowds, I sat that day by a swimming pool, just out of eyeshot of the television set, and reviewed a folder of information I had been gathering on the spectacle I was missing. The file was thick. It showed in no uncertain terms that the Super Bowl was big stuff to the citizens of Greater Miami.

I had had an inkling of what it had previously meant to the citizens of Greater New Orleans earlier in the month while in that city for the Sugar Bowl. The reliable voices of Bourbon Street — strippers, street-hustlers and shills — had complained to the *Times-Picayune* that the college crowd, mostly Alabamans and Pennsylvanians, were not the sophisticates that the professional championship game drew and were "pikers" by comparison. I remember being vaguely pleased by their complaints, as one might be by the complaint of a proprietor of a pornographic book store who has been visited by an arsonist.

The stories in the Miami papers, and others I had gathered, covered many column inches and asserted the Super Bowl's preeminence. NBC was paying $6 million just to televise it; each commercial minute would set a sponsor back $370,000. Each winning player would get $32,000; each loser $23,000. A source called "NFL spokesman" characterized the incoming crowd as "the goingest, the free-spendingest there is." There were a hundred extra flights, and eight hundred chartered buses, and each of the sixty-two thousand out-of-towners would spend $200 a day. By the time the last drunk had left town, the keepers of Miami's motel beds, stone crabs, and gasoline pumps would be $60 million richer.

I had missed, too, the Super Bowl party. Having been to other Super Bowl parties, I considered my forbearance a victory over beguiling gaucherie, but I was fascinated nonetheless by the glowing accounts. Instead of aboard the *Queen Mary* or at the Hialeah racetrack, this time they held it in a satellite terminal at the outer edge of Miami International Airport, accessible only by shuttle bus. This kept the party-goers to a select group of three thousand. A former All-Pro named Carl Brettsneider was denied admission. "Once you're through playing, it's over," groused Carl, and bullied his way in anyway.

The various NFL advertisers, media people, corporate executives, jocks, and ex-jocks sipped pineapple daiquiries and munched turtle kabobs and tried to get as close to Ethel Kennedy, the ubiquitous party-goer, and Howard Cosell, the folk villain, as they could. A special VIP section was carefully policed so that the milling crowd could not get too close. Mrs. Vince Lombardi was there. She said she remembered when the party was "small, intimate and elegant." The NFL bragged that the party cost $100,000.

Not all of the testimony was favorable, however. There were observations from heretics. Hunter S. Thompson described Super Bowl journalism thusly: "For eight long and degrading days, I skulked around with all the other professionals, doing our jobs — which was actually to do nothing except drink all the free booze we could pour into our bodies, courtesy of the National Football League, and listen to some of the lamest and silliest swill ever uttered by man or beast."

Fran Tarkenton, the quarterback, described the Super Bowl as "a manufactured, megabucks extravaganza with [traditionally] lousy play." He said, "Our championship has sold out to the dollar." He said that "no one cares about the purity of the game," and that the idea of playing in a "neutral city" was absurd. "Can you imagine the seventh game of the World Series being played in New Orleans?" Fran asked. He complained that the audience of pseudos had "taken the game away from the hardened fans — the partisan home crowd." He said at one Super Bowl he sat on the 50 yard line, "and no one was cheering."

Finally, I read in the *Miami Herald* a long personality piece on Commissioner Rozelle himself. How, since 1960, the one-time Rams publicity man had seen the league pass into a millennium of riches.

A picture accompanied the article, showing Pete tanned and smiling and, at fifty-two, looking good. I hadn't seen him in years, but I could tell he still had a winning smile, and even though I am one of those who never thought of him as Francis of Assisi (when *Sports Illustrated* made him Sportsman of the Year in 1964, I was not dismayed, but I could not for the life of me think why they had done it), I was pleased to learn that he was now making $250,000 a year. That in Washington he ran with the Kennedy types, and in Hollywood with the Hollywood types. And that, after all, his life's goal had not changed that much. He still thought covering high school sports for a California daily would have been a dandy life's work.

The story went on to credit Rozelle for the riches that were pouring in. The average player's salary was up to $62,000. The new four-year television contract was worth $656 million. The schedule was now bringing the game to the consumers on Sundays and Mondays and occasionally on Thursdays and Saturdays. The game, it said, had become an "American institution."

I offer these evidences of the brimming affluence of the National Football League neither to stimulate the reader's awe nor to applaud a fine example of the free enterprise system (which, of course, it is). I offer them, rather, to reaffirm a personal conviction that while the emperor is fiddling, the rest of football is burning down.

There are two very grim ironies at work here.

One is the fact that below the pro and major college levels (and all that money) the game is fast approaching financial ruin. The spawning ground of football is in deep fiscal trouble. It is getting by on charity, or by having its players sell pretzels on street corners. In the very county, Dade, that that Super Bowl was played, for example, high schools in the area were on a steep eight-year attendance decline, one that paralleled similar tailspins in almost every major city in the country — San Francisco, Philadelphia, St. Louis, and so on.

Fearing bankruptcy, the Florida high school athletic association announced that it was suspending spring practice. It cited the costs and the injuries, the one being entwined in the other. Coaches screamed — both high school coaches and college coaches. Florida, and Dade County in particular, has been a happy hunting ground for college scouts for years. The high school football there is excellent. But it had become a financial drain. The tailspin, however, was no worse than that being felt in other football hotbeds — Ohio, for one, and California. It is a national problem.

The second irony is the harder reality of the injuries themselves, and is worse because it is the reason for the first irony. Not because injuries happen, but because they have grown in number to epidemic proportions, and because the people who could do something about them, who have the money and the wherewithal to ferret out their causes, to scour the game for every trick and technique that has contributed to its present misery, prefer to ignore them. That is not just my judgment, which will not sting the pocketbook. That is the judgment of lawyers, who will. Lawyers who are taking the game into the courtroom. Except the lawyers say it tougher. *Trial* magazine charges that football is "hiding" its injuries.

But, alas, not hiding them well enough.

In the fall of 1905, during a football season of unparalleled brutality that included the death of nineteen players, President Theodore Roosevelt summoned the leaders of football — then mostly schools that later were to comprise the Ivy League — to Washington and demanded they clean up the game. Change its rules, protect its players, or find something safer for them to do.

Under that heavy duress, the rules were quickly and dramatically changed, and the game streamlined. Football had avoided almost certain self-destruction.

How close is it again? Close.

Although some casualty lists are available in football, no one source ever seems to know exactly how injuries occur or how many there are in a given period for all levels of the game. But all indications were that 1977 and 1978 were banner years for injuries in the sport James A. Michener called "the American form of violence."

In 1977, Navy coach George Welch complained of "more injuries than any time since I've been here," but didn't know why. Doctor Donald Cooper, the team physician at Oklahoma State, went onto the field thirteen times in one game, "and that never happened before." First-ranked Texas was down to a sixth-team quarterback by midseason. The *Detroit Free Press* characterized the Tampa Buccaneers–Detroit Lions game as an excuse for a "Go Blue" cheer — for Blue Cross and Blue Shield. The Buccaneers had lost twenty-two of their original forty-five players to injury. The Lions had had twenty-one knee operations in three seasons. Asked who on his ninety-five-man Maryland team had not missed a game or a practice due to injury, Coach Jerry Clairborne could name only one.

By mid-October, however, none could match the devastation of the La Porte, Indiana, High School Slicers. They had provided medicine a specimen football massacre: four broken backs, four broken legs, a mass of torn ligaments and cartilages. Fifteen lettermen had had major surgery. Coach Lou Famiano told the *Ithaca Journal* he thought at one point of moving practice to the hospital lawn.

At the end of one practice, Famiano called for one last play. "I shouldn't have. Our number-two punter broke his leg and our number-one receiver suffered a broken hand." In a junior varsity game, as one Slicer lay on the sidelines awaiting an ambulance for his broken leg, another was hit in the chest. His heart stopped. It took electroshock treatment at the hospital to revive him. Famiano said, "My only explanation is the kids have learned bad habits in the early stages of their career, and that's pure speculation."

In many respects, 1978 was even worse. The paralyzing injury of Darryl Stingley in August was a grim pacesetter for the pros. After thirteen weeks of the NFL season, 186 players were incapacitated, sentenced to the purgatory of the "injured reserve list," to which go only those players whose injuries are so severe they can't make it back in time to help out during the season. The figure represented 14.9 percent of the league's available roster spots.

At one point, season-ending injuries to players were occurring at a rate of fifteen a week. Some pro coaches blamed the sapping effect of the new sixteen-game season, up by two. Some looked at it from the other end of the process and saw it as a parliamentary problem. What they found needed was a higher limit on bodies. More troops to fill the breach. Forty-five to a team was simply not enough. "We have always been in favor of larger rosters," said Don Shula.

When Shula's Miami team played Houston in the playoffs in the Orange Bowl, advance reports sounded as if the match had been costumed by Johnson & Johnson. Miami quarterback Bob Griese wore a brace on his injured left knee; Houston quarterback Dan Pastorini was trussed up like a cop in a high-crime district — a newly created flak jacket covering his damaged ribs.

Miami running back Delvin Williams was hobbling with a knee sprain; Houston running back Earl Campbell had cracked ribs. Miami guard Larry Little had a bad knee and an ankle sprain; Houston guard George Reihner had an injured knee. Miami safety Tim Foley had torn stomach muscles; Houston cornerback Willie Alexander a broken jaw.

Perhaps in fear that the only thing sure was that the majority of the participants would not be in iron lungs, the Miami fans did not swamp the ticket windows. The game was the first playoff non-sellout in the club's history.

The Oilers, for the season, achieved their own club record in knee injuries. Rob Carpenter, George Riebner, Mike Renfro, and Billy ("White Shoes") Johnson underwent surgery. Eddie Foster missed the season. The Dolphins, who had established what was certainly an all-time record for knee operations (twenty-six) in the three previous years, cut their losses in 1978 to three knee operations. No one made a fuss over it, but the Dolphins were no longer playing on an artificial surface at home. In a blow for Nature over Technology, the Orange Bowl had ripped out its Polyturf rug in the off-season and planted grass.

The Baltimore Colts, meanwhile, lost twelve players for four games or more; six of those missed the entire season. Ten starters were lost to the team at one time or another. Coach Ted Marchibroda complained that the injuries came so fast and furious "we couldn't do things we needed to do" to compensate — and the once-proud Colts finished with a five-eleven record.

Quarterback Bert Jones missed the first six games due to a separated shoulder. After ten minutes of play in game seven, he hurt it again and was out another two weeks. On November 16, he came back to play against the Redskins — in great pain, he admitted later — but against Seattle the following week suffered another jolt when bounced out of bounds by cornerback Keith

Johnson. Johnson was awarded a flag and his team a fifteen-yard penalty, and Jones a spot on the reinjured list.

Eleven NFL teams lost ten or more players for the season. The snakebit Tampa Bay Buccaneers led in this woeful category with eighteen. (Actually, snakebite was about the only ill the Buccaneers did not suffer.) The Buffalo Bills had twenty-one significant injuries, compared with seven in 1977. In one game, at Denver, six Oakland players wound up in the hospital, three to a room: John Vella, Cliff Branch, and Otis Sistrunk, and Jack Tatum, Randy McLanahan, and Phil Villapiano.

But for those pragmatists who were not moved by purely humanitarian concern, the best example of how injuries can screw up a club was provided by the Denver Broncos. The Broncos won fourteen games and went to the Super Bowl in 1977, losing to Dallas. That year only two Denver starters missed games. In 1978, the Broncos went 10 and 6, and in sixteen regular season games and one (losing) playoff had twenty-six man-games lost by injuries to starters and alternate starters.

Among the colleges, a growing concern for the causes of injury was not enough to reverse the trend. There was one particularly frightening statistic among early returns from the 1978 season: a survey showed that injuries resulting in surgery had more than doubled since 1974.

Otherwise, the carnage was routine. Eleven players at the University of Kansas had to have knee surgery. A fourth of the Kansas squad was incapacitated at one time or another. Minnesota lost twenty-five players for a total of forty-one games. Losing three *centers* cost talent-rich Southern Cal the Arizona State game and a clear-cut national championship, at least in the opinion of head coach John Robinson.

In two games — against Notre Dame and Syracuse — Navy

lost its number-one tailback, its number-two tailback, its fullback, its wide receiver, its tight end, a defensive end, both defensive tackles, a middle guard, and a defensive back. The fullback needed surgery. "Our medical staff has meant a great deal to us, especially this season," said Coach Welch.

And so it went, down the line, on and on. Lord only knows how far. There is no such thing as a running, comprehensive, sport-wide "official" injury survey in football — no certified breakdown of the causes of injury, unanimously accepted and fully funded. Figures vary, depending on who has conducted the survey and with what resources.

To dissect injury statistics — to get to the root of the injury problem — one must therefore build a colossus from fragments. I found in dealing with the good people who do the research (mostly on a shoestring) that they tend to question each other's findings. The one consistency in all surveys is that they are grim. A Consumer Product Safety Commission report estimated that every year more than half of the players of the game beneath the professional level suffer injury that at least forces them to miss practice, and a quarter are out for a week or more. Jules Bergman of the American Broadcasting Company quoted a report that indicated 86 percent of all high school players were likely to suffer some kind of injury. Another study said that playing the game through college represented a 95 percent risk of serious injury, and that each year thirty-two college and high school players become paraplegics as a result of football.

The projection that injury will strike a million high schoolers, seventy thousand collegians, and cause a 100 percent casualty rate in the pros (at least one injury per player) was challenged by Brice B. Durbin, executive director of the National Federation of State High School Associations. Durbin said the only way those figures could have "basis in fact" would be to count "strains, bruises, blisters and scratches."

Indeed, in the lexicon of coaches many injuries are "minor" — meaning no game time lost. But just as sure as there will be "minor" injuries, there will be many others that will curtail seasons. Some will end careers. Many will have side effects that will grow more painful and restricting with age. Others will be immediately crippling.

Relatively speaking, football is no longer a killer sport (eight deaths nationwide in each of the 1977 and 1978 seasons) and should not be condemned on that basis. The real issue is not dead bodies, but wounded ones; the systematic wasting of men and boys within the boundaries of "legal play." Injuries are endemic to a physical sport, and certain risks are implied. The issue is not the risk of injury, but how much injury is "unavoidable," and therefore acceptable.

Apparently a lot.

In a survey for the *New York Times* Special Features, Dr. James Garrick, then of the University of Washington Sports Medicine Department, said: "If the United States ignored an annual epidemic striking a million and a half youngsters each autumn, Americans would revolt. Yet they cheered while that many college, high school, Pop Warner and sandlot players were injured this season." Dr. Garrick put the more celebrated Sunday mayhem of the pros in a stark perspective: "More high school kids get injured every Friday night than pros do in a year."

The *Times* survey was made in 1975. Football turned a deaf ear. The few rule changes that were made over the next three years, though in some cases very good, were not applied throughout the sport, and made no appreciable impact on its perils. The game was not turned around. No Teddy Roosevelts rode out of the sunset to protest the slaughter.

Some lawyers did, however. Lawyers were doing something about football injuries. They were filing suits, and collecting.

They had found football vulnerable to judgment in several areas, but they were collecting most profitably over the use — or misuse — of the modern hard-shell football helmet, a device Dr. Donald Cooper calls "the damnedest, meanest tool on the face of the earth." The myriad threats to football can almost be capsulized in the helmet. In a hat, it is:

— a focal point of coaches' intransigence in teaching dangerous techniques;

— the piece of equipment with which players are most likely to do damage (to themselves and their opponents) — and cause 80 percent of the game's fatalities;

— the wedge that has opened the sport to the current boom in negligence suits. "We used to have ambulance chasers before no-fault," says Dr. Cooper. "Now we've got jock chasers — and we better not take 'em lightly. If coaches don't wake up, the lawyers will eat 'em alive."

Cooper is a onetime 5-foot-1, 105-pound waterboy who professes a thirty-five-year love for football that is not diminished by his outspoken desire to straighten it out. I have met him only by phone, but I would not care to be in the path of his righteousness.

As medical consultant to the NCAA Rules Committee for five years (1969–1975), Cooper was credited with leading a hackle-raising charge that got college coaches to adopt three important safety measures: prohibiting the "crackback" block (the legal clip at the line of scrimmage), making mouthpieces mandatory, and outlawing below-the-waist blocking on kicks.

(The NFL did not get around to legislating against the crackback until two years later, and has not yet awakened to the need for the mouthpiece. As we shall see, safety is not first in the National Football League.)

On a day in 1976 that Cooper railed against the helmet in the *Topeka State Journal*, another story in the same paper told of a lawsuit brought by Mrs. Ruth Hayes of San Diego against Riddell, Inc. of Chicago for "unspecified damages equal to one-fourth the total assets of Riddell," the nation's largest helmet manufacturer (Riddell makes 70 to 80 percent of helmets sold in the U.S.). Mrs. Hayes's seventeen-year-old son Kip had been paralyzed from the neck down playing football. Mrs. Hayes's lawyers blamed the helmet.

Six months later, in May 1977, and a year and a half after *his* lawyers won a record Dade County judgment of $5.3 million against Riddell, twenty-one-year-old Greg Stead settled out of court for a reported $3 million. Stead's lawyers charged Riddell with producing a "potentially hazardous helmet."

The suit's success apparently was inspirational. In Dade County itself two suits nearly identical to Stead's were filed, one for $5 million against Medalist Gladiator Athletic, Inc. of Leesburg, Florida, on behalf of Leroy ("Butch") Jenkins, paralyzed in December 1975 while playing in a sandlot game in a black Miami ghetto, and the other against Riddell and a sporting goods store on behalf of a high schooler named George Cunningham.

By the end of 1978 helmet manufacturers nationwide were facing between $116 million and $150 million in negligence suits. The suits represented five times the size of the industry itself (annual gross: $24 million) and one hundred times its annual profit. They had caused a near panic. At the time of

Stead's suit, there were fourteen helmet manufacturers in the country. There were now eight, all operating on thinning ice.

Riddell's president, Frank Gordon, said his company would "stick it out to the end," but it is "a safe bet others will not." Riddell's liability insurance was up more than 300 percent— from $40,000 to $1.5 million in premiums. Fear of litigation had forced independent manufacturers to play a kind of fiscal Russian roulette: they couldn't afford a lawsuit and they couldn't afford the insurance, so they canceled the latter and prayed about the former, knowing they could lose either way.

The larger equipment manufacturers are owned by conglomerates (Riddell by Wynns International, Rawlings by A-T-O, Wilson by PepsiCo), but the conglomerates were not likely to throw good money after bad forever. For the time being, the manufacturers were passing on some of the costs to buyers, raising the price of helmets. They were also contemplating forming their own insurance companies.

The immediate dilemma is twofold:

1. Can a parent company, with much to lose, justify a potential catastrophe by a subsidiary whose profits are chicken feed in the corporate picture?

2. Can football be played without helmets?

It was not always. Coach Glenn ("Pop") Warner of the Carlisle Indians argued in 1912 that playing *without* helmets "gives players more confidence, saves their heads from many hard jolts and keeps their ears from becoming torn and sore." Gerald Ford took that advice to play without his helmet at Michigan in 1932 (a fact not lost on his rivals in Congress later on).

But helmets then were little more than leather pancakes, flapping down over the ears. The modern hard-shell helmet, introduced as a safety breakthrough at the All-Star game in 1939, and later improved with permanent face masks to reduce the risk of broken noses and cracked jaws, had subtle but far-reaching psychological effect on play. "Courage was a lot easier to come by," says Dave Nelson, the Delaware athletic director and secretary-editor of the NCAA Rules Committee. "Before [hard-shell helmets], you had to slip blows like a boxer slips punches. You blocked with your shoulder, you tackled with your shoulder. You didn't put your head in places they do now."

Soon enough, coaches learned something else about the hard-shell helmet: it was an effective weapon. As good as a blackjack, only legal. But its use had to be taught.

Techniques known as "butt-blocking" and "butt-tackling" got wide circulation, along with their wicked antecedents: "spearing," "spiking," and "sticking." Players rammed head-first into pileups, into defenders, into hapless quarterbacks, and into immobile running backs to put the finishing touch on tackles. The helmet became the game's principal article of intimidation.

Today, plastered with decals like the fuselage of a World War II fighter plane, it is a stylish-looking engineering marvel in two parts: a three-pound-plus artillery piece of polycarbonate, styrene, and leather, honeycombed with pods of rubber, water, antifreeze, or foam, and costing up to $100. A player could stand on it. He could grow tomatoes in it and it wouldn't leak. If he wanted to, he could drop it off a tall building and fracture the skulls of passersby.

Many coaches who first taught helmet hits never felt one in their ribs. Bear Bryant did. He used to practice with his players, "get down in the dirt and grunt with 'em" — until the hard-shell helmet came in. "I began to wake up the next morning with bruises. I gave it up. I tell our people to buy the best helmets available, the safest ones, but if I had my druthers we'd still have those old leather things. They didn't allow a player to bang into something as hard as he could."

Bryant says the helmet now is "so heavy I don't think I could wear one and walk." Doug Dickey, the former University of Florida coach who played when the metamorphosis was just beginning and a "hard" helmet was no more than a plastic mold suspended on the head by a webbing of elastic straps, picked one up at practice years later and was "astounded how heavy it was. It was like lifting a bowling ball."

That is exactly its effect at impact, says Dr. Cooper. Like being hit by a bowling ball. "If a kid isn't seriously hurt by it on a game Saturday, on Sunday he has so many bruises he looks like he's been tattooed with a ballpeen hammer. There's nothing wrong with the helmet itself. You could wear it every day and night for a week and it wouldn't hurt. Doing what it was intended to do — protect the head — it performs adequately. We seldom see a fractured cheek or skull anymore. We get fewer concussions. What's wrong is the *way* it is used. The head was not meant to be a battering ram."

But batter it does. *The Physician and Sportsmedicine* journal, citing figures supplied by the National Electronic Injury Surveillance System, estimated that forty thousand interscholastic football players were treated in emergency rooms in 1976 for injuries involving the head and neck. The Stanford Research Institute's study of NFL injuries showed that 9.4 percent of all injuries were caused by helmet blows. Neither of those studies took into account the severity of injury.

A far more revealing figure was obtained after a five-year

study of college players by Dr. Carl Blyth at the University of North Carolina. Dr. Blyth found that *29 percent* of football's most serious injuries — brain and spinal cord damage, broken ribs, ruptured spleens, bruised kidneys — came as a direct result of external blows by hard-shell helmets.

In April 1979, the *Journal of the American Medical Association* presented the most damaging evidence of all: a study that showed a "marked increase" in neck fractures and spinal cord injuries.

The study was conducted by Dr. Joseph S. Torg of the University of Pennsylvania Sports Medicine Center in Philadelphia. It assimilated data from principals, athletic trainers, doctors, and other sports medicine centers over a period from 1971 through 1977. Of the 1,129 injuries that resulted in hospitalization, surgery, fractures or dislocations, permanent paralysis or death, 550 were neck fractures — and 176 of those resulted in permanent paralysis from the neck down.

The last previous survey of this type had been made from 1959 through 1963. In that one, only thirty cases of paralysis had been found.

Torg attributed the dramatic increase to blocking and tackling techniques "that use the top or crown of the helmet as the primary point of contact." In those instances, the player drops his chin to his chest and directs the force of his blow from the top of his head down the straightened spine. In that hyperflex position, there is almost total rigidity and little "give," and the blow cannot be absorbed by the elastic structures of the cervical spine. A broken neck results, leading to paralysis when one or more vertebral bones that incase the spinal cord fracture and exert pressure on the cord.

The timing of the Torg-AMA report was ironic. A 103-page

study by Penn State's National Athletic Injury/Illness Reporting System (NAIRS) had just "exonerated" the helmet from blame in head injuries, citing a figure of only ninety-six "significant concussions" in games involving forty-seven high schools and eighty-nine colleges from 1975 to 1977.

The NAIRS result sounded contradictory, but wasn't. The reports covered different areas of injury. The helmet is designed to keep the brain from rattling around in the skull when a player's head is struck. It is designed to cause fewer concussions or subdural hematomas. In that, as NAIRS reported, it "performs quite effectively."

Again, it is not the helmet, but the way it is used that is the fault.

The results do not all make headlines or bring eye-opening judgments. The damage can be insidious. A two-year study at the University of Iowa of incoming freshman football players revealed that 32 percent had evidence of previous neck injury. One doctor treated high school players "with cervical spines that looked like those of arthritic ninety-year-olds."

Doctor Butch Mulherin of the University of Georgia told me that 30 percent of the injuries he sees are directly related to helmet blows. "You see older athletes now with chronic pinched nerves and degenerative arthritis that we never had when I played at Georgia in the Fifties, when the technique was to slide your head past and put a shoulder into it. It'll be worse for them later on. Maybe not surgery or paralysis, but a gradual incapacitation."

"Think about it," says Dr. Cooper. "Everything that has to do with a meaningful existence runs through that four-inch segment of your body [from head to shoulders]. Do like the coaches tell you, jam that helmet or face guard into something, force that helmet down or back [to compress the spine] and it's worse than a karate chop."

There is no question in Dr. Cooper's mind where the blame belongs. He blames coaches, and the "madness" of their desire to "punish the opposition." He thinks the coaches' belief in the power of punishment is the worst influence on the game. One Saturday stands out in his memory for its impact on the Big Eight Conference: the star Kansas quarterback, hit by a helmet, had to have knee surgery. The star Oklahoma cornerback, hit by a helmet, had to have shoulder surgery. The star Oklahoma State fullback, hit by a helmet, had to have his left leg set in a cast. Cooper did the work on the last. He recalled that the year before the same fullback had his *right* leg fractured by a helmet.

A collision with Nebraska running back I. M. Hipp put Colorado linebacker Tom Perry on an Omaha operating table for five hours in 1977. To save him, doctors had to drill a hole five-eighths of an inch in diameter through the skull and evacuate blood clots.

In Dallas, Washington Redskin back Bob Brunet, blocking on a running play, smacked headfirst into the knee of a Dallas defender and was knocked out. The spinal cord compressed as the neck tried to "climb" into his helmet. Brunet suffered a post-game numbness and tingling pains. It was first feared he had suffered a cervical fracture, but the injury was later diagnosed as a bad bruise and swelling on the spinal cord.

Both Perry and Brunet survived, but with their football futures in doubt.

There is no future for Ricky Luciano of Fulton, New York.

In October 1977 Luciano was apparently struck solidly in the chest by an opponent's helmet during a kickoff, according to accounts in the *Syracuse Herald-Journal*. He continued to play until the final quarter when, short of breath, he asked to be taken from the game. A coach volunteered to take him to the hospital, but on the way Luciano decided to go home instead. Later Luciano complained of "chest pains" and was rushed to Lee Memorial Hospital in an ambulance. He died in the emergency room shortly after midnight. The county medical examiner called it "accidental trauma" due to "chest injury."

Players learn dangerous techniques such as "butt-blocking" and "butt-tackling" in the littlest of leagues, where coaches have imitated things they saw or were taught at higher levels. Coaches are notorious copycats. They search endlessly and frantically for better mousetraps, and even the worst of their discoveries travel quickly, like dirty jokes. The added peril of helmet use for the younger player, says Dr. Cooper, is that he has not had time to develop the powerful neck muscles post-teens have. "The heads of some of those skinny kids are no more than knobs on the end of a whip. They ram that helmet in there and it makes you cringe."

The emphasis on weight training as a key element in basic fitness formulae for football began to grow rapidly after the Korean War and coincided with the growth in helmet-first techniques. It had to. Team trainers recognized that if a player was going to use his head as heavy artillery, the head needed to be anchored in something strong enough to keep it attached to his body.

The result was the common if somewhat grotesque appearance easily identified with football linemen and Mister America types: necks that were no longer merely swivels for the head but part of a superstructure rising from the shoulders in a sinewy column extending to the scalp. If the helmet were the glistening tip of the shell, the neck was the burly cartridge.

But whereas a lineman might develop a powerful 23-inch neck by the time he reaches the pros, the high schooler might still be working with a rickety 14-incher, a discrepancy not always appreciated until the lights go out. Tests by physicists on a group of pro players showed that when a 240-pound lineman capable of running one hundred yards in eleven seconds hit a 220-pound back capable of doing the one hundred in ten flat, the kinetic energy released could move thirty-three tons one inch. The force of the blow approached one thousand G's (one thousand times the force of gravity). Pilots black out at twenty G's.

Incredibly, I found in talking with many players that they were either blind to this potential or so accustomed to living with it (having, after all, been *taught* to live with it) that it did not scare them at all. Once expert in using the helmet as a weapon, even the brightest defended it as the "right way." Dick Anderson, the former Miami Dolphin All-Pro safety and president of the NFL Players Association, is now in the Florida legislature and is certainly no dummy. But he told me he thought the game would be "spoiled" if helmet-hitting were eliminated. "You need to tackle with the helmet sometimes," he said. "Injuries are the risk you take."

After being sidelined by a helmet hit in 1977, Texas Tech quarterback Rodney Allison said he "didn't think it was possible for a defensive player *not* to use his helmet." The Eagles' Frank LeMaster was quoted as saying: "You've got to use [it]. It's part of your head and . . . if you don't use the head butt, if you go in with your shoulder, the guy'll grab you and hold you. If you go in with your head, you have both hands free to shove his hands off. The way the new holding rules are, you're almost forced to. The helmet is one of my weapons."

But once you have given a player a loaded gun and released him to use it, there is no guarantee what he will do. Not every player overlooks the gravity of that responsibility. "The helmet's a killer," says Jon Morris, a former Bear. Light the fuse, he says, and the bomb will go off. "It's one hell of a weapon," says Mike Barnes of the Colts. "We do all our tackling with our heads now, where they used to do it with just the shoulders. You take that helmet and drive it straight up into a guy's chin, and drive forward. It scares me to think what it's doing to the guy's head who I tackle, but what really scares me is what it may be doing to *my* head."

It scares Larry Bethea of the Cowboys, too. Bethea told Jim Dent of the *Fort Worth Star-Telegram* that while in college he went to visit a teammate whose neck was broken in a game, and when he saw him, strung up "in so much traction he looked like he was in a cage," Bethea broke down and cried. Bethea recently helped put Dallas teammate Jim Eidson on a stretcher after a collision. He said it was like looking down on himself. "I think all football players at one time or another feel that shock of electricity through their spine after a hard lick. You think, 'This is it. I've finally done it. I've finally crippled myself.' When you get back to the bench you think, 'I've got to get out of this game. I've got to do something else that will not jeopardize my ability to walk.'"

John Bunting of the Eagles told the *Philadelphia News* of visiting a boy in the hospital who had fractured his spine making a headfirst tackle. It reminded Bunting of a time in college when he went to see a teammate who "had things drilled in his neck," how frightening that had been. The boy in the hospital "had a pipe in his throat, and the nurse told me there was little chance of him living, let alone walking again, and here his parents were telling me what a great tackle it was. That really bothered me."

Yet, as bad as the consequences of "ordinary," "acceptable" helmet use can be, they are only half as bad as the perversions that go beyond that use — the ear-holing, the rake blocks, the spearing — techniques of barbarism that were inevitable in the game the first time the coach chose to let the first player get away with a deliberate act meant to hurt another player. Two graphic accounts of the joys of helmet abuse are provided in the tell-all books written a few years back by maverick pro players Bernie Parrish and Dave Meggyesy.

Meggyesy, a former St. Louis Cardinal linebacker, describing a technique he developed while at Syracuse University under the tutelage of All-Pro center Jim Ringo, recounted that "I'd fire off the ball and stick my opponent under the chin, straightening him up and neutralizing his initial charge. Then I'd let him start to go around me . . . and just as he got close to the quarterback I'd spear him in the legs just above the knees with my helmet. . . . Only problem with spear blocking was that I got kicked in the head a lot. I'd be pretty dingy by the end of the game and by my senior year I was throwing up after every game."

Parrish, a onetime Brown defensive back, wrote the following of a confrontation with the Steelers' Mike Sandusky: "Mike was set on revenge for my cleating him in the groin the play before. . . . [He] never broke stride. He drove his helmet into the right side of my unprotected rib cage and knocked me six yards in the air . . . the hardest lick I ever took, the first time I was laid out on a pro football field. I heard the Pittsburgh crowd cheer as I hit the ground. . . . No official dropped a flag. . . . That night, around 3 A.M., I rushed to the bathroom with fierce stomach pains. I threw up a solid whitish ball of food the size of a grapefruit. I thought it was going to split my esophagus. . . . I was deathly afraid I was going to strangle. My throat was sore for three weeks."

The cancerous effect of such tactics dawns slowly on the men in charge. After surveying his squad of out-patients in 1977, then–Washington Redskins coach George Allen said, "Coaches are not the reason for injuries. Football is great the way it is." A coach at Vanderbilt offered the following testimonial on one of his injured players in 1978: "The advantage Ed had playing with a bad shoulder was that he always leads with his hat [helmet] so he never really feels the full blow to the shoulder." A less sympathetic member of the brotherhood told a newsman in Boston that he "resented people trying to make football injury-free."

The influence filters on down. In San Antonio, a five-day hearing was held to investigate butt-blocking charges against coaches in the Pop Warner League, where the tactic was outlawed. The incriminating evidence was on film: coaches teaching it in practice. In San Jose, California, a Police Athletic League coach said, "When you teach a kid to lead with his helmet, you're teaching him to break his neck" — and leading with the helmet was exactly what had been taught in that league "ever since I've been in it." He had been in it five years.

While guiding Notre Dame back to glory in his eleven seasons at South Bend, Ara Parseghian was one of the few coaches who crusaded openly against head-on tackling and blocking techniques. We discussed it over coffee at dawn one morning in a small cafe in downtown South Bend, where Ara remains a hero.

"I'd go to clinics," Parseghian recalled, "and hear coaches

say, 'You block with your helmet.' 'You tackle with your helmet.' I'd say, 'No way! You block with your shoulder. It's a lot stronger blow, and you don't risk nearly as much, so why be stupid about it?'

"I had one assistant coach I finally had to threaten to fire. He wouldn't stop teaching our kids to use that damn helmet. You get different mentalities in coaching. You get some defensive guys who want to kill the other guy, that's the way they did it, that's the way it oughta be done. It's tough to turn them around."

In 1970 the colleges outlawed spearing, which was defined as "the deliberate and malicious use of the head and helmet in an attempt to punish a runner after his momentum has been stopped." Later the prohibition was broadened to include *any* deliberate use of the helmet to punish an opponent, whether he had been stopped or not, and to make illegal "striking a runner with the crown or top of the helmet."

Face-to-numbers blocking and tackling (the front of the helmet or the face guard making initial contact) is still legal, however, and it is estimated that eight out of ten coaches teach it. The pros have no rules specifically intended to prevent spearing. Art McNally, the NFL's supervisor of officials, said when I asked him about this apparent oversight, "Spearing has never been a problem in the NFL."

The evidence does not support him. The evidence does not support any contention that spearing and other forms of helmet-hitting, legal or not, has abated at any level over the last half of the 1970s.

Parseghian said he watched the pros on television and saw "some of the most vicious helmet hits ever. This kid, Doug Plank of the Bears? His head comes flying in there with reckless abandon. It's awful. When Terry Bradshaw got blind-sided by Gerald Irons, I thought he was cut in half."

Russ Francis, the All-Pro New England tight end, had three ribs broken when spiked in the side by Buffalo defensive back Steve Freeman in 1977. By pro rules, Francis admitted, "it wasn't illegal, but you don't do that to somebody's ribs."

Nor have the colleges' fine-line definition of what is and what isn't legal stopped spearing. "It's more prevalent than ever," SMU defensive coach Steve Sidwell said in 1978. The SMU trainer, Cash Birdwell, said he had sent protesting letters to the Southwest Conference "every year, and every year it's the same. The officials just won't call it. Evidently they look upon spearing as part of the mechanics of tackling."

"You see it all the time," said Joe Paterno, "you just don't see it called. What is worse, you see it as the third and forth hits on a player."

Watching the 1977 Liberty Bowl, Dr. Donald Cooper was outraged: "Early in the game, a player digs his helmet right in the kidneys of a Nebraska runner. No flag. Two minutes before it's over, a North Carolina player is flat on his back when this Nebraska guy comes and just *spikes* him. Again, no flag. They should have thrown 'em both out of the game. But don't kid yourself—when players play like a bunch of billygoats, it's because they're taught to play that way."

In mid-1978, I flew to Chicago to meet with Herman Rohrig and Gene Calhoun of the Big Ten Conference. Rohrig is supervisor of Big Ten officials and Calhoun is considered to be his number-one referee. Calhoun had been telling me for months about a film that Rohrig puts together annually to educate coaches and officials on what is going on in the game. Calhoun assured me there were no tributes to forbearance in the film — that it was a collection of hard realities, not meant for the squeamish. He said it would be good therapy.

We settled into a small conference room in the bowels of the main offices at Big Ten headquarters, together with a clacking projector that Rohrig operated — stopping to make points, going back, slowing the film speed at crucial intervals. What I saw was a twenty-minute horror show of flying elbows and slashing forearms, of questionable blocking practices, of quarterbacks being smothered with late hits, of receivers getting ripped unmercifully. Time after time in the film a helmet could be seen making hard first contact — spearing, butting.

"Coaches say, 'We don't have a problem,' " Rohrig said as the prodigals flickered on the screen, "We say, 'Oh yeah? Look at this.' "

Gene Calhoun is an attorney, practicing in Madison, Wisconsin. A onetime high school football player and former Wisconsin baseball coach, he has officiated in the Big Ten for fifteen years. He is a large, balding, cherub-faced man who wears the Great Lakes on his speech, and only looks soft.

Calhoun knows football and football coaches — and he knows lawyers. He said, sitting there, that the two groups were on a collision course. That if somebody did not stop the coaches from teaching helmet-first tackling and blocking, by whatever name they go by, "the courts are going to step in and start making football rules." Coaches would wake up to find themselves side by side in the dock with helmet manufacturers.

While his voice was calm almost clinical, Calhoun's words cut like a knife.

He said, "The thing that is extremely critical is this: why was the NCAA formed? Roosevelt said, 'Clean up football or abolish it.' What was happening then is happening now. Boys are getting hurt unnecessarily. Number one for all of us is the safety of the players. I think the men on the rules committee are intelligent, honorable men who have the best interest of the players at heart. But changing the rules is not enough, and our calling more penalties is not enough if the coaches don't change their habits. It has to be a cooperative venture, and there's more at stake than coaches realize.

"When people get hurt a chain of liability could very well be triggered to involve everybody — the players, the coaches, the officials, the schools, the conferences — even the NCAA itself. If they haven't done everything expected of reasonable people to prevent the type of injury that makes an individual a quadriplegic, they are all going to find themselves on the hook.

"You don't think it can happen? A high school coach in Thornburg, Iowa, was named along with a school district and a sporting goods store in a $2 million suit. A Milton College player whose neck was injured in a head-on tackle named the school and its insurance company in a $3.1 million suit. The kid's lawyers proceeded on the theory that the boy was not coached in the dangers of this type of tackling. In fact, he was taught otherwise — stick that head in there, make contact."

Calhoun got up to leave. He had a speaking engagement in Wisconsin, and a long drive ahead of him. He had been traveling the Midwest like a tent preacher, taking the message to benighted officials, coaches, and athletic directors, at both the high school and college level. He said his warning was consistent, but it was the coaches he felt needed it most. For their own good.

He said, "I tell coaches, 'Go right ahead. Teach using that helmet. See what happens. You could lose your job, your home, your stature in the community — everything you ever worked for.' "

It is not hard to find evidence that lawyers are, indeed, closing in. From both sides. Three in Phoenix, Arizona — Richard Black, Richard Ball, and Steve Copple — successfully defended Riddell in a $2.5 million product liability suit by enlisting a firm specializing in safety engineering tests, to find that the helmet was *not* at fault, that the court would have to look elsewhere for a villain in the case. The suit had been filed years before on behalf of an Arizona high school player who was paralyzed as the result of a football injury.

Dynamic Sciences, Inc. of Phoenix made two life-sized dummies, dressed them in football uniforms, placed one on a helmet, from a car traveling on a monorail at thirty feet per second. According to data gained from the test, Dynamic Sciences determined that there was not a helmet on the market that would prevent *all* head and neck injuries because, Black said, "coaches ignore rules" that prohibit a player from using them improperly.

Even if tempting, it is unfair as well as imprecise to characterize lawyers as vultures hovering over football, waiting for the chance to pick the body clean. A Chicago lawyer named Phil H. Corboy put into a reasonable perspective how many of them feel. He said he would be "tickled to death to close down the sports end of my work, because there is nothing entertaining about looking across your desk at an eighteen-year-old paraplegic. It sickens me to have to do so. To look at a young man who has been rendered helpless and hopeless in a football accident is to look at slow death itself."

Frank Gordon of Riddell said it would be unfortunate if helmet manufacturers were forced out of the business because that would surely kill football.

Lawyer Corboy wondered if that would be so bad, losing only a game.

Can the helmet be defused? Moreover, can it be defused in time?

Predictably, with so many special interests involved, there is no general agreement. Even what would seem the most obvious first step has consistently met resistance: the recommendation, made as early as 1972 by the American Medical Association, that helmets be padded with a "soft outer covering." Today's helmets are so hard that Maryland quarterback Mark Manges broke his hand on one just following through on a forward pass in 1977.

Paterno has long advocated padded helmets, but does not get much support from his fellow coaches. Coaches resist, says Dr. Cooper, "because a padded helmet doesn't give 'em that big *whack* they want when somebody gets hit. It's the same reason they don't like padded shoulder pads. All they get is a soft thump. Coaches want to hear noise. They love noise. Equipment makers are aware that coaches, not physicians, buy helmets.

"Most coaches today never played in the helmet that is being used. They don't realize. Cornell used padded helmets for twenty years. Teams were thrilled to play Cornell. Head and neck injuries were reduced, and when they went home they weren't all black and blue. Cornell would still be using 'em, but McGregor [the manufacturer] quit making 'em. McGregor's lawyers told 'em to get the hell out of the helmet business because it'll burn your tail. They sold the molds to Bill Kelley [president of a firm in Grand Prairie, Texas] and Kelley still makes 'em for Gene Upshaw and two or three other pro players. They won't play without 'em.

"Coaches say padded helmets are dangerous because the padding increases torque stress. They say it causes pinched nerves. That was Ohio State's excuse when they quit using 'em after a couple years. Baloney. If that were all there was to it, they could coat the padding with Teflon. The coaches wanted their noise back."

Commissioner Rozelle, stumping for the status quo, called Dr. Cooper's remarks "naive." He said helmet manufacturers had made "all sorts of studies" indicating a padded helmet would cause other serious injuries — the pinched nerves from torque stress. For his audience, Rozelle provided a visual aid to demonstrate how the padded helmet would hang up. He pressed a pencil eraser against the glass top of a coffee table. The eraser, naturally, dug in under friction.

But the NFL's own injury report made by the Stanford Research Institute had already revealed other "reasons" the pros had for not padding helmets. Teams objected, the report said, "because manufacturers couldn't paint the team logos on soft helmets," and because they were "afraid of increased equipment costs." Also — the most unconscionable rationale of all — teams "did not wish to protect members of the opposition unless their own were also protected."

Checking further, Kaye Kessler of the *Columbus Dispatch* found that Ohio State did not abandon padded helmets because of friction, but "because no other school would adopt them." As one player at another school put it, "I'd rather hit somebody with a hard helmet. But I'd rather get hit with a soft one." It was found that the University of Oklahoma used padded helmets in practice, but switched to the hard shells for games.

The eraser-on-glass argument did not square, either, with the findings at Cornell after twenty years of padded helmets. Former Cornell team physician Dr. Alexius Rachun confirmed that there was "no increase in the number of pinched nerves." Any excuse not to pad the helmets, said Dr. Rachun, "is a terrible injustice to the player. Those tough football coaches just feel the only way to play the game is to beat the hell out of the opponent."

Manufacturers were also pushing for permission to have face guards removed from the helmets, having been burned in the courts by the supposition that the guard acts as a lever to drive the helmet back against the spinal cord. Dr. Richard Schneider, head of Neurosurgery at the University of Michigan, studied the case histories of 225 helmet injuries (66 deaths) in high school, college, pro, semipro, and sandlot games and concluded that the guard did indeed act as a lever and recommended its removal. Doctor Schneider said it would be better "to lose a few teeth than snap a spinal cord. No player would dare try it [any helmet-first technique] without a face guard."

With some surprise, I found there were many face mask detractors. Some objected on purely aesthetic grounds — the masks are an eyesore. They contribute to the anonymity of players by hiding the players' true expressions, not to say their identity. Players are recognized not by their faces but by their general configuration, as one might identify a prominent edifice or, say, the Bronx-Whitestone Bridge. With the advent of the face mask the player became, finally, truly, a knight in armor, to be seen from afar as expressionless and deadly.

Face guards originally were added to cut down the incidence of facial injury. But like the helmets themselves, they became helpers in mayhem. Orthopedic specialists traced minor problems to the mask because of impact pressures, and began treating a steady stream of whiplash victims. Tacklers had found the guard a convenient handle for interrupting the progress of ballcarriers. This, of course, resulted in a new penalty for officials to call.

No less a figure than George Connor, a seventeen-year pro veteran and College Hall of Famer, campaigns against face masks through the columnary aegis of Bill Gleason of the *Chicago Sun-Times*. Connor never had a broken nose, never suffered a serious facial injury — and never wore a face mask. He believes the modern player gets closer to an opponent than he would dare if it were not for that cowcatcher. Elroy Hirsch, University of Wisconsin athletic director and another Hall of Famer, said he agreed — in spite of having his own handsome skull cracked, and suffering a depressed cheekbone fracture while with the Rams.

And so did Elmer Angsman, another ex-Bears runner. Angsman said he lost nine teeth and suffered a broken jaw in pro and college play. But those things don't bother him now, he said. What bothers him now and sends him to the doctor "at least once a week, every week of the year," is a neck that he "twisted so often wearing that mask. I have cervical damage caused by tacklers grabbing the face bar. I have numbness in each hand." Angsman said the masks bring out the chicken in players, that "false bravery" would be replaced by proper technique if they were cut off.

In 1978, Maryland linebacker Peter Haley Jr. came within a millimeter of permanent paralysis, according to doctors, when his face mask rammed into the knee of a ballcarrier. The blow cracked vertebrae in his neck. "I was aiming for his waist," said Haley. "He moved, and I changed my angle." Without the mask, doctors said, Haley probably would have suffered a broken nose. With it, he was almost paralyzed. Maryland coach Jerry Clairborne joined Connor in advocating the removal of face masks.

Slicing across all these arguments, however, is an inescapable conclusion, steeped in irony: the helmet is used as a device to injure football players. What difference does it make which portion of it is more lethal if such use is allowed?

"What appears to be going on here," says *Physician and Sportsmedicine* "is a game of semantics, in which coaches and rule-makers are saying that the only danger to the head and neck is when the top of the helmet makes initial contact, and physicians and other concerned persons, including a minority of coaches, replying that it makes little difference whether it is the face guard, side or top of the helmet that makes the initial and forcible contact."

In 1976, the National Federation of State High Schools Association ruled that no helmet blow, from any position, not even "face-to-numbers," could be the first contact in blocking and tackling. Doug Dickey, then at Florida, thought it a rule worth looking into because it might stop a player from burrowing into a falling ballcarrier or quarterback, requiring him to at least look where he is going.

Some concerned coaches, like Paterno, thought it might be unrealistic because the head "tends to fly around and get in the way anyway." Doctor William Clancy at Wisconsin argued that because of that rule he has treated an unusual number of "stingers" — a momentary partial paralysis caused by the transitory stretch of the nerve running from the neck down the arm during a shoulder tackle — among high schoolers at the Sports Medicine Clinic in Madison.

But a stinger is not a permanent injury. All twenty-four cases Dr. Clancy treated were fully recovered within six months. The high schools' experiment may still be open to judgment, but results were encouraging: the high school federation reported that deaths and catastrophic head and neck injuries were at a twenty-five-year low in 1977–1978. Despite this, no move was made in NFL and NCAA rules committee meetings to follow the high schools' example.

Rules of sport are not graven in stone. They are changed frequently, and, through the years, have been changed expressly in football to make it a safer game. Colleges usually lead in these reforms, with the pros' fear of a commercial-image failure causing them to lag behind. In any case, says Joe Paterno, "We have an obligation to try things, even if we don't agree that they're the final answers."

On that basis, and as a kind of compilation-distillation of ideas and suggestions I had gathered, I wrote in *Sports Illustrated* that it seemed logical to try these across the board, from the sandlots to the pros:

• Make all deliberate initial-contact helmet hits illegal, by any part of the helmet. "Deliberate" would allow for strays and be a judgment call officials could make, says Gene Calhoun.

• Pad the helmets and shoulder pads, or produce a study to show it would hurt more than help.

• Remove face masks, or produce a study verifying their safety.

• Make mouthpieces mandatory. (They already are in college and high school football.)

• Make all hits above the neck illegal.

• Make any flagrant foul involving the head (hits by it, hits to it) punishable by immediate disqualification, and a team penalty exceeding fifteen yards.

• Spot-check practices to see that coaches are not teaching or condoning dangerous techniques.

Would such changes mar the game's attractiveness, or make it more difficult to coach? No more than rules against clipping, flying tackles, hurtling, and turtleback formations did. Most rules concerning players' safety are first pushed by physicians, not coaches, anyway. Coaches squeal, but they adapt. They got along fine without blocking below the waist on kicks in the colleges. They got along fine without crackback blocks, head slaps and goalposts on the goal line. Not a fan was heard to complain.

Coaches will always resist change, says Dr. Cooper, and doctors do not vote on rules changes. He found as a consultant that when doctors come around, coaches get the whim-whams. "As long as I talked strictly about injuries, they didn't mind, but when I started talking about *preventing* injuries, they called it 'meddling.' They said, 'Why the hell don't you stick to practicing medicine and quit trying to act like a goddam coach.'

"Some coaches resisted the mouthpiece legislation to the bitter end. They said their quarterbacks couldn't call signals through them. After three or four years of coming back [from the meetings] frustrated, I got my dentist to custom-fit a mouthpiece. The next year I gave a thirty-minute report with the mouthpiece in. Nobody noticed. I said, 'Did everybody understand me?' And I pulled out the mouthpiece. They turned around and voted it in. Our dental bills have dropped to practically nothing."

Helmets used at the college level now must meet standards laid down by the National Operation Committee on Standards for Athletic Equipment (NOCSAE), a group made up of sporting goods manufacturers, the NCAA, junior colleges, and trainers. The standards are an attempt to unify against faulty manufacturing practices, and would seem a step in the right direction. But *Trial* magazine, a monthly journal of the legal profession, has already called the NOCSAE standards "dismally inadequate" and "low-level," a sure harbinger of litigation to come. Says Calhoun: "The lawyers smell blood."

The issue of *Trial* in which the helmet critique appeared was devoted entirely to sports litigation, leading with a grisly cover painting of two red-eyed hockey players banging each other with sticks. Various bases for lawsuits and how to prepare them were presented. Cases were made against the helmets and the use of synthetic turf.

Trial said that if "coaches are willing to buy inferior helmets, then industry stands willing to participate [for profit] in the crippling of our youth." It recommended substandard helmets be banned, coaches who teach helmet-first techniques be fired, and that parents be apprised of the risk with consent forms. It said "alternative sports may be more attractive" for young athletes, but that "the coach or teacher, from Pop Warner [Leagues] on . . . in assuming his position has assumed responsibility for their safety and well being."

Finding the battle lines drawn, equipment manufacturers have pushed for a bill in Congress to provide liability-judgment limitation. Said Howard Bruns, president of the Sporting Goods Manufacturers Association: "The sporting goods industry itself is under attack. The question is, will football survive?"

"It won't," says Dr. Donald Cooper, echoing a prediction Joe Paterno once heard. "If we don't do something, everybody will be playing soccer."

No, not everybody. Jeff Boynton will not be playing soccer.

Boynton was considered to be the best football player Plum Borough High School ever had. Handsome and well built, he had been voted the most valuable running back in the Keystone Conference in Pittsburgh. He graduated in June 1978 with a football scholarship to attend West Virginia University in the fall. In July, however, he went to Mt. Lebanon, Pennsylvania, to play in a Shriners' High School All-Star game.

And on a routine pass play, Boynton made a fateful move.

From his position in the defensive secondary, he saw the ball coming. At first, he said, he "thought about intercepting. But in a flash, I ducked my head and decided to tackle. I was told so many times not to duck my head, to keep my head up and use my shoulders."

Boynton slammed headfirst into the pass receiver's hip. The receiver got up; Boynton did not. When his coach reached him, he said he had a "burning sensation" in his neck, arms and fingers; his body "tingled."

Rushed to Oakland Presbyterian University Hospital, Boynton underwent surgery to fuse the crushed vertebrae in his spine. Coach Joe Naunchik was there when the neurosurgeon came out of the operating room to give the report. "He said, 'Jeff is going to be a quadriplegic.' I couldn't believe it. I said, 'Do you mean Jeff's going to be confined to a wheelchair?' He said, 'Hopefully, a wheelchair.'"

Boynton's physician, Dr. Joseph C. Marroon, a consulting neurosurgeon for both the Steelers and the University of Pittsburgh football teams, said it would take "a miracle" to get Jeff off his back. Dr. Marroon himself was a scholastic All-America halfback and college player at Indiana in the early 1960s. He said he personally had seen "at least one player a year" become permanently paralyzed with spinal injuries in the last four years.

"It's tragic," he said. "These are young men in their prime. I'm not against football. I got through my undergraduate studies on a football scholarship and it helped me to get to medical school. But if something isn't done to make the sport safer . . ."

And John Manns will not be playing soccer. Or anything else.

A slender 6-foot 155-pounder, Manns played for Mergenthaler Vocational High School in Baltimore. On October 27, 1978, in a game with Northern High, he made a saving tackle on a runner returning a kickoff. Northern coach Joe Voskuhal had the best view of the play, occurring as it did on his side of the field. "He put his head right in there and tackled the runner right in the gut. If he hadn't made the hit, it would have been a touchdown."

Manns fell back, and the Northern runner fell back. The runner got up. By the time a paramedic got to Manns and had him on a stretcher for the ambulance, the boy was already paralyzed. "He kept telling me he had a hard time breathing," the paramedic said. "He was talking barely above a whisper."

Manns had suffered extreme damage to the spinal cord, caused by a fracture to the vital third vertebra. A break in that region is usually fatal within three to four days.

At six o'clock the following morning, Manns's uncle called Mergenthaler coach Paul Buckmaster. He said Manns was dead, at age sixteen.

The death of Manns and the paralysis of Boynton had a profound effect on their coaches. They both resigned, saying they they would never coach again. Vocational's Buckmaster had coached twenty-one years; Plum Borough's Naunchik, nine. They were considered good at their jobs, and enthusiastic supporters of the game.

Joe Naunchik told Bill Nack of *Newsday* that he "never went into those games subconsciously thinking anyone would get hurt. Then all of a sudden, the last couple of years it started happening around here."

He did not quit immediately after Boynton's injury. He returned for the 1978 season. But "every time there was a violent collision, I would be relieved when everybody got up and walked back to the huddle. That's no way to coach, is it? Every time you went to the field you were reminded of what could happen." After every game, he said, he would comfort himself, "Whew, that's one less."

There was another crucial effect. Naunchik found he could no longer "persuade a kid to play football." He could no longer recruit. He was "still a strong believer in football," but he said he had become "more aware now that the lessons football teaches — sportsmanship, fair play, self-discipline — can still be learned in swimming, basketball and tennis. Sometimes we think we are the only sport teaching that. But it's not true. You see players get hurt and go through the emotional duress of the family and then you say, 'I don't have to be here. What happens if it happens again?'

"I guess the bottom line is it has to happen to you. You read about what happens in Pennsylvania or across the street, but it has to happen to you."

Paul Buckmaster resigned immediately after John Manns's death. He said, "I can't send another player into the game when there is the possibility of this happening. John was a beautiful kid from a beautiful family and I don't want to have to tell another family that their son has been injured."

Buckmaster was at the hospital that Friday night when Manns asked for his father. "He told his father he was going to die, and to 'be strong.' That young man was so brave.

"It happened to me once and I don't want it to happen to me again. I love football and I'll miss it, but under the circumstances I have to do what I have to do. I've been to hospitals with parents to visit players who had bends of this and twists of that, but this is an ungodly type of thing. . . . And nobody, but nobody, knows what it's like unless they go through it."

The week before it happened, Buckmaster said, he was a "completely different person." On the very eve of the game he sat with his wife at dinner, giving her a pep talk about the benefits of football — "all the good things it does for youngsters. It teaches a kid loyalty, discipline, dedication, sincerity. Go down the line. It's tough, tough, a game of life. You get knocked down and you have to get up. You lose and you have to prepare for next week. It's what life is all about."

But on Saturday morning, he said, the whole world had changed. "I feel like a horse that has been broken," he said. He told his wife, "We gotta stop playing this sport. It's not a sport. We have to give it up."

The Mergenthaler team played its last two games without Coach Buckmaster. He never went on the field again.

In its report to the National Football League after a three-year injury study, the Stanford Research Institute made the following prognosis: "Without radical rule changes, and an equally improbable altering of coach and player attitudes, American football will continue to be the world's most injurious sport."

That is an overly optimistic view.

With changes, both in rules and attitudes, there is no reason to think football will ever lose its position in that cheerless estate. By design and nature, it is a rough game. None is rougher. *Somebody* has to be number one.

Hence, injury is easily assimilated and injury accounting (as opposed to injury prevention) is a popular topic in football. The first words out of a coach's mouth at the beginning of any postgame or postpractice press conference usually consist of: "Joe Crashly broke his collarbone today." Or, "Tom Smith has a 'knee,' Dick Jones has a 'shoulder,' and Harry Brown has a 'hip.' " Coaches do not have to specify what "knee" means. Football writers know it does not mean the player owns one, it means he has hurt one.

Football games are won or lost and are wagered on depending on a team's sick list. Betting lines rise and fall with the figures. Promising seasons are ruined by them. Arguments for squad sizes are based on them. Because of them, college coaches — some — lobby for 125-man rosters, instead of the 95 they are now limited to, so that they can have an adequate number of fill-ins for the lame and halt. Most pro coaches would like an increase — any increase — in *their* 45-man limit, for the same reason.

Those who despair of the weekend casualty lists have long been encouraged to look at the good football does. The lives it enhances, the financial sheets it balances. Injuries are considered a risk worth taking by healthy young men because many of the alternatives — surfboarding, trampoline hopping, driving in traffic — result in statistics far more baleful. Against the backdrop of society's more self-destructive pursuits, football actually holds up pretty well, the argument goes.

Doctor Donald Cooper of Oklahoma State, that dogged campaigner against the game's more libertine mentalities, keeps his own perspective by citing "the classic case of the kid in Florida who died in football practice. The next day, in memorium, they canceled practice. And at four that afternoon, when the kids would have been playing football, five of them were out hot-rodding around and got hit by a train. All five were killed."

But war mutilates many more than it kills, and it is the war ethic of coaches that contributes heavily to the injury problem in football, and becomes, in the end, a way of life. The coaches who teach it and the younger men who play by it are often indifferent to its polluting violence. If violence is accepted, how much injury must therefore be accepted? More specifically, if rules are meant to protect a sport's participants, and players are getting hurt at record rates, are the rules being tragically ignored, or are they just inadequate?

I once asked lawyer Gene Calhoun, the veteran Big Ten referee, if it were possible to strike a finer line between what is "necessary" and what is not in football, with the hope of strengthening the rules to cut the casualty rate. Or at least arrest its growth.

"We could do it with a thirty-second bulletin," he said.

"A thirty-second bulletin?"

"If they wanted to clear up all excessive violence in football, they could do it with one half-minute bulletin. 'From now on, no late hits. A guy's down, he's down. We're not going to let you demolish a player anymore. We're going to call "holding" every time we see it, so don't hold. Don't frustrate players into retaliating. No more hits out of bounds. No more extra hits on quarterbacks. No more piling on. No more gang tackling when a back is clearly in the grasp of a tackler and going down. We're going to put a greater burden on a player to know when to let up, when not to use his body or head as a weapon.'

"An official's first responsibility is to the players' safety. He gets a bulletin like that and he calls a game accordingly. An official can call a game as close as they ask him to. But he wouldn't even try if the coaches aren't going to go along.

"No official is going to martyr himself. He has to have coaches cooperating up and down the line by accepting rule changes or interpretations and giving the officials their complete cooperation. If that happened you'd better get up early because there'd be a star in the East. You show coaches a film on pass interference and in five minutes the room's in an uproar and they're at each other's throats. You'd be surprised how often they don't know the rules we've already got.

"You'll never make football completely safe, but there are changes you could legislate for safety. But you write a rule that says you can't block a guy below the waist, where he's most vulnerable, and you'll get coaches saying, 'You're making it a Sunday-School picnic.'

"Players do what coaches tell them. If you didn't have cooperation, you'd have six hundred yards in penalties and everybody would say, 'The officials are taking the game away from the kids,' and they'd be right. The pros started calling holding a lot closer a couple years ago. They had three-hour games and all the coaches and players screamed.

"I have a great respect for coaches. I've never had to call one of them for unsportsmanlike conduct on the field. I've never had one argue with me over a personal foul — the cheap shots everybody hates. But the trouble doesn't begin there. It begins on the practice field, where the player is trained. I've seen coaches in practice hold on to a boy's neck, then shove him onto a pileup. 'That's what I mean by being aggressive! That's what I want!'

"It's wrong, it's dangerous, and it's illegal, but when a player knows that's what the coach wants, he's going to do it. He'll take advantage of every chance. I had a game one year, the quarterback rolled out to pass and released the ball, and this defensive player was just about to deck him when he looked around and saw me. I was two steps away. The kid said, 'I wish you weren't there.' I said, 'Son, I'll be there every time.'

"You see a ballcarrier go down on a slip, and the defensive

player knows he's going down. But he comes up and pops him anyway, takes that free shot and hurts him. Aggressive play. Even if the flag had gone down, it wouldn't have prevented the injury. It had already happened. Flags don't prevent injuries. Coaching would have prevented the injury."

But coaches are under siege to produce. They know from experience, and by what the nobility tells them, that it is a cutthroat business. It has to be the only way because Vince Lombardi said it: "Winning isn't everything, it's the only thing." And Woody Hayes said it: "I used to think winning was important. Now I think it's everything." And Bear Bryant said it: "It beats anything that comes in second."

The energy of production is hard on coaches. Football is a time- and energy-eater. The game is constantly changing, and coaches must constantly adapt. It is man's nature as he gets older to fight change, particularly change for the better. But the coach has to ride with it. He can't afford to waste time swimming against the current.

Thus locked in, he can lose perspective. Because he is part of the whole, he has no time to step back and mentally sort out the procedural mass and isolate things that might be out of whack. Transferred to the field, to the game itself, desperation and win-or-else intensity combine with the high physical properties of the game to produce the bad philosophies and bad techniques that get people hurt.

Rare is the coach who sees this. Lee Corso of Indiana does. Like Gene Calhoun and Donald Cooper, Corso puts the injury problem squarely in the coaches' laps — in effect, his own.

"When you have a cancer, you cut it out," says Corso, "you don't put a bandage over it because it won't heal. When you get a bum coaching, he'll have bums in his program. When players try to get away with things, it's because they're doing it in practice, and you have to lay that to the coach. What coaches do dictates what the players do. But we don't cut 'em out. We find a coach is a crook and we put him on probation and the next year he's coaching in an All-Star game."

Most coaches accept injury. They complain about it, alibi it, and pay respects to its seriousness, but they accept it. They stand sympathetically over the fallen bodies of their players and call it "the breaks." As the casualty lists mount, they become even more stoical. The Steelers' Chuck Noll, after losing six players in one game in 1977, and the University of Pittsburgh's Jackie Sherill, after losing Heisman Trophy candidate Matt Cavanaugh and twenty-four others for one game or more, called it "the normal risk of football." Villanova's Dick Bedesem said of the rising tide of injuries: "I don't think there's anything much you can do." At Dave Nelson's own University of Delaware, coach Tubby Raymond said he thought "Everything that can be done to make football safe is being done. I personally feel there's a great deal more made out of the danger of football than there really is."

Doctor Cooper is not surprised by this attitude. He believes the pressure gets to coaches. "I've seen what it can do. We had a coach who came on the field down in Austin to drag me away from a Texas player who was hurt. I was too flabbergasted to say anything. The next time it happened, we were playing in Lincoln. One of the Nebraska kids got hit not more than ten feet from me, around the thirty-yard line. I could see he was unconscious, so I went right to him. The coach came down the sidelines from about the fifty. 'Get the hell away from that guy, he's not your responsibility.' I could see he was about to grab me and I said, 'Don't you touch me. There'll be a fight if you do. It may not last long' — he was twice as big as me — 'but by God I'll slug you.' That guy isn't here now, but I have an agreement with Jim Stanley [the Oklahoma State head coach]. I won't try to coach if he won't try to practice medicine."

Compounding this reluctance to face reality is an inherent suspicion coaches have for rule changes. Broached on the subject in the face of his own list of out-patients, Redskins' coach George Allen said, "Too many rule changes haven't helped before." The result is that coaches maintain a death grip on dangerous tactics long after their prescribed use — wiping out a linebacker, cutting down an end — has been distorted into something that intimidates or injures.

Coaches clung to spearing when it was clearly a peril to athletes. Clipping was first taught by Walter Camp in 1908, but it was not outlawed until 1949. The crackback block, murderous on knees and nothing more than a legal clip, was not outlawed until 1971 in the colleges, 1974 in the pros. Fearful of having "proven" methods taken from them, coaches, it has been said, would defend a blackjack to the base of the neck to stop a third-and-one if it had been "done that way" in the past.

The exaggeration, of course, is ridiculous.

Or is it?

Consider the knee. According to the Stanford Research study, 25 percent of lost-time injuries to pro football players involve the knee. It is the athlete's most susceptible part, and not even suited for hard dancing, much less football. The Detroit Lions had twenty-two knee operations in three years; the Miami Dolphins had eleven in one season. Of the twenty-six lost-time injuries that ruined a good Maryland team in 1977, eighteen were below the waist. But, "I don't know how we could have eliminated them," said coach Jerry Clairborne.

In a game with Texas A&M in late October of that season, underdog, undermanned SMU took a 21–7 lead in the second quarter — and then suffered knee or leg injuries to six defensive starters and lost, 38–21. "We were going down like chopped wheat," said Mustang coach Ron Meyer.

Don Shula had a film put together of forty knee injuries to the Miami Dolphins. In review, the *Miami Herald* said that seeing the film was "almost guaranteed to create a fleeting sense of revulsion, even in those who haven't felt a knee grind, rotate and lock unnaturally." The variety of causes was shown to be endless: pileups, clips, leg-whips, players falling into one another.

Shula pointed out that there were no "cheap shots" among the culprits, that the injuries resulted from mostly routine happenings. His only conclusion was that "injuries occur when the player has his weight on the leg and he's not aware that the blow is coming."

Knee injuries are death on careers. In his eight years with the St. Louis Cardinals, defensive back Jerry Stovall broke his nose, lost five teeth, fractured his cheekbone, broke a clavicle, ripped his sternum, broke seven ribs, broke a big toe three times, and suffered eleven broken fingers. But it was a knee injury that ended his NFL career in 1971.

Knee operations are a dime a dozen — not in cost, in frequency. Miami Dolphin defensive stars Dick Anderson and Mike Kolen had three apiece in four years, and they both retired before their time, unhealed. Kansas City's E. J. Hollub still limps after a record twelve knee operations. After four operations and an abrupt retirement from the San Diego Chargers, Kevin Hardy, then twenty-nine, told the *Washington Post* in 1974 that he experienced almost constant pain, could not run, could not enjoy a round of golf without a cart, could not join his non-football-playing friends skiing or playing tennis or frolicking with their sons. He said he now knew "what all those coaches meant when they said you had to pay the price."

Knee injuries are also an increasingly popular basis for lawsuits. Dick Butkus sued the Chicago Bears for $1.6 million over his crippled knee in 1974, charging improper medical treatment had caused irreparable damage. He settled for $600,000. In 1977, Bill Enyart won a $770,000 judgment against the Oakland Raiders and their orthopedic surgeon because of failure to diagnose a torn ligament that ended Enyart's career in 1972. Bubba Smith sued the National Football League, two game officials, one of whom was the down-marker holder, and the Tampa Sports Authority for $2.5 million in 1977, claiming that a damaged knee — hurt when he hit the yard marker in an exhibition game in Tampa in 1972 — had rendered his 270-pound dreadnought of a body ineffective for anything except weather forecasting. Smith said he now could tell twelve hours in advance that rain was coming because of the arthritis that had set in.

Yet, says Art McNally, the NFL's supervisor of officials, "it has been shown by studies that only one percent of injuries to knees were on plays that were illegal." McNally had been asked if perhaps NFL officials had been lax in calling certain plays — piling on, late hits, forward progress, etc. — tight enough and with sufficient concern for players' safety. He was defending his officials, but in doing so was leaving the game itself wide open: if 99 percent of these injuries are from "legal" hits, wasn't it time to ask why they are legal?

In *Out of Their League*, Dave Meggysey described a legal hit on an opponent's knee that should be required reading for every football coach: "[On a kickoff return], my man must have thought someone had blown their blocking assignment, or maybe it was because he was a rookie, but he was making a bad mistake: running full speed and not looking to either side. I knew he didn't see me. I gathered all my force and hit him. As I did, I heard his knee explode in my ear, a jagged tearing sound of muscles and ligaments separating."

Over the years, coaches have been led to accept rule changes on the basis of safety. Usually they are led by physicians armed with hospital charts. Sometimes they are led by other coaches. Ara Parseghian and Joe Paterno were leaders against blocking from the waist down on kicks, which, like the crackback, was murder on knees. Other coaches, Parseghian recalled, said, "Gee, we can't do that, it'll ruin the game." But they did. And it didn't. And the fans never noticed. The game remained unruined.

Nevertheless the knee continued to take a fearful beating. By one study, surgery required in knee injuries had actually gone up, from 43 percent to 58 percent in the years since 1973.

Middle guard Dan Relich of Wisconsin found out one reason why.

Relich was considered one of the best defensive linemen in the Big Ten going into the 1977 season. Wisconsin was playing Ohio State. The Ohio State quarterback rolled out, the center blocked into Relich, "straightening him up." Relich put his hands on the center's shoulders to fend him off. He was rigid from the waist down when an Ohio State guard pivoted and blocked down into his knee. The tactic is called a "chop block" by some coaches, a "cut block" by others. It finished Relich for the season.

Ordinarily, players suffer in silence over such injuries. They check into the hospital, take their medicine, count their stitches, and keep their mouths shut.

Not Relich. "It was a bush thing to do," he said. "It comes with the uniform, you expect to get hurt, but you don't expect it to happen like this. Ohio State has so much talent that you wonder why they have to resort to things like this. It shows a real lack of class. I'll remember it."

Relich said he experienced the same kind of block against Michigan State. "They were on the back of my knees every other play. My knees were so sore and swollen I couldn't practice until Wednesday. Michigan would never do something like that, and Illinois didn't."

The chop block is legal.

Darrell Royal has watched the chop block grow in favor in college football and says, "The coach who teaches it ought to have it done to him once or twice. Coaches have to ask themselves. 'Are we trying to keep this guy off the passer, or are we trying to put him on crutches?' It's the philosophy we have to find out about. If we don't have sportsmanship, we don't have a game. The players aren't fooled. They know the destruction they can do with those things. If it's not taught, it's condoned, and that's the same thing."

The question of what is "necessary" is a ticklish one. Coaches are apt to say that almost everything they teach is "necessary"; certainly coaches should know. Doctor Clancy, while decrying dangerous practices, admits that the problem of changing the game without "reducing it to tag ball" is a rightful concern of coaches. "They're afraid doctors will go off half cocked."

But left to their own devices, coaches are not likely to go off at all. How many ribs were crushed and spleens ruptured before spearing was disallowed? How many more will go before the helmet is legislated out of the hit business entirely? How many ligaments were ripped before crackback blocks were outlawed, and how many more will go before all downfield blocking below the waist is eliminated?

Given the growing prospects of intervention by the courts, coaches can no longer afford to ignore medical evidence. To paraphrase Dr. Clancy, "We're not coaches, but they're not doctors, either." The rules of football are not immutable. Administration of any sport has as its first tenet of rule-making the question: Is it safe for those who play it? If, says the NCAA's Dave Nelson, an unfair advantage is legalized by rules, rules have to be changed. To keep a sport healthy as well as attractive, the question of what is "legal" often has to be based on what is "necessary."

If only coaches can answer such questions, let them answer these:

Is it necessary to block any player below the waist on any downfield play?

Ara Parseghian doesn't think so. Parseghian says below-the-waist blocks outside the legal clipping zone — five yards on either side of the center, three yards on either side of the line of scrimmage — are not necessary at all. "On any play where there's a scramble of twenty-two men, blind-side hits and unprotected hits on knees occur." Doug Dickey, the former Florida and Tennessee coach, thinks the more effective block in that circumstance, anyway, is "the one where you go through your man, not down at his knees."

Is the "chop block" necessary?

No, says Indiana's Corso. No, says Doug Dickey. No, says Parseghian, Royal, and Washington's Don James. Within that six-by-ten-yard legal clipping zone, considerable force can be generated, and dangerous practices are tolerated. The "rollup block," in which an offensive lineman "rolls" up the back of a defender's legs, is similar in concept. It also is not necessary.

Is it necessary for a third and even a fourth 260-pound lineman to help two other 260-pounders put away a ballcarrier or quarterback when he's already trapped or on the way down?

Norm Evans, the retiring Seattle tackle and All-Pro, thinks not. Evans is "bugged" by all the piling on he sees in football, the redundant hits on ballcarriers and quarterbacks. He thinks a greater burden should be put on defensive players to make them more aware of the obvious. Should they not know when they deliver that extra blow that they might be doing unnecessary harm? That because they're in the neighborhood doesn't mean they have to crash the party? Should they not be as aware of bounds markers as offensive players? Would it be too much to ask that they realize the ballcarrier is going there anyway and that it is not necessary to ride him another five yards out of bounds?

Late, redundant hits go hand in glove with gang-tackling, a tactic spawned by southern college coaches years ago and given widespread respectibility under the euphemism "pursuit." Pursuit is an incontrovertible virtue of defense. The trouble with pursuit is that it often translates into vicious finishing-off blows on backs whose momentum has already been stopped. Contrary to popular belief, the whistle does not have to be blown to signify a player is down. The whistle is to alert everybody that the play is over, not to signify that a ballcarrier's momentum has been stopped.

Once gang-tackling became widespread, it was increasingly difficult to distinguish late hits and piling on from momentum. Coaches teach getting to the ball; officials know that. Too often, says San Diego State trainer Bob Moore, the late hit is regarded as "a sign of team defense instead of a potentially dangerous act of overaggression."

The game, says Moore, is "wrapped up emotionally" in these tactics. "Combine that with officials not calling the late hits, and you have a dangerous situation. The injury does not always happen then. It takes a toll for later on — the aspect of prolonged punishment. A player who has been hit head-on for three quarters might try to make an unusual dodge to avoid repetition late in the game, take a clumsy step, get hit awkwardly and tear up a knee. I've seen it happen. All this could have started with a piling-on early in the game."

Woody Hayes once said that a player good enough to make the Ohio State team "is good enough to change directions in mid-air." When John Ray was defensive coach at Notre Dame, he said that players like Alan Page, "as good as they are today, can be taught anything — to stop on a dime if you tell them." That being the case, would it be politic to ask them to do exactly that — to turn away from a pileup, to resist taking that "free shot" momentum allows?

According to almost every study, the players most injured in football are, ironically, the game's most skilled — the running backs, the quarterbacks, the receivers. They are, appositely, the most likely to suffer unnecessary hits — hits meant to punish and intimidate. Officials can see these things. Pete Williams, the former Navy halfback who is now the top referee in the Southeastern Conference, says an official "can judge intent." He says it would be easier, however, if coaches told players "you can't do this anymore, it's against the law," because then the ones who deliberately pile on or hit late would be that much easier to spot and penalize.

Is it necessary for a defensive player to unload on a receiver when it is obvious the ball is overthrown?

The colleges now have a rule against this practice, making the defender responsible for knowing where the ball is. The pros do not.

Is it necessary to tackle players who don't have the ball, just because they might get it?

Jerry Claiborne of Maryland and Lou Holtz of Arkansas can tell you why they don't think so, although this is a favored tactic in the college game where blind-side hits on tailbacks in the option play are allowed. The option may be the most exciting play in football, and its most dangerous. Since its evolution out of the split T in the early 1950s, coaches have puzzled over defending it. What they came up with early on has many refinements now with the advent of the triple-option (wishbone, veer) offenses, but basically it was this: wipe out the quarterback on every play, whether he keeps the ball or not, and blind-side the tailback. If this procedure were suddenly dropped into the game as a surprise tactic, its lethal qualities would probably be condemned, but evolution has given it favor.

"Coaches teach their defense to tear that pitch man's head off," says Claiborne. "The pitch man is looking back at the quarterback, watching for the ball, and he's vulnerable — and here comes the strong safety (or linebacker) across to blind-side him." Claiborne lost his star running back, Steve Atkinson, in 1977 on such a play. "He got annihilated," said Claiborne.

"It's legal," says Holtz, who lost *his* star back, Ben Cowins, the same way, "but it's not ethical."

Is it necessary? If you are a defensive coach having to face an Alabama or Oklahoma wishbone, you might say yes, but Doug Dickey says there's another way. He thinks a defensive player responsible for the tailback should be made to play the option as he would a pass receiver: go for the pitch if you wish, but if you play the man, just establish your ground until he gets the ball. If he runs into you beforehand, that's his fault. "There's no need to hit the pitch man on every play. Look at it from his standpoint. How would a linebacker like being blind-sided time after time, sometimes when the play is past him?

The overall picture is clear enough. The rules of the game do not protect its players. The rules are not always "fair" to both parties in the two thousand separate one-on-one hits that make up a normal football game.

Ironically, the rules are especially unfair to quarterbacks, the most important players in the game.

Of all the ill-begotten, ill-advised apologies for the plague of injuries in football, none beats the one about quarterbacks.

The quarterback is, at once, the most esteemed and assailed of football players. As the game's foremost expression of skill and leadership, he can aspire to be a campus king, and a quarter-million-dollar-a-year pro. But he must pay for this status. He is a likely (if not logical) focal point of fan abuse when his team loses, and, as he goes about his business, the recipient of some of the most conspicuous acts of savagery the grand old game can muster.

This is as it should be, the apology goes. Football is the ultimate he-man's game. Football does not coddle gifted players. Quarterbacks are particularly gifted and should not expect special handling. Thus: 1) the quarterback when injured is merely getting his fair share of the lumps, and 2) nothing can be done about it because if you tried you would "hurt the game."

Some good and sensible men subscribe to this foolishness. Even those who know the lumps first hand.

After his quarterback, Lynn Dickey, was wiped out of the 1976 season with a shoulder separation on a particularly hard hit by Bears' tackle Jim Osborne, Green Bay coach Bart Starr attempted to still the outrage of his own side (Dave Roller called it a "cheap shot" and vowed revenge on Osborne) with what might be called the party line. Starr did some gutsy quarterbacking for Green Bay in the 1960s, and went down a few times himself. He said, "It's a violent game. You have to live with that sort of thing."

After being hit by Houston end Elvin Bethea in 1977, Pittsburgh quarterback Terry Bradshaw managed to escape with only a fractured navicular bone in his right wrist. The wrist was "dented," Bradshaw said, but at least got in the way of perhaps greater damage. When Bradshaw got up, he was a magnanimous casualty. Elvin Bethea was just doing what comes naturally. "These are aggressive, physical men in an aggressive, physical game," said Bradshaw. "When you take away the things people can do — the linemen rushing the passer, linebackers blitzing — you take away from football." He said he didn't think they could do any more to protect the quarterback "without taking something from the game."

"Take away" from football? How ironic a choice of words.

Here is a sample of what was "taken away" from football in 1977 because of that kind of talk.

In the first televised college game of the season, Matt Cavanaugh, the Pittsburgh quarterback and a prime Heisman Trophy candidate, was buried by Notre Dame's defensive end Willie Fry just as he released a second-period touchdown pass. Forced backward under Fry's 242 pounds, Cavanaugh put his left hand back to brace the fall and snapped his wrist. He was through for six weeks. Good-bye Heisman.

On the first Saturday of play, half the teams in the Big Eight Conference lost their starting quarterbacks. One other Big Eight quarterback was playing hurt with a practice injury. By midseason, eight starting Southwest Conference quarterbacks had been put out of commission. Texas was down to a sixth-stringer as it held desperately to the number-one ranking. The Longhorns lost two quarterbacks in one game — in the same quarter.

Georgia, suffering its first losing season in fourteen years under Vince Dooley, was down to its fourth quarterback by the time it got to Georgia Tech for the final game. In that one, number four sprained an ankle and number five, a freshman, dislocated a fibula. Dooley finished up with still another freshman who had been a reserve on the junior varsity.

Almost every potential All-America quarterback was injured in 1977. Besides Cavanaugh, Houston's Danny Davis, Texas Tech's Rodney Allison, Stanford's Guy Benjamin, Harvard's Tim Davenport, and Brigham Young's Gifford Neilsen all went down for varying periods.

But that was child's play compared with what the pros were dishing out.

On a memorable Sunday in November, Fran Tarkenton of Minnesota, who had never had a serious injury, spun away from a rush on a busted play and was submerged by Cincinnati's Gary Burley. Tarkenton's ankle snapped. On that very same "day at the butcher shop," as one press dispatch called it, James Harris of San Diego was helped off the field with a sprained ankle, Lynn Dickey with a broken leg, Brian Sipe of Cleveland with a shoulder separation, Bill Munson of San Diego with a fractured leg, and Bradshaw with a shoulder injury to go with his dented wrist.

Bradshaw seemed to be getting it every year. In 1976, he suffered almost the exact same kind of terrifying hit that the Rams put on Minnesota's Kramer in 1978. Caught running out of the pocket by Cleveland defensive end Joe ("Turkey") Jones, Bradshaw was grabbed by the waist and was struggling like a fish on the line as the whistle blew. At that point, Robert F. Jones wrote, "it looked like a take from *King Kong*. [Jones] upended him as if he were a stuffed panda, then pile-drove him head first into the ground."

X-rays showed that Bradshaw was unbroken, but his vertebrae were compressed to near the cracking point and he missed two full games as a result. Jones's team was penalized fifteen yards, and he had his name announced (to cheers) over the loudspeaker. Pittsburgh coach Noll called it, generously, "an enthusiastic tackle." Steeler linebacker Jack Lambert was not so generous. "I told Jones that I thought what he did was the cheapest thing I've ever seen in football. . . . I hope he gets his neck broken."

At one point in 1977, twenty quarterbacks in the twenty-eight-team NFL had suffered incapacitating injuries. In addition to the above, Jim Zorn, Richard Todd, Ken Anderson, Dan Pastorini, Billy Kilmer, Steve Barkowski, and Joe Namath were sidelined. Tampa Bay, the league's worst team, was also its hardest hit: four starting quarterbacks lost to injury.

As doleful figures go, those would seem a stiff enough price to pay for being sure quarterbacks are not "coddled." Not everyone agrees they are "something you have to live with." Not everyone believes you would "take something from the game" by providing quarterbacks more protection within the rules

—protection not against the normal risks of a physical sport, but against legal loopholes and dubious ethics that have allowed a twisted rationale to spread in the game. That have made it possible for larger, heavier-muscled, less-talented players to take violent aim at quarterbacks, not just to stop them in their normal duties, but to intimidate and brutalize them.

John Madden, who retired as Oakland coach after the 1978 season, raged for years against rules that allowed the quarterback to become "not only our most valuable player, but our most vulnerable. We protect our kickers with good rules. You can't run into a kicker legally unless you also block the kick. But you can run into a quarterback any time after he throws the ball as long as the referee thinks you were in the act before the ball was thrown. That doesn't make sense to me. It doesn't make sense to protect the kickers more than the quarterbacks."

John Pont, the former Yale, Northwestern, and Indiana coach, is not convinced, either. Pont wonders about a "new mentality" of coaching where "you make the quarterback the target and kick the hell out of him whether he has the ball or not."

And neither is at least one quarterback, Seattle's Zorn. Zorn doesn't think it's necessarily "part of the game" to wind up under half a ton of voracious "defenders" just because they happen to be in the neighborhood when he lets go a forward pass. "If I don't have the ball," he says, "I don't see why the hell I have to get knocked on my tail."

Zorn has been in the NFL only a few years, so his temerity can be excused. He is not, however, an unscarred heretic. He suffered a broken cheekbone in 1976 when he "stepped up to throw and at the same time a guy rushing in hit me in the face with his helmet." Zorn didn't think that was so "necessary."

Most of the admittedly fragmentary reports of football injuries in recent years indicate how fair the "fair share" of injuries to quarterbacks really is.

The Stanford Research Institute's computer work-up for the NFL indicated that of players on offense, quarterbacks were the second (behind running backs) most likely to suffer injury. A study of 1,002 high school and college players by the National Athletic Injury Report Systems (NAIRS) indicated that quarterbacks suffered one-seventh of all "significant injuries" (those that cost game time). Quarterbacks were hurt twice as often as wide receivers, secondarymen, and offensive linemen, and substantially more often than linebackers, tight ends, or defensive linemen.

The problem of protecting the quarterback is as old as the T formation, and is linked directly to its growth. In the T, the quarterback first became prominent as a passing threat, and soon enough gained the recognition defensive players are wont to give those they think are taking the bread from their mouths.

The Browns' Otto Graham popularized the use of a permanent face mask on a hard-shell helmet because of the "recognition" he got in the 1940s and 1950s for the completed passes he inflicted on opposing defenses. Graham's jaw was fractured twice.

One of the classic photographs of football is the one that shows Y. A. Tittle of the Giants on his knees in gloomy Yankee Stadium, his helmet ripped away, his balding head bowed and bleeding. Former Commissioner Bert Bell's immortal line, "I never met a dirty football player," was delivered right after (and in reference to) the blind-side tackle of Lions' quarterback Bobby Layne by Chicago's Ed Meadows that sent Layne to a Detroit hospital and moved his coach, Buddy Parker, to suggest: "Meadows should have brought a blackjack."

Through the years, not every quarterback has been willing to concede these batterings as *quid pro quo*. Some objected on purely practical grounds, appealing to greed (an injured quarterback is bad business). Jack Nix, a Santa Ana, California, insurance man who played end for the 49ers and refereed in the NFL for ten years, remembers Frankie Albert giving opposing linemen sales talks on the subject. "He'd scream at 'em, 'Don't hit me like that! It's stupid! You put me out of the game and you're cutting your own paycheck! People come to see me play!' "

In the days when a player went both ways — played offense and defense — he could occasionally retaliate for the liberties taken by defenders, Nix says. "Bob Waterfield had another way. One guy kept plowing into him after the throw, and Waterfield got tired of complaining. The next time the guy charged in, Bob threw a spiral right into his face, as hard as he could. It was doubly effective in those days because we didn't wear face masks."

Nix is one of those radical thinkers who believe the open season on quarterbacks today is the worst kind of hoax because it is self-inflicted — a cream pie football is throwing in its own face. The hoax is complicated, however. It begins with the logical premise most coaches and players swallow willingly: that the quarterback is just one of twenty-two on the field, protected in the same way by the same tidy rules.

That is logical, but is also nonsense.

There are, to begin with, unmistakable physical inequities. Football players have changed markedly since World War II. Everybody is bigger for sure, but intense weight-lifting programs — in some cases augmented with chemicals — and various strength machines have bulwarked the muscle positions (defensive and offensive linemen, linebackers) with men who are not only bigger but infinitely stronger. Quarterbacks don't lift weights. Coaches make them stop when the season starts, says Bill Yeoman of Houston, "so it won't affect their throwing motion. Linemen, of course, never stop."

The consequence is that what used to be a fairly minor weight differential has grown radically; the quarterback now stands out in every team picture as the one who looks underfed. The Missouri team that played Georgia Tech in the 1940 Orange Bowl had a backfield that averaged 180 pounds — and a line that averaged 189. Wallace Wade's 1926 Alabama Rose Bowl team had an interior line that averaged 195. Fifty years later, Pittsburgh's backfield in the Sugar Bowl averaged 195.6.

In the last fifteen years, the weight of All-America interior linemen has risen an average of 1.3 pounds per year, while backs' weight stayed about the same. Projecting figures, the NCAA estimates that the average interior lineman will weigh 280 pounds and be 38 percent larger than all other players by the year 2000 — and considerably more than that when compared to quarterbacks.

The contrast in the pros is even greater. Pat Haden of the Rams weighs 182 pounds. When he goes against the Dallas front four, he faces one 270-pounder in Ed ("Too Tall") Jones, 255-pound Jethro Pugh, and two 250-pounders in Harvey Martin and Randy White. The laws of physics still apply. $F = MA$: Force equals Mass times Acceleration. As the well-conditioned athlete grows, his capacity for meting out punishment multiplies proportionately, and the athlete whose size remains almost constant is at that much more of a disadvantage. Worse, says Johnny Majors, the Tennessee coach, the 265-pounder "used to be fat and slow. Now he's *fast*. In some cases, faster than the quarterback. That means he can deliver a terrific blow."

The more disproportionate the blow, the more likely the

injury. Doctor Fred Allman studied 43,000 Pop Warner Leaguers at the Atlanta Sportsmedicine Center and found that the injury rate among football players with similar height and weight and skill was "very low." A study made by Dr. Carl Blyth at the University of North Carolina showed that injuries increased proportionately with age, as *dis*proportions widened. At age thirteen, 25 percent of the players surveyed suffered injuries. At fourteen, the injury percentage went up to 28, and advanced dramatically from there until, at eighteen, there was a 68 percent injury factor. The difference in foot-pounds in blows delivered by a 270-pounder and a 170-pounder, traveling at the same rate of speed, is roughly 60 percent.

Doug Plank of the Bears is a likely source of testimony. Plank calls it "a complete mismatch." You have, he says, "on the one hand an offensive player who really isn't conditioned to take hard hits — and maybe doesn't really know how to take them, or to fall." On the other, "defensive linemen coming in who are usually in great shape, are quick, agile and weigh 250 and above. Any time they hit someone who isn't built like themselves, they're going to do some damage."

Defensive players are aware of this mismatch; in fact, they drool over it. The increased emphasis on, and recognition for, the "sack" — a lamentable statistic at best — only intensifies their hunger. Baltimore's Fred Cook once said, "When I get a sack, it really fires me up to get another. I guess I get myself into a sadistic state of mind." Added teammate Joe Ehrman, a 6-foot-4, 254-pounder, "Sacking a quarterback is just a real high altogether. It's like eating a big chocolate sundae." (Ehrman once made Joe Namath's head his stated life's desire, but later mellowed to where he "still likes to hit quarterbacks, but not Namath more than any other.")

Does this mean "bigger" players should not be allowed to

tackle quarterbacks? Of course not. But the disadvantage of an overwhelming size differential dovetails with other, largely overlooked factors that increase the risks.

Contrary to Plank's evaluation, the quarterback's main problem is not that he does not know how to take a hit, but that he is expected to take hits no other player is asked to take. A defensive tackle does not get slammed in the chest by two 270-pound quarterbacks just as he releases a forward pass. A linebacker does not get "sacked" by three 250-pound quarterbacks while he is stumbling backward, sometimes awkwardly, after throwing, in anything but the fetal position.

Quarterbacks are expected to be immune to pressure. If they do not stand in a disintegrating pocket, waiting until the last split second for a receiver to work free, and then release a perfect spiral just before the cave-in, they are said to "hear footsteps."

But consider the position quarterbacks are in. Go to a mirror and throw a facsimile forward pass. If you are right-handed, your right foot is planted as you throw, but your weight transfers to the lead foot as your arm comes around. Everything is moving forward on the follow-through. Freeze there, and ask yourself: is this the position you'd like to be in when the avalanche hits?

For that matter, review the whole procedure. Is there any position at *any* time when passing that you would feel up to receiving "Too Tall" Jones? Especially when you know from experience that Jones will arrive unconstrained by mercy and bent on burying you? Says Jim Zorn: "I'm the most vulnerable to injury when going backwards, in the grasp of a defensive lineman. That's when I'm the most helpless." That is also when the second and third "defenders" arrive to get in on the fun.

Would a defensive end like to take such a hit?

Fred Dryer of the Los Angeles Rams answered the question

for Charley McKenna of the *Milwaukee Sentinal.* Under the circumstances, Dryer said, he could think of a lot of places he'd rather be than in a quarterback's shoes. "The rush that goes through your mind is the same feeling [you get] when you've almost been hit by a truck," Dryer said. "A feeling of what could have been. If you have the ball in the NFL, you're in trouble. I really enjoy hitting somebody. But being hit is no fun. . . . When I get up off a good tackle, I wipe my brow and say, 'Thank God it wasn't me.' "

Compassion does not come with appreciation of this one-sided state of affairs. When he put 200-pound Tampa Bay quarterback Mike Boryla in the hospital with torn knee ligaments in 1977, 280-pound Green Bay tackle Mike McCoy was asked if he felt bad. "No," said McCoy. "It sounds cold, doesn't it? But I didn't feel sorry for the guy. I've never felt guilty about things like that."

Well, why should he? To date, no 180-pound quarterbacks have put any 280-pound tackles in the hospital. He has nothing to fear in retaliation. And he is, after all, only doing his job in the accepted way. Coaches teach players to "get the quarterback." Coaches *want* quarterbacks to "hear footsteps." Quarterbacks under duress make mistakes. Coaches shriek with pleasure when game movies show a particularly heavy hit on a quarterback. They award helmet decals for such feats in college, and in the NFL they keep statistics on "sacks" and give bonuses.

A crackdown on late and redundant hits on quarterbacks was begun in the NFL in 1977, according to Art McNally. McNally instructed his referees to call out when a pass was gone to let charging defenders know the quarterback was no longer fair game. But only forty-seven roughing-the-passer penalties were called, compared with forty-three in 1976. By the same token, coaches certainly do not coach "late hits." A late hit means a fifteen-yard penalty. Coaches would rather have an abscess than a fifteen-yard penalty.

But what, really, is a "late hit"?

What it is and what people think it is are two different things.

The rules make broad allowances for "momentum" in tackling. Some coaches now believe that may be their biggest flaw. Many brutal hits on quarterbacks and running backs are excused under the vagaries of "momentum." Many hits are not tackles at all but vicious exclamation points. Even the quarterbacks are conditioned to excuse them.

"Defensive linemen are brought up to rush the quarterback," says Matt Cavanaugh. "That's what they're trained for from the time they start playing. They can't stop the instant the quarterback releases the ball. . . . Most of the problems come once the momentum is up and the lineman can't pull back, and I don't think it's possible to take that out of the game. I don't think it's possible to change the rules. You can't do that and be fair about it."

Fair? Can't stop? Impossible to change? Conditioning is complete when the street victim sympathizes with the mugger.

Cavanaugh had broken from the pocket and raced to the right sideline to loose his crossfield touchdown pass against Notre Dame. His momentum unchecked, Fry ducked his head and slammed into Cavanaugh just after the release. Texas quarterback Jon Aune suffered a fractured fibula when hit by an Oklahoma player's helmet — *three steps* after he had made a pitch on the option play. ("Someone had blocked him and then he got up, but I guess he didn't see I didn't have the ball," said Aune.) Ken Anderson had thrown the ball, his weight forward, when Pittsburgh's Steve Furness "kind of fell on my leg." Fran Tarkenton was "trying to go down when Burley jumped on me." Tarkenton said it "wasn't dirty."

None of these were. "Dirty" is not the factor, momentum is the factor. Can momentum be legislated against?

John Madden thinks so. "Why not? We tell a guy he can't plow into the kicker, we can sure as hell tell him he can't plow into the passer."

Coaches who argue against equal protection under that rule, however, say a quarterback is a more likely running threat than a punter and can't be made sacrosanct. He is liable to tuck the ball in and scramble away, as Tarkenton did so often. Coaches don't want to give quarterbacks license to steal.

But what is really being served by "momentum" and to what actual purpose is that momentum built up? Pete Williams was a Navy halfback in the late 1940s, when he was known as Pistol Pete. Williams says any schoolyard dodger knows that the tougher man to elude is *not* the one who has built up momentum, but the one who is in control and not fully committed to the charge. A defender rushing headlong at a ballcarrier is in much the same position as a bull rushing a matador, and is just as likely to get the run-around.

Momentum does not make tackles, it finishes them. The tackler who builds up momentum to clobber a quarterback knows full well the quarterback will be there when he arrives and that he won't be embarrassed by a sidestep. Thus what is often allowed as momentum is actually the infliction of the greatest possible punishment.

Says Jack Nix: "Maybe that's been our biggest mistake. Maybe we've bragged too long about the 'killer instinct,' and made everybody think it's the only way. Hit hard, sure. Body contact, sure. But common sense should tell us we're hurting more than just a quarterback when we put him in the hospital. Is that the way we want to win?"

If coaches are willing to say no to that question, it is not as difficult to solve the dilemma as some think. You must, however, be willing to assume certain things: first, that most defensive players can see. If they can see they can be made to do things. Every coach boasts that defensive players are better than ever — bigger, faster, more gifted. John Ray, the former Notre Dame defensive coach, used to say Alan Page "could do anything I asked him." Ray thinks that if Fry had had his head up, and had been coached against plowing into quarterbacks who didn't have the ball, he could have pulled up before steamrolling Cavanaugh. "We can demand more of defensive players than we do," says Ray.

That being the case, says Ara Parseghian, and acknowledging the fact that a defender advancing with more caution in the manner of a screening basketball player is less likely to get fooled, a "grab" rule might be put into effect for quarterbacks, at least on a trial basis. If the defender gets there and the quarterback still has the ball, the defender has the same tackling rights as he has in regard to the kicker before the ball is gone: no holds barred. "But if the ball is gone, and he's got his head up instead of down in that ramming position, he can see enough to hold up, and just grab the quarterback. A grab is a lot less likely to break a rib." (John Madden would add an aural aid: he would equip referees with air horns to sound the instant a pass has been released.)

A rule to protect quarterbacks the way punters are protected would not be difficult to write. But granting the quarterback's added potential, a "grab" rule would be more appropriate. It might also help mitigate the damage being done to quarterbacks on option plays.

The option presents a thornier problem, however. In its

many forms and formations (split T, veer, wishbone), it is probably the most difficult to stop in college football — but it requires that the quarterback be a runner and therefore puts him in greater jeopardy. This is why pro teams don't use option plays.

The evolution of defending against the option has passed through many nuances, but one gambit is now consistently applied: keep the quarterback an east-west runner (laterally along the line); don't let him turn upfield and become north-south. Tackle him *every* time — before, as, or after he releases the ball. Be aggressive. Lower the boom. If a wishbone team runs fifty option plays on a Saturday afternoon, make him get up fifty times.

San Diego State trainer Bob Moore says the option "has become the most dangerous play in football" for this reason — everyone rips the quarterback. "I don't see how he keeps getting up," says Moore.

Sometimes he doesn't. The night before the 1977 Oklahoma–Ohio State game, Oklahoma defensive coordinator Larry Lacewell promised that the Sooners would "make Rod Gerald get up on every play." Nothing malicious was implied, just some good old down-home strategy to stop the slick Buckeye quarterback. Oklahoma pounded away at Gerald, a 6-foot 175-pound stringbean. The battered Gerald was taken out in the third quarter, and Oklahoma won the game.

The quarterback's relatively unprotected moves make him as vulnerable on an option play as they do on a pass. He comes to the point of the pitch with his eyes averted to the tailback, his arm extended, his feet committed. If he executes well he will draw a tackler, which is the whole idea. But in that position he is wide open for trouble from his chin to his thorax to his knees.

Trouble comes in the form of a 220-pound linebacker with fire in his eyes and an artillery shell on his head and a release from his coach to let his frustrations go on option quarterbacks. If the quarterback is put out of commission, so be it. Give that man another decal.

It is obvious to the most casual observer when a defense is sent out to destroy a target, says John Pont. "Officials could call it," he says, "just as any good athlete could be made to back off a little. They call roughing the passer, they can call that. Coaches should look closer at game films. Some of the hits on the quarterbacks after a pitch are brutal. But one coach teaches it, the next coach does it. It's one-upmanship. Somebody has to say, 'Hey, wait a minute, there's a difference between a tackle and finishing off a guy.'"

It would seem a simple enough equation to work out: coaches and officials acting together to decide what is "necessary" in football. But the deeper issue at the bottom of such carnage on quarterbacks is sportsmanship. When a coach plots the incapacitation of another player, it is profanity to call him a sportsman.

To argue that what is happening to quarterbacks is "just football" is double-talk. "Intimidating" a player is permissible in football. Is it, however, sporting? How far should you be allowed to go before it's determined that you've crossed the line and become profligate?

A certain amount of concentrated effort against a star player is familiar in sport. It is acceptable to guard him relentlessly, double-team him, pitch him a certain way, shift or zone a defense for him, neutralize him. But "concentrated effort" is not license to indulge in perversions of the rules.

The line is crossed with the first deliberate attempt to hurt or weaken a player.

Would the following be likely to happen next New Year's Day? In 1965, Texas played Alabama in the Orange Bowl. It was the last college game for the Tide's Joe Namath. He had just come off knee surgery. Bear Bryant himself told how Darrell Royal warned his Texas players, "If anybody hits Namath's knee, he's on the bench. We'll win without that." Namath lasted the game and came within a foot of a touchdown that would have beaten Texas in the last minute.

In commenting on the current atmosphere, Royal, who is now Texas's athletic director, said, "So-and-so [the coach of a rival team] was showing films on his highlight show last season. He came to a really vicious hit on a player. The player's helmet flew off. So-and-so laughed and ran it again."

Such attitudes become license, says Royal. License leads to injury. Brigham Young's Gifford Neilsen found himself "a marked man" in 1977. As the season progressed he was hit with "more intensity" every game, and took "more cheap shots" than he thought necessary. There were times, he said, when he took a beating all day "without getting the benefit of the doubt on judgment calls" by officials. "I think the officials could have seen this, especially with a dropback passer like me [who is] a sitting duck."

Against Oregon State, Neilsen faced "a relentless rush — brutal, but clean." He said he "never took such a beating." It is at such times that a quarterback is most vulnerable to injury — doing something he would not ordinarily do to avoid punishment. In Neilsen's case, he was "very weary" when he passed late in the game, was hit, responded too late, and suffered a fractured knee. He was through for the year.

Not only star quarterbacks are beaten down in this manner, of course. It is a common practice, differing only in the degree demanded by the coach and the level of acceptance of officials. New England Patriot tight end Russ Francis was also "singled out" in 1977.

"I've never seen a guy get worked over like they're working on Russ," said Pats receivers coach Ray Perkins.

"I'm getting mauled out there almost every play," said Francis.

Films showed his weekly struggles to get downfield through a hail of extraordinary bumps and blocks and elbows. A helmet into his side cracked three ribs and finally put him out.

Those who think of football as a game of attrition defend such tactics as perfectly legal. You shouldn't be in the game if you can't take it. Others, however, see it more for what it is: an injury-inducing breakdown in sportsmanship, and they see it as at least partly traceable to the failures of, and the failing respect for, those who officiate the game.

NFL officials have, in recent years, suffered considerable on-field abuse. Players challenge them, fans throw things at them, coaches curse them. "Some [coaches in the NFL] get up real close to you and call you every name in the book," said one, a ten-year veteran. "And they're not words you use around the house." John Madden was pictured on TV making an obscene gesture at an official over a decision. Ted Marchibroda of Baltimore was televised ranging up and down the sidelines in Miami, storming at an official. Oakland receiver Fred Bilitnikoff breasted one and had to be restrained after a pass interference call.

NFL officials earn as much as $17,000 a year (at a rate of $325 to $800 a game) in part-time employment. Their counterparts in college believe trouble lurks when such a handsome subsidy becomes built in to a way of life, making an individual vulnerable, even acquiscent, to such abuse. College officials don't usually "need" the $150 to 250 a game they get in the major conferences. Pete Williams, an engineer, says "half the officials in the Southeastern Conference probably make more than the presidents of the schools" whose games they officiate. Referring to the NFL's pay scale, attorney Gene Calhoun says, "I suspect that you can get pretty dependent on $17,000 a year."

The implication is clear enough: NFL officials are willing to put up with more. Says one coach: "As you progress up the ladder from high school to college to pro, you see officials grow more liberal in their interpretation of the rules, and that is a dangerous thing."

Players obviously sense this. Once they know the cops won't shoot, the looting begins for real. The most prominent recent example of disrespect has been demonstrated by Pittsburgh's Mean Joe Greene. Not caring for calls made against him in a game with the Colts, Mean Joe said of the officials that if "given half the chance, I'll punch them out." He claimed he was "on a crusade against the striped shirts, and I will be until I get out of this game." The NFL did not take him out of any game, it merely fined him. In 1977, Greene had to be fined again for his punching episodes against the Denver Broncos. He said he was merely going "outside the law" to get justice.

Players and coaches seeking justice in this manner may get more than they bargain for, says Calhoun. They may be promoting an atmosphere made to order for disastrous consequences. "An NFL official [Armen Terzian] got conked by a whiskey bottle in a game at Minnesota. It knocked him out. It could have killed him. Even after the game the Minnesota coaches were still complaining about the officiating and the bad calls, and officials who 'blew it.' Well, is that an excuse for violence? It would have cost the NFL $200,000 in lawyers' fees alone just to defend itself if that guy had been badly hurt.

"Listen. No one is immune. Bo Schembechler [of Michigan] in our league criticizes officials all the time. Dan Devine [of Notre Dame] had some pretty rough things to say about the officiating in the Atlantic Coast Conference. We put up with our share of 'terms of endearment,' too, because we hate to penalize kids for something coaches say, and I'll tell you, some of the things would curl your hair. We put up with it as long as it doesn't affect our judgment, then we throw the rag. But I've heard kids say after a penalty like that, 'Why doesn't that so-and-so shut up!' meaning his own coach.

"There's a time and place to criticize officials. If they're bad, they deserve to be criticized. That's why we have meetings and review film. But on the field is no place to go crazy. I tell coaches, protest, sure, if you have a gripe. But do it right. Blow your damn stack, do something outside the scope of your authority, and you are very likely to find yourself individually liable. Outside the protection of the school, outside the protection of the conference. Go ahead and berate officials. Incite the crowd. Start a riot. But when the damages are counted, you may lose everything you worked for, and face the possibility of a criminal charge as well."

In 1977, two separate but similar messages went out from the offices of the National Football League and the NCAA. One, from Commissioner Rozelle, warned that playing-field viciousness and misconduct "do not belong in professional football" and would bring "disciplinary action." The other, from Dave Nelson, secretary-director of NCAA officials, said the tactics being practiced were "humiliating college football." Nelson said the "football code and rules governing unsportsmanlike conduct are being ignored by players, coaches and officials." He said there was no place in college football for maneuvers "deliberately designed to inflict injury."

After a subsequent USC–California game, Stanford's Walsh reviewed the films for his upcoming game with Cal. He said that the things he saw in that game "were not in the best interests of college football." USC coach John Robinson had complained about Cal's "dirty play." Cal end Ralph DeLoach had bragged that Cal "intimidated" USC flanker Randy Simmrin. Cal coach Mike White said DeLoach "spoke very well for our program."

Wayne Hardin of Temple said he saw more "dirty football" that fall than he had seen in years — "guys throwing elbows, a guy sticking a helmet in the middle of another guy's back. I saw Michigan playing a team, up by a big score, and sent in a guy and three plays from the end he really clocked this guy with his elbow. He wasn't even involved in the play. On the last play of the game, he tried to do the same thing to another player, but missed."

Coaches allow those things. They are a "coaches' problem" instead of a "players' problem" or a "commissioner's problem" because football is a coaches' game. If they do not teach good sportsmanship, they must be responsible for the acts of bad sportsmen.

Johnny Unitas says the best way to stop the more brutal players is to "throw their ass out of the game. That would end it." Earl ("Red") Blaik, the former Army coach, suggests a penalty box, arguing that nothing makes a player more reflective than sitting on a bench. Doug Plank, although perhaps an unlikely advocate, agrees. "It would be like enforcing the death penalty. Right now you practically have to hit somebody on the back and trample on his head to get thrown out. If an official came up [and warned me what would happen], I might not like it but I'd make darn sure that whatever he was watching I didn't do in that game."

But those are the flagrant fouls. What of the others? What good is a fifteen-yard penalty for clipping if your player is on his back with a torn knee? Herman Rohrig, the Big Ten's supervisor of officials, says, "We have to impress on players and coaches that football is not an exercise in annihilation." Coaches get more safety conscious when it costs them fifteen yards. A way to impress them further might be a twenty-yard penalty. Would a player think twice before aiming a forearm at someone's neck if he knew it would cost his team twenty yards — or even thirty? Would a thirty-yard penalty make a coach more conscious of his humanity?

Football coaches are fadists. Successful coaches believe strongly that it is not original thought but hard work and dedication and an appreciation for the finer points of the "fair advantage" that will get them home. They have such strong, successful figures as Lombardi and Bear Bryant to emulate. They demand as much of themselves as they do their players. It is the logical way.

But to be logical is not always to be right. A coach may ask too much. He may be on actionable ground when he tells a player he has to block in a certain ruthless way, or tackle in a way he knows is meant to intimidate and hurt. He cannot delude himself anymore that the charge that he may be going beyond his bounds is an infringement on his coaching prerogatives.

Trial magazine, in their special sports litigation issue, warned that "what coaches teach can be held against them. The mere act of putting on a uniform and entering the sports arena should not serve as a license to engage in behavior which would constitute a crime if committed elsewhere."

Fanaticism within a philosophy of action is always dangerous, but it is especially dangerous when it involves something as physical as football. Chip Salvestrini is a high school coach in New Milford, Connecticut. When he played in college, Salvestrini says, "One of the coaches would come up to me and say, 'Salvestrini, there'll be twenty-five dollars in your back pocket if you break that quarterback's arm by halftime.' I see guys now who'd do anything to win if they can get away with it. I drill it into my players all the time — you can be nice and win. You can play clean and win. You don't need all that other crap."

In 1977, an eighteen-year-old linebacker at Virginia Polytechnic Institute died after being given a series of "punishment" exercises. For having beer in his room and taking part in a "ruckus," Bob Vorhies was made to complete ten fifty-yard sprints, ten hundred-yard sprints, fifty pushups, fifty situps, two hundred-yard "bear crawls" in which he had to scuttle on his hands and feet without allowing his knees to touch the ground, four other hundred-yard runs of various kinds, and an undetermined number of laps around the field. All this after the normal practice day.

Vorhies collapsed in his dormitory room and was found dead there. The county coroner blamed "cardiac arrhythmia," and said there was "some relationship between the drill and his death." The boy's father, Jerome Vorhies, sued, producing a letter from his son that said "they treat us like animals." The father said "they pushed him too far." But two months later a grand jury found "no neglect or wrongdoing."

The assistant coach who ordered the punishment was not identified. VPI's head coach, Jimmy Sharpe, a thoroughly decent young man whom I have known since he played for Bryant as a watchcharm (180-pound) Alabama guard in the 1950s, was later fired, but the university said it was unrelated to the incident. No one from VPI's official athletic family or Alumni Club attended the boy's funeral. The school sent flowers.

The death was a terrible, tragic fluke. The severity of the boy's training, examined in cold print far removed from the daily rigors of the football environment, seemed excessive, but in relationship to what? The trouble with judging football from the outside is that there is nothing to compare it with, except perhaps war (a favorite comparison of Woody Hayes's), and while some may be revolted by "what it takes" to play the game, others glory in it and take to it without a qualm, like frogs to swampwater.

An astonishingly large number of the letters I received on the brutality series for *S.I.* were from lawyers. Many of them were seeking information; some were offering to trade. Though many of them sounded naive about football — a little scary in itself — none sounded less than dead serious. And, of course, they all sounded eager.

A combative lawyer, armed with a cause, can be a terrifying human being. Doctors, for example, are terrified by lawyers and malpractice suits. Doctors make a lot of money. They also make mistakes. Lawyers make mistakes, too, but it is much more profitable to sue doctors. To minimize their risk, they present as low a profile as possible. But football, as the Mount Rushmore of sports, does not offer doctors much in the way of camouflage.

Thus, one more crisis grows in the game: doctors flee from it. Team physicians and game-day volunteers run for cover. After the death of John Manns in Baltimore, the director of interscholastic athletics for city schools there acknowledged that he was having "great difficulty" getting doctors. It was, he said, virtually impossible to have one at every game.

It is not, however, a Baltimore problem or a Philadelphia problem — it is a national problem. In Jefferson County, Kentucky, the medical society was unable to provide physicians for eight county teams. Dr. Kenneth Eblen of Henderson, a twenty-four-year "volunteer" at football games, said that he frequently had to act as physician for both teams.

"There are a heck of a lot of doctors who won't even *go* to a game," said Dr. Eblen. "They're scared of the liability situation. It's something they can't control. Parents and coaches put too much pressure on doctors to let kids play." One Kentucky physician had a patient who suffered a broken neck. His parents insisted the boy be allowed to play because they were afraid he would miss out on a college scholarship. The boy played. The physician quit as team doctor.

At the higher levels, lawyers have taken cognizance of — in their words — team doctors acting as "house men." They charge that when employed by a professional team or college, doctors are apt to be more concerned with the coach's needs than the player's. When Dick Butkus collected $600,000 in settlement of a suit that alleged his knee was irreparably damaged by drug injections, his lawyer, James Dooley, said NFL doctors were engaging in "conflict of interest." Attorney Bob Baxley, who represented Houston Ridge in a successful suit over a leg injury that was allegedly aggravated when Ridge was given pills enabling him to play without pain, said, "Players should hire doctors, not owners."

Lawyers have fairly leaped into the controversy over artificial turf. *Trial* magazine quoted surveys that showed the turf "reduced players' careers three to four years" and was condemned by "80 percent of the NFL players," and offered unblushing hints as to what its readership might do about it. Doctors, of course, have been leading that chorus for years. Nobody paid much attention because the doctors didn't sue anybody.

There are unmistakable advantages to an artificial playing surface for outdoor sports. It doesn't have to be cut, watered, or fertilized. It looks as good in December as it does in August and shows up well on television. When it rains, the players don't get muddy. And tests show players *do* run faster on it.

But all that does, says Dr. Donald Cooper, is make for more violent collisions. "We've already got enough trouble with violent collisions."

Players also get better traction on it, but they hardly need that, either, when a ligament can tear in the act of falling down. Roman Gabriel once complained that his *helmet* clung to the turf, causing a concussion. When Bert Jones separated his shoulder on AstroTurf in 1978, he said his shoulder pads actually "grabbed" the surface and had his right arm pinned just before he was hit by a 260-pound defensive end. The inopportune combination finished poor Bert off.

Besides the blackened feet, infected elbows, and mangled toes ("turf toes," in the vernacular) that are common punishment for those who play on artificial turf, the incidence of more serious injury on it so alarmed Georgia team physician Dr.

Butch Mulherin, himself a former Bulldog player, that he got coach Vince Dooley to cut practice time on the school's AstroTurf field to thirty-five minutes a day. "We get more shoulder separations, more fractured wrists, more ligament sprains on AstroTurf—no question," says Mulherin. "The foot gets so well fixed to the stuff, gets so much torque, it won't release. That means more ankle injuries, more pulled hamstrings, more groin pulls."

Former Redskin coach George Allen says that not even extra knee, elbow, and arm pads offer enough protection. "Players get bumps, bruises, and abrasions that take weeks to heel. Ankle and knee joints take a beating. Just *standing* on it is like standing in a hotel lobby. It tires the legs and takes away their spring."

"As far as I'm concerned," says Dr. Mulherin, "artificial turf has no place in football."

With such endorsements as these, you would think football administrators would have the bulldozers out in force. Not at all. Fifteen of the twenty-eight NFL teams play at home on carpets. Since the Stanford Research Institute report in 1974, four new fields were laid in NFL cities — in Detroit, Seattle, New Orleans, and New York. Every one was artificial.

It can be argued, of course, that three of those are in domed stadiums, where natural grass cannot grow, and that two of the three synthetics — Polyturf and Tartan — are no longer produced. But if fields in domed stadiums cannot be made as safe as grass, why dome the stadiums? Are the warmth and dry hairdos of fans more important than the health of the game's players?

It could be argued on the other hand that only one percent of the reported injuries in football are to NFL players, and they have been alerted. Let them take their chances. The football field construction news among colleges, where there was no particular alarm, would seem more worthy of concern. While Monsanto was installing those four AstroTurf fields in the NFL, it was also installing thirty — count 'em, 30 — in college stadiums, including ones at Arkansas, California, Iowa State, Kansas State, Kentucky, Boston College, Michigan State, Virginia, and West Point.

A report by the National Athletic Injury Reporting System covering the 1975–1977 seasons indicated that college players spent 41 percent of their field time (practice and games) on artificial turf, resulting in a higher injury rate for knees, feet, and ankles, as well as a higher overall rate of "significant" injuries, those which restricted the player for more than seven days.

It would seem, therefore, that Monsanto's multimillion-dollar bonanza has been extracted at a terrible price. But surveys being what they are (mostly suspect), and given the demands of the consumer, it is pointless to blame the manufacturers. Manufacturers can show you their own surveys. They are, after all, in the business to provide what people want.

Administrators of football want better land economics and lower maintenance costs. Ironically, not all of them have found artificial turf to be as practical as they first thought. Three cities — Miami, Denver, and Washington — went back to grass in their municipal stadiums when they determined it was cheaper than tearing out their carpets every five years. Ed Garvey said that it proved a point: practicality is easier to sell than humanity.

Charlie Krueger, the former pro tackle, was quoted in *Trial* as saying, "Nothing will be done until someone dies." That's not entirely true. Kent Waldrep, a TCU player injured in a 1974 game at Alabama, filed a $3.5 million suit against the city of Birmingham charging that the artificial playing surface (Polyturf) then used at Legion Field in Birmingham caused him to suffer spinal cord damage.

Waldrep was tripped as he went out of bounds on a play. He landed on his head, broke his neck, and wound up in a wheelchair. His lawyers claimed the field wasn't properly padded. Now someone else dresses Waldrep and combs his hair. Reluctant to face an end to an active life, he made a trip to Russia, looking for a miracle cure. Bitterly, he said, "It's hard to imagine building up my body for twenty years, then zilch. I can't make it do anything. It's frustrating to command the leg to use and it just sits there."

If the players' interests came first, Waldrep said, administrators would "rip up all this artificial turf. Studies prove it causes more injuries. The players say they don't like it. But nobody does anything. . . ."

The sad fact is that studies do not "prove" anything. *Trial* charged that the lack of expertise in tracing the causes of injury in football today ("instead of hiding these injuries, they should be ferreting them out") is in itself a terrible offense. It suggested a central registry of injury information for the sport.

That such information is not available is, if not criminal, a sad commentary on the good intentions of football. Despite the fact that it is our most injury-filled game, there are no "centers" for data, no computerized feedback to high schools, colleges, and professional teams, no telling them that this or that ruptured tendon was caused by such-and-such a blow in the fourth quarter in the rain on a grass field in Ames, Iowa. Worse, says Dr. William Clancy, the Wisconsin team physician and orthopedic surgeon, "no organized medical input [is made in the rules-making process] by the people who are the best authorities on injury. A lot of people who really don't know are making the input. Rules committees are afraid doctors will change the game."

In view of the rising casualty lists, this attitude is shocking. Doctors and trainers need to be armed with data; so do coaches. The elements of peril to those who play the game need to be examined on a regular basis.

A number of attempts by concerned medical men have been made to bridge this gap. Dr. Clancy is active in the American Orthopedic Society for Sports Medicine and the College of Sports Medicine. Sportsmedicine clinics, acting as centers for treatment and rehabilitation, are now operating in twenty-four cities. In some, such as Dr. Joseph Torg's clinic in Philadelphia, injury studies have been undertaken (Torg's on head and neck injuries). Though limited, they are commendable.

But at best it is a disjointed effort, resulting from a common, basic flaw in the administration of the game: people don't care enough. Or, rather, *enough* people don't care.

In January 1974, Dr. Kenneth Clarke, then at Penn State, "out of desperation" formed the National Athletic Injury Reporting System and began funneling injury reports on twenty-five high school and college teams into a computer. His aim was to provide a "continuous awareness" of the definition of injuries, the degree of their severity, and the solutions they demanded.

The aim was high, the response low. For two years the research was funded mainly by the sporting goods manufacturers, with small grants from the high school federation and the NCAA. Dr. Clarke now computes "175 to 180" reports from high schools and colleges. NAIRS, in turn, furnishes subscribers monthly reports and a year-end summary. Clarke also kept tabs on three NFL teams, but found "the league was not interested in our findings." He said NFL owners told him "they didn't need any more data."

Dr. Clarke is now at Illinois. Penn State still provides the computer for NAIRS, and Clarke still gets nominal support from sporting goods manufacturers for a six-person staff, but he is "very discouraged." The NCAA continues to shovel money into the program by the teaspoonful — a $1,500 grant in 1978 — and without more funding Clarke "doubts the program will go on much longer."

He says his is a "realistic discouragement" because the commitment to keep injury records "has never been part of our sports heritage." He says people think "what they are doing is all they can do. Our concept of sport is that everybody is an expert, therefore we don't need all these sophisticated studies. It's an attitude problem."

NAIRS is handicapped further by an intricate injury-gathering process that relies entirely on the input of its subjects. The trouble with intricate surveys is that they can be overwhelming. The NAIRS procedure calls for a team trainer or physician (or whomever the school designates) to follow a 133-page book of instructions, cataloguing for the computer the most intimate details of individual injuries. Dave Nelson at Delaware found it a "mind-boggling process," easily discouraging the nonprofessional fact-gatherer. After being assured by his physical rehabilitation people that a 72-page report NAIRS provided on the 1976–77 season "didn't help a bit," Nelson dropped from a weekly NAIRS accounting to a monthly report.

The last sanctioned study made by the NFL was the Stanford

Research Institute's report in 1974. Through 1978, there had been no updating. The NFL's weekly rundown of league-wide injuries is not meant for medical evaluation, but for use by coaches who don't want to lose an edge, and to keep bookies from getting one. Why would a multimillion-dollar business that dispenses volumes of nonessential information on every conceivable aspect of play not bother to update something so important as the whys and wherefores of its injuries? Because, said Jan Van Duser, NFL director of personnel, "we feel they would give us the same results. Rules, playing surfaces and the number of players have not changed that much."

Exactly, said Joe Grippo of Stanford Research. Without change, what's the use? Grippo believes that "labor problems in the NFL" have created a reluctance to face up to the problem and do precisely that — make dynamic changes in the rules and in the conditions of play.

"They [players and management] have been at each other's throats for years," said Grippo. "They're afraid to tamper with the underpinnings of the game. You need labor harmony to make sweeping changes."

The NFL player strike of 1975 accomplished two things beyond the inflation of a linebacker's value on the open market: it raised the level of distrust between owners and players, and it made players more aware of the value of their broken bones. A widening no-man's-land developed between management and labor as the players resorted to the harsh business ethics owners themselves had used for so many years.

In business, you take your grievances to court, not to the locker room. Increasingly, injuries have become reasons for litigation. Nick Roman sued the Kansas City Chiefs for back pay and damages because he was "released when hurt, violating the contract." The Oakland Raiders' Terry Mendenhall was awarded $91,500 in 1975 because the Raiders' team physician allegedly concealed a knee injury before Mendenhall was traded. Raymond Hickl of the Oilers, who had a history of head injuries, was hospitalized after being hit on his helmet by a player's knee. When he decided to quit football, the Oilers decided not to pay him. Hickl went to the newly formed arbitration committee, which awarded him $4,000 — finding that the Oilers had made "little or no attempt to determine if Hickl had any previous injuries."

In 1977, Miami Dolphin defensive end Bill Stanfill took owner Joe Robbie to arbitration. A four-year All-Pro, Stanfill was suffering from a chronic neck injury. He consulted three or four doctors, all of whom confirmed that he should not play. Stanfill told a Miami newspaperman that the Dolphins' offer to settle the remaining three years on his contract was such that he felt obliged to go to court. The arbitrator ruled in his favor, holding that the contract should be honored. A settlement was made.

There are no brass bands or waving pennants in courtrooms and emergency wards. With a gangland mentality allowed to fester on the field, and with a sport whose leadership is more responsive to Nielsen ratings than injury reports, it is small wonder that the wolves (mostly lawyers) are at football's door. In the end, money itself will have to intervene. "Litigation," says Kenneth Clarke, "is waking people up. Litigation will be the cause of change." When owners are convinced that injuries are costing them money, an NFL referee told Jack Nix, the former player and official, they will push for reform.

The NFL didn't respond at all to the Stanford Research Institute's report and its recommendations. The pros made no appreciable rule changes for 1975 and the high injury rate continued. In a grand show of concern for the game, the NFL made two rules changes in 1978: it made it possible for linemen to "hold" a little more convincingly (to extend their arms and open their hands), and second "bumps" on receivers once they were five yards downfield were prohibited. Injuries did not bring about these changes, however; according to the league communiqué, Commissioner Rozelle was "concerned" that the scoring average in the league was at a thirty-six-year low. The NFL had "to put more offense back in the game."

The SRI report said a lot of things in 1974, but one of the things it said best echoes like a graveyard voice today. According to the SRI findings, only 1.3 percent of all injuries in the NFL involved illegal acts that drew penalties. Those in the blood bond who excuse the violence consider this proof that players are basically rules-abiding fellows and ought to be left alone. There is another way to look at that percentage. If "illegal acts" are not responsible for the outrageous number of injuries, then the fault lies *within* the rules, in things that are happening that *ought* to be illegal.

Those who say you would "hurt" football by changing the rules hurt it infinitely more by doing nothing. No one thing will magically render the game injury-free. Part of its attraction, both in the playing and the watching, is the physical intensity.

Furthermore, it is an intriguingly complicated game, made even more complicated by the fact that it is really three different games — high school football, college football, pro football — with different rules, interpretation of rules, philosophies, and styles of play. Things forbidden at one level as too dangerous are allowed at another. The game is not even officiated the same way from level to level, or, in some cases, from region to region.

In trying to analyze exactly what has caused all of football to suffer an unacceptable injury rate, I explored many sources, tapping the minds of concerned coaches, physicians, and officials. At the conclusion of the *Sports Illustrated* series, a number of proposals for changes in rules, equipment, playing conditions, and coaching philosophies were offered. Perhaps not all of these changes would work, but there is no doubt that changes have to be made if football is to remain the prototypical American sport. As a game, it must be played within civilized boundaries, for if it is a game, you do not maim.

On that unarguable basis the following rules were suggested. In some cases, they were already in effect at one level of football or another, but if they are worthwhile, they needed to be instituted across the board:

1. Outlaw all deliberate helmet hits — if the helmet makes initial contact in blocking or tackling, it is wrong.

2. Outlaw blocking below the waist on all downfield plays, or outside the "legal clipping" zone. Ban the "chop block" and its relatives at the line of scrimmage.

3. Instruct officials to enforce more stringently the rulings on late, redundant, or unnecessary hits, be they on ballcarriers, receivers, or quarterbacks. The criterion at its most rudimentary would be to make tacklers responsible for knowing when a player is stopped, helpless, or already going down.

4. Institute a "grab" rule for defensive players tackling quarterbacks in the act of passing, in which only the arms and hands would be used if the "momentum" has caused the tackler to hit the quarterback after he passes. If this proves unworkable, give the quarterback the same protection the punter is given.

5. Institute a no-hit rule on receivers (until they catch the ball) and on tailbacks in the option play. An offensive player without the ball should not be fair game.

6. When it is evident that quarterbacks are being hit on

certain types of plays simply as a form of intimidation, warn the coach of the team responsible. If the practice persists, call personal fouls.

7. Crack down on all "momentum" tackles involving out-of-bounds plays and forward progress. A player on offense knows where the boundary lines are; the defensive players should, too.

8. Outlaw all forms of "clubbing" or forearm blows on ballcarriers and receivers; outlaw all head tackles save in interior line play.

9. Penalize all overt forms of bad sportsmanship, including end-zone dances, gestures, and taunting.

10. Increase the penalties for flagrant fouls and unsportsman-like acts to twenty yards (minimum) or thirty yards; eject repeat offenders and coaches who repeatedly dispute officials' calls.

Administratively, the following was suggested:

1. Standardize the rules throughout the game, allowing only for differences dictated by age and physical development (e.g., length of quarters).

2. Make mandatory the representation of physicians and game officials on rules committees.

3. Establish a central registry for injuries, with input on their causes and computer readouts available for high school, college, and pro teams. Allow the NFL to fund this project as a token of its appreciation for having the colleges and high schools as its farm system.

4. Establish a crew of rules committee members to conduct clinics in which coaches and players would receive instruction on rules and injury-causing tactics.

5. Pad the outside surfaces of helmets and shoulder pads; make mouthpieces mandatory; study the face guard's value, and if it is truly a cause of spinal injury, prohibit its use.

6. Make some form of lightweight knee brace mandatory equipment (e.g., the 8-ounce plastic model used at Oklahoma State).

7. Outlaw artificial turf.

8. Outlaw strong chemical stimulants and institute urine or saliva tests as necessary to ensure that players obey the rules against the use of drugs.

9. Monitor practices to make sure techniques being taught are legal and ethical.

None of these recommendations would affect the aesthetic qualities of the game. None would lessen its appeal. They *would* make life more difficult for coaches, and more costly for administrators, but if they saved half a dozen players from wheelchairs, they would be worth it.

Teddy Roosevelt never intended to abolish football when he inveighed against its excesses seventy years ago. He said in an address at the Harvard Union that he did not in the least object to sport because it was "rough." He emphasized that he did not wish to have colleges "turn out 'mollycoddles,'" or "men who shrink from physical effort or from a little physical pain."

But, he said, "I trust that I need not add that in defending athletics I would not for one moment be understood as excusing that perversion of athletics which would make it the end of life instead of merely a means in life."

Unless there are sweeping changes in football, a storm of litigation is coming. Doctor Cooper said to me, "If you love the game, you have to be concerned. You can't put your head in the sand. We've got a crisis of broken bodies. If we don't do something about it, we're going to wake up in five or ten years and there won't be any football.

"There are a lot of enemies of football now. They're frothing at the mouth because of all the litigation and all the problems.

They think it's so good because they're finally going to get this son-of-a-bitch out of the way. Get rid of it. We've got a professor in the philosophy department who hates the game, hates the coaches, hates the players — and he's with those who see this as a golden opportunity: don't *improve* football, eliminate it."

I talked with B. shortly after the *Sports Illustrated* series came out. He said the college administrators he knew had taken the series well, that in some corners, notably the executive offices of the Big Ten Conference, a rallying cry could be heard. He reminded me, however, that change sticks in the throat.

"People have to be coaxed into change, especially change for the better," he said. "More so when they are told to look in the mirror for the causes. If the acts that bring on injuries were no more than the sins of a few twisted minds, blame would be as easy to pinpoint as a flash flood or some other natural disaster. But the problem is not with twisted minds, it's mostly with educated people who think they've been doing right all along."

To be sure, some of the game's leaders recoiled at the charge that they were remiss. Pete Rozelle said he "resented" the insinuation that the league was "callous" to injuries, and resurrected the hoary argument that 99 percent of the injuries in the NFL happened on plays where no foul was committed. As for the unfortunate casualty statistics such as those involving busted-up quarterbacks, he said the NFL did not feel there was anything that could be done "without changing the basic character of the game." In effect, he did not want to "make it touch football."

Brice Durbin resented having his high schools lumped with Rozelle's pros in the indictment — or with the colleges, either, for that matter. It was a legitimate resentment, considering the high schools' superior record for safety rules. Dave Nelson objected at first along classic comparative lines (e.g., that water sports produced more quadriplegics than football). He rightfully pointed out that *all* coaches were not to blame (I had not blamed *all* coaches), and that some very conscientious ones had worked with him on the rules committee for the past twenty years, including an old favorite of both his and mine, Fritz Crisler.

The 1978 season passed fitfully, and with enough blood spilled to cause tremors of fresh indignation in newspaper columns from Boston to Los Angeles. Some, like George Will, wrote extensively on the brutality question, and others asked embarrassing questions every time a body went down. There were outcries from surprise sources. Howard Cosell, champion of the common man and the bloated phrase, said that the NFL had "first merchandised violence, next it merchandised sex. And it failed on both counts." He said the league was "now suffering from that violence."

Meeting in Hawaii in early 1979, the NFL opened an eye. In a flurry of rules activity (meaning, in the lexicon of publicists, three or four decent changes) the pros announced that "quicker whistles" would henceforth help prevent quarterbacks from taking late hits. Blocking below the waist on all kicking plays was prohibited, bringing the NFL to parity with the colleges at last in that part of the game. The rule against the crackback block was extended, and it was decided that players should be penalized for punches or kicks even if the punches and kicks did not land.

Tex Schramm of the Cowboys said the key to the changes was "defining what is unnecessary. Even in the case where it's a legal hit, if it's unnecessary, it's going to mean a penalty." Schramm said that "violence used to be a part of our game," but that people "who used to watch football for its violent hits now question whether those hits are necessary."

No action was taken in Hawaii on helmet use, though I knew from talking with Don Shula that he and other coaches and officials on the competition committee had recommended making it illegal to plow headfirst into a receiver, a quarterback in the act of passing, or a ballcarrier already stopped and otherwise helpless. Perhaps that would have been too much too soon. Or perhaps it would have been construed as an admission. In any case, when the owners reconvened in New York in June 1979, they added the helmet limitations Shula had outlined. A step in the right direction.

As usual, the colleges went a step further. Meeting in Dallas in January 1979, the NCAA rules committee voted to restrict blocking below the waist on *all* plays in which the ball changed hands, exempting only normal scrimmage plays. A new rule penalized any defensive player who charged into a passer when it was obvious that the ball was already thrown. A rule was passed to assess multiple penalties when more than one foul is committed by a team on the same play. For example, if three clips were called on one play, the offending team would be penalized forty-five yards.

I learned early in 1979 that there was a chance the NCAA was going to set up a central agency, probably at the NCAA offices in Kansas City, to survey and research the causes of injury. It sounded promising. After the NCAA Council met in April, however, there was no announcement.

I called B.

He said they had tabled the motion in order to "talk about it further."

4.

OF COLLEGES AND COACHES

I am a rube for college football. I admit it. I think it is superior
entertainment to the professional version for a number of techni-
cal, aesthetic, and emotional reasons. I came to this conclusion
young and have been influenced by experts. Maturity has not
cured me. It is a terminal case. I expect to die a sucker for the
game, unreconstructed.

Technically, the college game is better because there is more
diversity in it. It is not stereotyped, and does not fight change
the way the pros do. College coaches adjust their game to the
players on hand. The pros pick through the talent and make it
adjust.

College coaches try anything — single wing, double wing, I
formation, veer, split T, wishbone, spreads, flea-flickers,
double and triple reverses, tackle eligible passes — whatever is
legal when it is legal. If a mode of attack phases out, they
quickly go to another. As a result, they score more points, make
more yards, raise more blood pressure. They do not need
personalities in the television booth to tell people how exciting
they are. Each team has a personality. It varies from coach to
coach, from section to section, and from conference to conference. Every Saturday there is an interesting new match-up.

The pros do not change because they cannot afford to risk failure at the box office. All pro teams look alike; the differences are in the subtleties that make the better coaches stand out — e.g., Don Shula and Tom Landry — and in the unique physical abilities of the individual stars. Offenses and defenses are otherwise interchangeable. Switch uniforms and you wouldn't know the difference.

The college game is better because it engenders more spirit and emotion among participants and spectators, and an intimacy the pros can never hope to achieve. It operates on a more exalted plane, because of its traditions and because it is involved in the education of its players. Football is important to America because it was first important to the colleges. United States presidents and Supreme Court justices are counted among its by-products.

The college game is better because it is, simply, more meaningful, for everyone involved. College football is an engrossing, all-encompassing thing. I once walked across the snowbound campus of Dartmouth College with the president of that great school, and when we reached the football stadium he said, "It is no accident that it is here, in the middle. Everybody identifies with the football team."

I like it that college players respond to halftime talks. That it gets you *here* when the band plays "On, Wisconsin!" and when Alpha Tau Omega wins the prize for the best homecoming float. I like it that college football has card sections and crowded fraternity dances, and leggy majorettes and cowbells. And cheerleaders who actually lead cheers, and do not just provide them like pro cheerleaders.

The game began with the colleges, and the history of it is wonderful. I like to hear the story about KF-79, Columbia's secret play, beating mighty Stanford in the Rose Bowl. I like to read about the bowlers, the toppers, and the pneumatic headgear, or the time when the players parted their hair in the middle and wore it long to cushion the blows. I like the things they wrote about the Poes of Princeton: "Arthur Poe is back, smaller than ever." I like to think that Ted Coy of Yale really did say, "The hell with the signals. Give me the ball."

And those nicknames. "Germany" Schultz, "Mr. Inside," "The Gipper," "Choo Choo" Justice, Pat ("The Kangaroo") O'Day, "Slinging" Sammy, "Whizzer" White. The idea that someone would say, "Fight fiercely, Harvard," actually chokes me up. Once I heard a gray-haired old lady, a professor of astronomy at the University of Michigan, give a rousing speech to a pep rally on the quadrangle in front of the university library. She was no bigger than an ice bucket. She had a soft saintly voice. The snow was coming down on her gray head. "Go, Blue!" she cried. It sent shivers up my spine.

The essence of college football is something the pros cannot duplicate. There is a spirit to it, a drawing together. People *do* identify with a college team, and it is totally unlike that tenuous identification a pro fan may feel for two and a half hours on a Sunday afternoon. College football is the alumni, the parents of the boy down the street who made the team, the girl sitting next to you in the library, the restaurateur who rides around with "Beat 'Em Bucks" painted on his station wagon.

It is a game of ancient rivalries that inspire genuine loathing, not for a weekend but for a lifetime. It is traditional games, whose meaning is deep — Army vs. Navy, Ohio State vs. Michigan, USC vs. Notre Dame, Alabama vs. Auburn — no matter how bad the records may be, how low a team is in the standings. In Texas a rule of thumb for years has been that you dress up for the college game and down for the pros, because the one is heavy drama, the other fun but of no great consequence.

College football is Mormon schools, Quaker schools, Baptist, Catholic, neo-atheistic schools; poor-boy and rich-boy schools. It is a game for towns like Boulder, Colorado; Austin, Texas; Fayetteville, Arkansas — far away from the blackened cities and the skinned infields of baseball parks, up where you can see Mount Rainier in the background, or look out over Lake Cayuga, or just get on top of the stadium, up there on the last row, and look out on a campus like Wittenberg, Colorado Western, or Kansas State. The people in Cleveland Municipal Stadium on Sunday afternoon would never understand that.

Football is rooted in the colleges. It has done its best work there, and, I think, its chances for survival are there.

But there is a basic flaw in the college game, one that courses through its body like an infection. It is called recruiting, and it is the bane of college football.

Auctioning ballplayers is accepted in the professional leagues. I wouldn't say it's a bad thing there and it gives us a chance to know how a good catch of tuna might feel when the bargaining begins at Fulton Street. The colleges do not hold player drafts. Instead, they recruit. They allow their coaches to roam the countryside like snake-oil salesmen, trying (sometimes desperately) to win within (and sometimes without) the rules the best players for their schools.

Young assistant coaches revel in recruiting, with its glamorous travel and expense account dinners. But, by the time they've been in it for a while, most recognize it for the tiring, often degrading thing it can be. They learn to despair of the long drives in the night. The lonely hotel rooms. The phony backslapping. The pandering to drunken alumni. The white lies — like telling Junior he's a cinch All-Conference, and telling Mama what a fine meal that was when they almost choked on the okra.

Recruiting is the root of almost every problem coaches have, including the ones that get their teams thrown in the slammer by the NCAA. Alumni, coaches, and admissions people cheat over recruiting. Head coaches demean themselves recruiting. Some of them make asses of themselves. And besides all that, it's expensive.

Recruiting in its present form suckles the caste system, helps keep the downtrodden down. The operational word is "expensive." Every coach wants the best material, so he can win and go to bowls and get a five-year extension on his contract. It would be un-American to want otherwise. But it is absolute lunacy for forty or fifty coaches to spend thousands of dollars on phone calls and jetting back and forth across the country to recruit one solitary athlete.

Miami is a mere 1,800 miles from Norman, Oklahoma. But forget what it had to do to Elvis Peacock's eighteen-year-old head, having the illustrious coach of the Oklahoma Sooners make two cross-country trips to see him. And the coach's assistants eight trips (one brought his wife just to take Elvis to supper). The irony of it is that they couldn't pay Peacock $10,000 to play for them, but could spend $10,000 to *get* him to play for them.

The recruiting rules, as laid down by the National Collegiate Athletic Association, are a very carefully worked out, very complicated order of confused priorities and pusillanimous mumbo-jumbo. Through this sieve the coaches venture forth, making players hypocrites. They say, "You're a good athlete, so here's an academic scholarship. You are now a student-athlete."

Coaches believe, but seldom say, that the scholarship athlete is a contracted employee of the university. He is paid to produce, to represent the school as an entertainer and emissary, paid in the currency of the "free ride" — an all-expenses education consisting of tuition, board, books, laundry, walking-around money, etc. The package comes roughly to $30,000, but the value of the education, if the athlete gets it, is limitless.

There are two ways to look at this. Traditionally, that's what college athletic scholarships are for — to provide a gifted athlete a chance to get an education he would not ordinarily have been able to afford. But in reality,if they had to pay O. J. Simpson what he really meant to the athletic department — in terms of gate receipts and television dates — USC would have had to take out a loan.

The basic terms of the scholarship (or "grant-in-aid"), as well as various recruiting restrictions, have been arrived at painstakingly over the years. Ostensibly, schools submit to these restrictions to keep their athletes in a state of purity, holy and acceptable unto the NCAA. But the real motive is economic: colleges can't afford to have price wars for athletes. To offer more than scholarships and "fringe benefits" is to risk financial disaster. Hence the "student-athlete" myth.

Why this is so hard for the NCAA membership to swallow is a perpetual mystery. The members certainly know better. The athlete is not a normal student. There is, furthermore, nothing wrong with him being special, and his services paid for in the most meaningful way a university can pay a boy: by educating him. It does not taint the athlete any more than it does the scholarship piccoloist in the marching band.

Once it is established what the college athlete on scholarship really is, then his relationship with the coach can proceed along

more clearly defined and better-appreciated lines. The relationship is, essentially, that of employer–employee, with a dash of
father–son.

I have heard a number of coaches complain about the
system, some of them after they have gotten out of it. Not all of
them hated the idea of being a fifty-year-old man kowtowing to
an eighteen-year-old child; some of them actually thought their
best coaching was done in a mother's kitchen. But they all
admit that the key to success is getting boys to come to their
school in the first place, when they might not be at all inclined.
Or maybe they might have *been* inclined, but got talked out of it
by a better salesman.

The process is a phenomenon worth looking into.

Johnny Majors, head coach of the University of Tennessee,
parked his car on the back side of the hangar, where it was partly
obscured by a row of light planes. He said he didn't like to be
seen driving a Cadillac. "If you get your tail beat, it doesn't look
good driving a Cadillac," he said. They had tried to give him a
Cadillac prematurely at Pittsburgh, too, he said, but he held out
for an Olds. Now that he was back in Tennessee, his resistance
had apparently weakened, but he still had qualms. When I had
come to Knoxville the week before, Majors had traded cars with
Henry Lee Parker, his administrative assistant, so I wouldn't
make something of it. "Henry Lee is more the Cadillac type,"
Majors said, grinning to expose the division in the front teeth of
what he calls his "ruddy farmer's face."

The pilot of the orange and white (Tennessee's colors) Piper
Navajo was waiting in the warmth of the hangar together with a
younger man with wispy red hair, a Tennessee assistant coach
named Robbie Franklin. Franklin had alerted Majors to the
emergency. A coveted high school prospect, a defensive

lineman living just south of Bowling Green, Kentucky, had signed a Tennessee grant-in-aid but was now wavering. Woody Hayes of Ohio State had paid the boy a visit which set off vibrations. The player was good enough for Majors to take to the air.

The university-owned Navajo and its pilot had been Majors's steady companions since early January. There had been Coach of the Year banquets from Boston to Los Angeles. Majors had swept the more established of these honors, but presumably because of the magnitude of his championship season at Pitt, new honors had been conceived, and accepting them had kept him flying around. He had been in demand as a lecturer, too, and there had been rush trips like this one to help get some meat on the bones of a Tennessee team that had gone 6–5 in 1976 and got coach Bill Battle fired.

"I wake up in a motel room and I don't remember if it's Humboldt, Tennessee, or Kalamazoo," Majors said. "I feel like a schizophrenic. How's it look, Charlie?"

The pilot plopped down a salt-stained pair of rubber boots. "It's snowing in Kentucky, Coach," he said. "Not supposed to stick, but . . ."

Majors looked at his patent-leather shoes with blue suede tops. He was dressed handsomely, if not ruggedly, in a light orange sports jacket, matching striped shirt and tie, gray slacks, and a polished leather suburban coat. He shrugged.

"When I went out to take the Iowa State job in 1968, all I wore was a thin brown suit, like crepe paper. I was ducking in and out of doorways to stay warm.

"My first head coaching job — what did I know? I was a bundle of nerves. I couldn't sleep. I didn't know anybody. I was in the *North*. I was scared to death I'd fail. I'd always had that fear of failing. My first day at school, six years old, I told my mother, 'I'm not going.' She said, 'What's wrong with you?' I said, 'I can't read!'

"You should see the official picture they took of me in Ames. The expression on my face — miserable. I'm finally a head coach, and I don't know what the hell to do. I know I can't go back to Arkansas. Frank Broyles has already filled my old job. I know I have to recruit. My dad had told me, 'Lay your ears back and go to work.'

"I got a map of the state and took a ruler and divided it into four equal parts — one each for me and the three assistants I'd hired. I said, 'Okay, we'll each take a quarter.' And one of my new assistants said, 'Better make that thirds, Coach. I'm leaving.' I didn't even look up. I said to Jimmy Johnson, 'Take him to the airport, Jimmy.' I was discouraged enough without having to look at him."

Majors laughed and led the way outside to the plane. The flight to Bowling Green would take more than an hour, bucking head winds. From there, Robbie Franklin said, it was another thirty minutes by car to where the prospect lived on a dairy farm. Robbie carried an overnight bag. If necessary, he would spend the night to get the boy's signature on a national letter the next day, when binders became final. Majors was carrying only a briefcase.

"What's the story on this kid?" he asked as they buckled in, facing forward in the six-seater. "I thought he was ours."

"I think he needs to be reassured, Coach. Woody Hayes came in with both barrels and now the boy's confused. I think he just wants to hear you say you want him."

"Well, we want him, all right. He has the size we need."

Majors dug into his briefcase for his list of recruits, looking for statistics.

"Six-four; two-thirty-five?"

"Yes, sir. Probably make a noseguard. He saw your Pittsburgh defense in the Sugar Bowl and was impressed."

"How about academics?"

"Not too strong, but we can help him. He's no dummy. He read where you said you wouldn't win the national championship with this year's crop of recruits."

"Well, that's right, isn't it? We've done okay, but we were late starting. If we could have brought in the numbers we did at Pitt . . ."

His first season at Pittsburgh, Majors said, he signed seventy high school seniors. The NCAA limit is now thirty a year, ninety-five total.

"At Pitt, we already had our staff," Majors said, "and we knew what we were going to do, so I just turned the coaches loose to recruit. We were ten weeks on the road. I told everybody to report on the weekends to see where we stood. We didn't get many blue-chippers, but we did get guys with fire in their eyes. They were *desperate* to succeed."

With the plane airborne, Majors loosened his seat belt and took out a cigarette, exposing hands surprisingly large and big-boned for a small man. As the Tennessee tailback in the mid-1950s, he played at 162 pounds and led the team in rushing, passing, and punting; played safety; was a unanimous All-America and second to Paul Hornung in the 1956 Heisman Trophy balloting.

The pilot turned the Navajo north and west, sliding above threatening clouds and into open sky.

Recruiting, Majors said, is never easy, but the degree of difficulty varies. "At Iowa State they hadn't won in so long — a 2–8 record the year before I got there, no tradition, no enthusiasm. That first year we got nothing but nubs. We busted our tails for seconds and thirds. You'd talk to a kid and he'd look at his watch.

"Iowa got all the good state boys. We had to become a national institution to cope. I sent Joe Madden to Pennsylvania. I didn't know anything about Pennsylvania, but I sent him. Joe brought back a newspaper clipping. It said, 'Some schools soft-sell their program, but some don't. Iowa State sends in the Music Man — drums pounding, pamphlets flying around.'"

Majors leaned forward and slapped the armrest of the facing seat. "We had to be like that, like the Music Man. We had to do tap dances just to get their attention. We were living on air, fighting for our lives. Trying to outrecruit teams like Kansas State. But it was a good time to be in the Big Eight. I don't believe you ever knock the opposition; you praise what you've got. One year the Big Eight was 28–8 against outside opposition. I didn't have to say anything against Iowa or Michigan. I could say, 'You play in the Big Eight, you have a chance to play with the best.'

"The second year we ran out of recruiting money while our guys were still on the road. I got my back up and said, 'Stay out. If we don't do it now, we'll never do it.' We spent fifteen thousand dollars over budget. Not much by Tennessee's standards, but Iowa State couldn't throw money around. We signed George Amundson, the quarterback from South Dakota. About five good players come out of South Dakota a year, and we had one of them. The third year we played Oklahoma to a standstill and lost 29–28. It made our program. The last two years we went to bowl games. Iowa State had never been to a bowl game."

Majors studied his list of recruits. Of the twenty-eight who had signed Tennessee grants, seventeen were from within the state. He said you could usually count on at least a dozen and no more than twenty-five good players a year in Tennessee, so it was necessary to mine the bordering states — Kentucky, for one — and to go into Pennsylvania and Ohio and east to the tidewater area of Virginia. The mathematics was inescapable: in Tennessee, 296 high schools field football teams; Pennsylvania has 567.

Franklin said they had just missed one hot number in West Virginia, a halfback who billed himself "Alexander the Greatest." Alexander, he said, had signed with West Virginia — in the state's Capitol Building with Governor John D. Rockefeller IV on hand.

Majors said he contacted some of those he had cultivated in Pittsburgh the previous fall. "I told them I wasn't about to bad-mouth Pitt, it's too good a school. But if they had a visit or two left, come down to Knoxville and see us.

"Most schools can give you a good education. Tennessee has fine engineering, medicine, business, law. But all things being equal, I think a kid wants to know he has a chance to play, maybe a chance to play for a championship. A successful recruiter doesn't lie. He accents the positive. At least I can tell them we're starting out in the middle instead of rock bottom. Tennessee hasn't had losing seasons; it just isn't satisfied to go 6-5."

The rental car that Robbie Franklin had ordered was not at the tiny airport in Bowling Green. Neither, however, was the snow. The storm had lifted and in its wake temperatures had fallen. Robbie, scouting around the airport for a substitute vehicle, found a set of keys that had been turned in, but he couldn't find a car to fit the keys. "How do you like going first class?" Majors asked me.

The rental agency finally delivered a car from town, and

Robbie took the wheel, heading south on Interstate 65 with his foot hard on the accelerator, hoping to regain some time. Majors laid his coat over the seat.

"I don't want a kid whose arm you have to twist," he said. "I want one who it means something to to wear that orange shirt. Even outside Tennessee, it means something. I didn't have that at Iowa State, and not much of it was left at Pitt, either, but I can appreciate the importance of it. I told the Tennessee players at our first meeting, 'It should mean a lot to you to play here, where there's tradition. That orange shirt meant something to the great players who were here before you. Regardless of when we become champions, and I don't have any idea when that'll be, you can play like champions. Like Tennessee teams have played before. This is a fresh start.'"

He slapped the seat with his hand.

"That's why I say, 'Don't come here if it doesn't mean something.'"

He slapped the seat again.

"And that's why recruiting is so important in the fall, when you can bring a boy in on game day, let him hear the whooping and hollering. He has to think, 'Boy, I may be just another student on Friday, but on Saturday I'm special to a whole lot of folks.'"

We left the thundering interstate at the junction of State Road 100, a much narrower ribbon through blood-red strips of raw land opened for seed, and rode past glistening silos and crushed, beaten-looking farmhouses.

"I go into very few wealthy homes," Majors said. "I see kids who are hungry, who see football as a means — an education, a career. I don't like arrogance. If I see a father living his frustrations through his boy, or a boy trying to get a guarantee, I tell them, 'You have a chance,' period. Not many kids have their hands out, not as many as you'd think. But I've seen kids who were tickled to death to see you the first time, and two months later you had to crawl in there on your hands and knees."

The car passed quickly through downtown Franklin, population 6,500. A weather clock on an office building indicated it was 27 degrees. In the open on the other side of town, the wind got up and shook the car.

"I've always enjoyed recruiting. I like the challenge of winning a boy," Majors went on, "the chance to look him in the eye, to communicate. They asked me at Iowa State, 'How are you going to deal with blacks?' I'd never played with blacks or coached them. I said, 'If they're men, I'll treat them like men. If they're kids, I'll treat them like kids. I'll treat them the way they want to be treated.'

"Every recruit is not a man. We brought in that group four years ago at Pitt — blacks, whites, Polish kids, Italian kids, guys from the South, from the North. They weren't at all close. They were doubtful. Suspicious. We were tough on them at times. Four years later you never saw such respect and love among a group of young men. They'd have practiced till midnight if we'd asked them. They grew up. How much farther, Robbie? Hell, you said thirty minutes."

"We're close, Coach." Afraid he had passed the boy's house, Franklin had made a premature turn, become disoriented and was too embarrassed to confess. He kept driving, hoping for a familiar landmark.

Finally, he pulled off into a narrow dirt drive and came to a stop in front of a squat, cinder-block house the washed-out color of an underdeveloped sepia-tone photograph. No shrubbery enhanced the landscape. A solitary swing suspended between two barren trees turned slowly in the wind.

The boy's father met Majors at the door, a hulking, frowning figure with glasses thick as windshields over hollowed-out eyes. He was wearing green coveralls and was in his stocking feet and his graying hair was almost shaved, causing his bullet-shaped head to appear to thrust up from his shoulders.

Without fanfare, he invited Majors and Franklin inside, as if Coaches of the Year dropped by regularly, and turned down — but not off — the living-room television. A thickset boy, wearing glasses indicating eyesight as poor as his father's, came out of the kitchen. The father introduced him as Buck, the brother of the boy they had come to see, undoubtedly a relief to Majors, who took a chair under a large print of *The Last Supper*. On the opposite wall a 1977 calendar advised to "Insulate Now." The house had the pungent smell of raw sewage. The father explained that the pipes had frozen and the toilets were backed up.

"Donnie," the father said, "is still milking the cows. Buck'll get him." Robbie Franklin followed Buck out the door.

Alone with Majors, the father said he had become an avid football fan since Donnie became a sports-page item. His own enthusiasm had surprised him. "I don't understand the game, but I watch it all the time." He said he even took a portable television to the barn on weekends to watch the games. "I been milking those bastards all my life," he said. "The least they can do is let me enjoy it once in a while."

They chatted amiably. The father said the family "didn't have to live in this dump, we got another place, a nicer one, not too far away," but it was a way to assure Donnie a better school district for his football. Abruptly, the father turned solemn. Tilting his head forward, he said earnestly, "Coach Majors, I think we got a problem. Woody Hayes was here last weekend and sold Donnie a bill of goods. I want him to go to Tennessee, but Donnie's like his mother. Every time he hears something new he changes his mind."

A flicker of surprise crossed Majors's face (he admitted later he was stunned by the finality of the news), but he spoke calmly. "I appreciate your telling me," he said.

Donnie himself led Buck and Robbie Franklin back into the living room. Even in stained work clothes he was plainly an athlete — powerfully built and lithe, with pleasant good looks. A protruding upper lip made him appear petulant. Brown curls spilled from a red and white cap he left on as he took a seat on the sofa, a vantage point from which he could see both the Tennessee coaches and the television set. A Jerry Lewis movie had come on, apparently one the boy had missed. Even without the sound, and in the middle of talking, he seemed able to follow its progress.

Majors started slowly, making a conversation piece out of his winter travels. "I tried to get up here a couple times, Donnie, but our schedules got fouled up. I think you couldn't make it the last time." Then he said how pleased he was that Donnie "had decided to come to Tennessee." The boy did not react except to say he had made a last-minute trip to Auburn. Majors said he remembered Auburn as a place where there were always nice-looking girls.

"I felt like I was in heaven for two days," the boy said, releasing the television from his gaze and offering his first, small smile.

Majors carried the conversation, saturating the room with the vitality of his personality. It nevertheless seemed clear enough that Donnie had been sorely tempted by Ohio State. He was defensive on the subject of opportunity, of where a lineman might go "to get a pro offer." He said he had been led to believe Ohio State was such a place. He said he had been worried over "stories" about all the big defensive linemen Tennessee had signed.

Majors leaned forward. "Who? What big linemen?"

The only name the boy gave him drew a smile. "Yeah, that boy's from Ohio — and Ohio State didn't even try to get him," Majors said. "Listen, young man, competition will make you a better player and us a better team. Did you ever think of that? I don't think you're the type who's afraid of competition, are you?"

The boy said he wasn't. He shrank from the issue. His gaze wandered back to the television. "That Jerry Lewis is something else," he said.

The visit that Majors hoped would be brief dragged into the second hour. Majors glided effortlessly into a lighter pitch. He expressed genuine bafflement that the boy would consider backing out of his agreement with Tennessee. He said he thought Donnie must be "kidding," just "trying to make Coach Majors's hair gray." He pointed out that Tennessee needed big, quick linemen like Donnie, that the need was "critical," that they were "counting on him," that he should remember the positives of playing "in your own backyard," where "we speak your brogue. Do they speak your brogue in Ohio?" He spoke of the pleasure of "getting in on the ground floor" of a building program. "We are undefeated, untied and unscored on — and we haven't won a game, either."

He pointed out how pleasant it is to have your friends come see you play, and to have your future formed "in your own backyard."

The boy looked up. "Coach Majors, that backyard is two hundred miles from here."

"How far is it to Columbus?" Majors said.

The father laughed and slapped the knee of his coveralls. "He's got you there, Donnie."

The phone rang and Buck hopped up from his listening post in the kitchen to answer it.

"Wish I had money for every time that thing has rung lately," Donnie said.

The father, who had slipped out of the room, reappeared in a large yellowish cowboy hat, grossly outsized for his shaven head.

"Hey, that's all right," Majors said, brightening. "But, uh, it's the wrong color."

"Well, hell no, it's not, this is Vanderbilt's," the father boomed. "Now, here —" He peeled the hat away like the leaf of a giant artichoke, uncovering a second one of a deeper orange shade. This one had a "T" on the facing.

"Ah, *that* is the model," crooned Majors.

As if a switch had been thrown, the tension eased. The boy began to respond more agreeably to injunctions, and to ask questions. He asked if it were true that the pros "find you no matter where you play." "Of course," Majors said. "And do you think they'd pass up a school like Tennessee?"

Sensing the change, Majors wound down his argument. "We want you at Tennessee, Donnie, and we're counting on you. But I'll tell you one last thing. Once you get there, don't think you won't have problems. You'll have 'em. I did; everybody does. When you do, come see me. My office is always open. If it's something pressing, and I'm in a meeting, they'll call me out."

Donnie remained noncommittal through the good-byes. Majors told him Robbie Franklin would be over in the morning for the signing. The boy said he would "take the night to think about it." An Ohio State coach was supposed to come too, he said.

Robbie Franklin seemed to breathe easier as he drove Majors back to Bowling Green. "I think you turned him around, Coach," he said.

"Maybe. He seemed tuned out at the start."

"He doesn't think he's big enough."

Majors laughed. "Yeah, a kid six-four, two-thirty-five, sees a kid six-six, two-fifty, as a 'monster.' Donnie's plenty big enough."

"You like him?"

"Yes, I do. I think he may be a little wary of the competition, but, hell, so was I. I was petrified. He'll be fine once he gets to Tennessee. Don't lose him, now."

It was dark when the little Piper landed in Knoxville. Majors said he had eaten exactly two suppers with his family since they had moved into their new house — a forty-year-old colonial on four and a half acres in suburban Topside — and now he had missed another.

His secretary left a note on Majors's desk the next morning. It read: "Coach Franklin called. Donnie signed. Coach Franklin wanted you to know your talk had a great bearing on our being able to sign him."

"I think Robbie's looking for a raise," Majors said, grinning.

Three weeks after Donnie enrolled at Tennessee, he quit and went home. He returned, briefly, and quit again. He wound up at another, smaller school.

I know Johnny Majors well enough to believe that what I saw in Kentucky was an honest example of the way he conducts his business. Besides being a fine coach, Majors is an open-faced sandwich. Even on the brink of rejection, he made no outrageous promises, hinted at nothing more inveigling than the chance to play for a good team at a good school.

We talked later about the boy's attitude. He had obviously become jaded with sales talks. Majors passed it off as a natural rural reticence and an inferiority complex. He said he could understand it, being a farmer type himself. Personally, I said, I would have asked the boy to remove his nose from the television set at least while I was into my pitch, but knowing the difficulties young people have in doing that I imagine the only way it would come about was if there had been an air raid.

I came away respecting Johnny Majors more than before, and feeling vaguely ill at ease with the process he and his fellow coaches must go through to assemble the raw material for their work. For one thing, Majors is a giant in the game, and deserved more respect.

More significant, and more sobering for me, was how heavy the professional influence weighed on the proceedings. Donnie's main interest in college — indeed, the only interest I could see that raised a spark in him — was the proximity it would provide him to professional scouts. He was not going to college to get out from under the udders of a cow and on the road to enlightenment, he was going to college to get a leg up on a big pro contract. In Donnie's case, it appeared to be a dead end. He seemed doomed to wind up one of the ninety-nine out of a hundred who never get a look.

But at the retail level, that likelihood was not discussed. Majors pandered to the dream-wish, something coaches should not do, he told me later, because most kids' dreams of a pro career are illusory. He said it was a change for him, too, and sad. He had gone to Tennessee some twenty years before, wishing to play football forever but knowing education was his first priority, not a fringe benefit.

I came away thinking there had to be a better way. Perhaps there isn't.

Some time later I received in the mail a page from a back copy of the Columbus, Ohio, *Dispatch*. A story about a famous coach covered the entire page, under a sixty-point headline: "Abolish Athletic Scholarships!" The coach's main message was in twelve-point italics: "I think it would be a wonderful thing if a coach could just forget all about the high school and prep school wonders of the world and develop a team from among the students of his institution who came to his school because they liked it best and not because of any attractive offers made for athletic ability. . . ."

The famous coach went on to say that "instead of the specialized football player, I think it would be wonderful if every student could develop in many kinds of sport. . . . Let the stadiums keep on getting bigger and let the crowds grow with them. Let the competition grow keener. But some day I hope that scholarships for college athletes will be a thing of the past."

The coach's name was Knute Rockne. The story appeared in the *Dispatch* on March 4, 1929.

In prosecuting the college basketball scandals of 1961, an assistant New York district attorney, Peter D. Andreoli, said that one pertinent thread ran through all the players' testimony: none of them had any loyalty to his school. A. Whitney Griswold, the late president of Yale University, so disliked athletic scholarships that he termed them "the greatest swindle ever perpetrated on American youth." Sociologist Reuel Denney of the University of Hawaii, a collaborator with David

Riesman in *The Lonely Crowd*, said that in the commercialized sports environment the athlete "is first turned into a robot, and then sometimes the robot becomes a burglar. I think the first stage, when the human being is turned into a robot, is worse."

These are not new views, by any means, and they are extreme. Football remains a major assimilating force on the college campus, and there are as many legitimate reasons for letting the superior athlete play his way through an education as for supporting a brilliant violinist. It would be a mistake to kill the athlete's chances of going to college because the process is given to excess.

Better to curb the actions of his elders.

Better still to curb the process itself.

As always, the mechanics and morals of recruiting mainly have to do with money. That the system can be corrupted is not new, either. Seven members of the 1893 University of Michigan football team were not even students at the university, and when Yale lured All-America tackle James Hogan to New Haven in 1902 it was by dint of free tuition, a suite in Vanderbilt Hall, a ten-day trip to Cuba, and a monopoly on the sale of scorecards. I suspect that some of the old recruiters, with a less intense light on their activities, could teach the new breed a thing or two.

In well-publicized infractions cases prosecuted by the NCAA in recent years, the promises delivered (and discovered by investigators) included the providing of illegal air and ground transportation, two-week vacations at Long Beach, phony transcripts, pieces of furniture, free auto repairs, fraudulent test scores, fake employment in summer sports camps, the co-signing of promissory notes, and, in one case, an up-to-date scrapbook of newspaper clippings.

Gifts were made of clothing, tickets to pro games, television sets, cash for athletes, cash for wives, cash for various relatives, contact lenses, record albums, rings, sports coats, winter coats, athletic equipment, refrigerators, and rods and reels. Recruiters arranged for the exchange of automobiles for season tickets, wildly inflated prices for single-game tickets, reduced apartment rentals, medical services, dental care, lodging for relatives, and credit cards. They got traffic tickets fixed, furniture moved, and bank loans repaid.

Lumped together like that, the indiscretions sound numerous, but spread out over a few years and cases they become little more than routine. That the recruiting of athletes is the most fertile ground for cheating is beyond question. The dilemma doesn't change: coaches, alumni, and administrators still cheat sometimes. What seems to have changed is the distance the modern college player has grown from the Rockne ideal (which is, after all, the Stagg ideal), and how unrealistic that ideal now seems. Money has done that.

When he was suspended a year by the National Football League for betting on games, Paul Hornung said he would "play for the Packers this year for nothing" if they would let him. Playing for nothing should never be asked of a professional player, of course. For a collegian it should never be questioned. But for the star college player today, his matriculation is often no more than a bridge in time, something to pass over to get to the real money.

The hotshot college player does not say he would gladly play for nothing. He says he would gladly play for a lot.

And he wants it coming in and going out.

Ottis Anderson of the University of Miami was the first running back chosen in the 1979 National Football League player draft. Preening before the draft, Anderson said he planned on "asking for an arm and a leg." Out of hand he dismissed Buffalo, Kansas City, Cincinnati, and Chicago as teams that "don't pay enough money for me." And because the St. Louis Cardinals "don't pay no money," he said it would be "best for them not to pick me. I don't want to play for them." He said he wouldn't want to play for the hometown Dolphins because "they don't pay no money, either."

When he was chosen by St. Louis, Anderson said, "Well, I'm happy. They [the Cardinals] are the best organization in the league."

As it turned out, Anderson not only accumulated a gift for hyperbole during his college career, he also accumulated an agent, against NCAA rules. In fact, he had accumulated three agents. They ran concurrently, like a play with three first acts. The summer before his senior year, aware that it was wrong and "nervous" about it, Anderson agreed to be represented by Michael Trope of Los Angeles, a twenty-seven-year-old wunderkind in the business of wheeling and dealing. He said he did it because "I was just a junior and I had nothing to look forward to my senior year."

Anderson's version of the events was that he then dropped agent Trope because "he doesn't get you no kinds of endorsements or manage your money." He signed on with an agent from Houston, borrowed money to buy a car, paid it back, dropped the second agent, and signed with a third. Agent Trope then sued him for $52,500, the amount Trope said Anderson would have had to pay him for agent's fees if he got the kind of contract Trope thought he deserved. Trope said he wondered how sympathetic a judge could be to have before him "a guy who got a car from one agent, loans from another, then signed with yet a third."

Trope was not through suing, however. Nor singing, either.

He filed $500,000 in claims against thirteen more of the nation's top college players, alleging that they had breached contracts by signing with other agents. He said that several had played their senior seasons after receiving cash loans and signing "offer sheets" from his office. Maryland's Steve Atkins and Texas A&M's Eugene Sanders admitted they had received loans from Trope or his representatives. The loans and signings were in clear violation of NCAA rules.

The surface issue was that of a relatively new problem in college sport: a plague of agents swarming over the game, promising to extract big money from pro teams in return for the athletes' willingness to suborn the system and break the rules. But the deeper issue is the progressive undermining of values, a process that converts the game's participants into mercenaries.

When Paul Hornung of Green Bay and Alex Karras of Detroit were caught betting on games in 1963, they were suspended from the National Football League for a year. It was not the gambling itself, but the gambling's implications, that made their conduct unpardonable. Naively, and perhaps unwittingly, they had destroyed a portion of faith in the integrity of the game that paid their way. Spectator sport, to remain sport, cannot afford to have the outcome of its contests questioned.

I met with Hornung shortly after this incident. I found him immensely likable, and properly contrite. He was, after all, not a criminal; his football playing was unassailable, and he had not thrown a game or taken a bribe. But one day he was merely the pal of a gambler-businessman and the next day, "scarcely before I realized it," he said, the man was his betting agent and confidant. He said he had no idea of the consequences when he placed that first hundred-dollar bet.

At the time, I found this incredible. Anybody old enough to

read a detective novel could fathom the suspicions that association could arouse. Hornung did admit that although he was not sure of all the implications of the rule he violated, and did not consider his action "immoral," he knew for sure it "wasn't kosher."

I asked myself later, what sorcery could make this Golden Boy risk his handsome neck and way of life by flouting as he did a rule he could read on every locker-room wall in the National Football League? The answer was not really so hard to find.

In a sense, Paul Hornung was indoctrinated to excess at age seventeen with the coming of the first high-pressure college recruiter. ("I wasn't offered a car or anything big like that," he told me, "but in some cases I was promised extra money.") So sought-after was he that Bear Bryant, then at Kentucky, brought the governor of the state to the modest Hornung apartment in Louisville to help charm Hornung into accepting a scholarship. Bryant said years later that he probably would have stayed at Kentucky a couple more years if he had landed Hornung. Hornung's mother, however, wanted her son to go to Notre Dame — it was her dream. She didn't bother to wake Paul when the governor came to call.

Used to special treatment as a college and a pro star, it seemed perfectly natural to Hornung that the United States Army obliged him with weekends off so that he might continue his career with the Packers. He could scarcely get out of the way of people wanting to do him favors and give him money. By and by it became quite easy to take lightly a "simple little wager" of one hundred or two hundred dollars. If the money didn't mean much to him, why should the rule? "After all," he said, "I'm just another one of the vehicles in this business."

The point is the same today as it was then. When sport is big business, the people who run it — pro team owners or college presidents — demand that it be successful. They are successful if they win, and they win when they have the best players. The players, of course, know this by the way they are treated. They may have only a vague intuitive sense of the pressure they are under, but they know they are indispensable to the process and are both manipulated by it and able to manipulate it. It is no wonder values become relative and rules become playthings.

The whole complicated mechanism begins with recruiting. Any coach or business manager would attest to the logic. The first buck spent has to be the one that brings in the talent. Recruiting costs for a major college football program run well into six figures, but are easily assimilated in an overall athletic budget that might reach $5 million or more. Some schools can (or must) recruit for less than $100,000; others, like Notre Dame, ranging far and wide for its harvest, would have trouble staying under three times that. The NCAA imposes no restrictions on how much can be spent, as there are too many variables to consider. With some, "How much?" is answered by "Whatever it takes."

The recruiting process — the ramifications of handing out valuable athletic scholarships to deserving youth — is the source of continuing controversy and regularly drives college administrators into paroxysms of self-analysis. Big money is never inconspicuous. Recently, a chairman of the economics department at one university was outraged when denied a request to bring three candidates for an assistant professorship to the campus for interviews. The football coach, he argued, was allowed by NCAA rules and by the college to bring in ninety outsized adolescents a year, wine them and dine them and schlepp them around campus. The chairman called it "rank hypocrisy" and "no joking matter."

Annually when the representatives of the disparate NCAA

membership convene in Dallas or San Francisco or Miami, they come in wringing their hands over the system. They set up caucus centers (with wet bars) in $150-a-day suites, make reservations for dinner, then advance onto the convention floor armed to the teeth with ways to "cut costs" in athletic programs. That really means "cut football," because football costs more and gets more attention. Football *is* the NCAA convention. Chairs scrape and the coughing is epidemic when they talk about anything else.

Football, however, is the only means most schools have to *make* money from and for athletics. And in recent years inflation has dictated that making money is more important than fielding good representative teams which lift a school's spirit and inspire its alumni. Big football schools would like to cut costs, too, but they would rather beat Notre Dame. You don't scare Notre Dame by taking laundry money from your athletes (which the conventioneers did a few years ago), or by reducing your chances to get them to your school.

No one is madly in love with the system, but no one seems to know what to do about it, either. The NCAA establishes the recruiting code, and pores over it painstakingly. In its present form it bears a striking resemblance to the income tax laws. It is a morass of patched-up restrictions and nit-picking dictums that determine, ostensibly, every move a recruiter makes — whether he can say hello to a prospect if he bumps into him in the St. Regis lounge, whether he can buy him a seltzer while there, walk him around the corner and get him a discount on a sports coat, or advise him on the sale of his free tickets, the status of the used-car market, the colors in the rainbow, the part in his hair, and the virtues of the steak au poivre over the veal oscar at Le Côte Basque.

It's a difficult code to know, much less to live by. In other words, it is a mess. The investigators in the NCAA office (a harried force of ten) who have to deal with it should get combat pay. Even coaches who are known in the business for being honorable tell me that, in one way or another, they break the rules — more or less as conscientious objectors. ("If I see a kid standing in the rain needing a lift, you think I'm gonna drive right past?")

And *every* coach I know, when he has had a couple, complains how hypocritical the system is. Unfortunately, this skepticism makes it easy for some to go over the line and become outright cheats. I have already mentioned the skulduggery used by this splinter group. The influence of their lawlessness, alas, filters down rapidly to the objects of their attention. An ex-SMU star, outlining for a Texas newsman the way the money flies around (if you can call under the table a flight), had this advice for youth: "Take it and run." Caveat emptor.

In that light, the first logical step for the NCAA would seem to be to crack down on the crooks operating within their imperfect system. Many right-thinking coaches advocate a tougher line: bust some heads, they say. Indiana's Lee Corso says crooked coaches "ought to be gotten rid of." He'd like to see "public censures," and have the cheats "run out of the profession." Bear Bryant says the punishments are too little and too late. He says, "You can buy a team, coach it, win a championship and be dead before they get the results" of an investigation. He advocates swifter justice.

Coaches who ravage the system deserve no sympathy, but I suspect the reason more drastic measures have not been taken against them is because the overseers of the game realize how difficult they have made it to police, and how generally baffled the membership is. In hearings before a House subcommittee looking into NCAA enforcement practices in 1978, what stood out consistently was how ineffective the NCAA is in clarifying its own procedures.

The hearings covered twelve months, fifty witnesses, and seventy hours of testimony, and although they did not prove (as they set out to do) that the NCAA administrative staff was a bunch of guys with dirty fingernails running around subverting due process and pursuing a "hit list" of weak and vulnerable schools, they did show that confusion mars the process. Even the finest minds the NCAA could muster on the subject — the Committee on Infractions includes such respected academicians as Professor Charles Wright of Texas and Dr. William Matthews of Kentucky — could not dispel the doubts and explain what all the whys and wherefores were there for. An "unimpressive performance," Wright said of his group's subcommittee appearance. It was worse than that.

The implications were clear enough: if the men who write the book and administer its justice cannot adequately defend the fairness of the system to a panel of United States congressmen, how can they expect a sophomore linebacker or a thirty-year-old coach trying to survive in the pressure cooker of big-time college athletics to embrace it?

The recruiting guidelines have become inextricably tangled because there's no set definition of what recruiting really is. Knute Rockne's plea for a return to the true student-athlete sounded utopian even in 1929 (especially coming from a Notre Dame coach) and may be even more unrealistic today, when monstrous athletic budgets could no more depend on a volunteer army than the highway patrol could depend on motorists writing their own speeding tickets. But there is a kernel of reason in Rockne's statement that might well be applied even at this late date.

The present-day recruiting process is a predator that devours loyalties to the school and to the region. It makes no concessions to where a boy lives or has grown up, or, for that matter, considers what his dreams might be. Wherever he is, if he is good enough, he is fair game for traveling brainwashers. And it usually boils down in the end to the best offer.

With no restrictions on their movement, college recruiters not only spend more and cheat more, but they are eager to make each of their institutions a national one. Joe Paterno has a line for it — "The farther from home a coach gets, the better the talent looks, and the more he'll want to cheat to get it."

The jet age has done that for the game. It is not just Notre Dame or the service academies or the insatiable Oklahoma Sooners who traipse around, madly following flight plans sketched in colored pins on the coast-to-coast wall maps back at the office. It is practically every major college in the football business. Ohio State may corner the market on talent in Ohio, but when the Buckeyes roar onto the field in September they will probably include mercenaries from Tempe, Arizona, Woodbine, New Jersey, and Orlando, Florida — not to mention a hoard of imports from Michigan.

The NCAA — which is to say, the colleges acting as a group — has let this practice grow until its limbs have gone through the roof. A Pacific Ten coach told me one time that, as a prized high school quarterback, he got so sick of seeing recruiters drinking coffee in his living room that he would call home first to make sure the coast was clear. "What could I do?" he said. "They were flying in from Dallas, from Philadelphia — from *Jackson, Mississippi*, for crying out loud."

A coach from Dallas, Texas, should never be caught camping on the doorstep of a kid in West Covina, California, this or any year. The trouble starts and the balance tips when they do this. I say balance because there is a practical consideration as well as an ethical one at work here — and when it comes to establishing policies, practicality is a more compelling factor than ethics any day. Parity — the equality of competition — is something every sport needs. The way it is now, the big and powerful can afford to send recruiters jetting back and forth across the country; the strugglers cannot. The imbalance is thus perpetuated as them that have, get. If parity is something to strive for, imbalancing factors have to be dealt with. Curbing the recruiting range is one way.

The National Football League solved the parity question years ago by instituting an equalization draft. Though a draft would, of course, be anathema to the college game, designated territories would be a palatable answer — spheres of influence drawn up by areas to include x number of high school players engaged in tackle football. An arbitrary base might be 150 high schools and 10,000 athletes. If a coach does not have that many schoolboys in his home state to choose from, the NCAA would draw a circle out from the university until it encompassed the specified number. The coach could not *physically* recruit outside the circle. If the circles overlapped, they would be extended concentrically until each school had the allowable number.

Besides establishing the spheres, the NCAA would be responsible for nabbing the trespassers. It would be easier then because coaches would scream bloody murder if they found a poacher in their area.

Such a scheme would cut recruiting costs by a staggering amount. It would also give the coach at Duke a word in edgewise with the kid in Asheville who can throw a football through a porthole at fifty yards, but who ordinarily would be entertaining Chuck Fairbanks and Bo Schembechler this weekend. With less pressure, the blue-chipper might wind up playing before the home folks, and making Mama proud.

Spheres of influence would not deprive an athlete of his choice; they would not prevent the boy in Asheville from going to Notre Dame if he really wanted to. They would simply keep coaches closer to home, and stop them from making bloody nuisances of themselves. A coach could still write a letter, make a phone call, or get some film shipped in. And if a kid in San Diego wanted to go to Notre Dame, his high school could get some film together and he could write Dan Devine a letter or let Devine write him one. A fifteen-cent stamp certainly beats a thousand-dollar air fare. It would not hurt to have the final offer in writing, and notarized.

When the NCAA reduced scholarship limits for Division I (Big Football) schools to thirty a year and a total of ninety-five in 1976, the motivation was, as always, to "cut costs." The surprise fringe benefit was that the talent got parceled around a little more evenly, and the 30–95 rule accomplished a minor miracle overnight. The sound of crashing giants was heard across the land. In one week alone, Alabama, Arizona State, Notre Dame, USC, and Texas were beaten and Nebraska was tied.

Some coaches feared the opposite would result — that the only way to turn a program around was to bus in seventy players a year, as Johnny Majors did his first season at Pittsburgh. But Majors was trying for a quick fall. He could have done it either way. Volume recruiting allowed big-budget schools with big staffs to recruit year-round, loading up the freezer with prime meat when the pickings were good. Their redshirts were better than most teams. Those who had that kind of leverage were naturally reluctant to give it up.

It was obvious the 30–95 rule was causing something

significant to happen when schools like Oklahoma started complaining about the seven or eight boys that got away to Tulsa, helping that program on the road to parity. Oklahoma coach Barry Switzer said there wasn't a great team in the Big Eight in 1977 because of the new rules. What Barry meant was that he no longer could be sure of beating Iowa State 45–0. The spoiled-rotten Oklahoma alumni cannot understand it when Barry does not go 11 and 0. But there is nothing wrong with other schools filling their stadiums and going to bowl games.

Those who were concerned that since thirty times four would not equal 95, coaches would assign hatchet men to run off the surplus, need not have worried. There was nothing in the rule that said a coach *had* to take thirty boys a year. Being limited, a coach had to be more selective. He couldn't slop around recruiting anybodies who could not hack the competition. Natural attrition took care of the rest, boys being boys. Upward of ten will quit a team every year, flunk out, or run off with the love of their lives.

The football scholarship itself has always been a source of protracted examination, not to say anguish, for administrators. In its many coats the scholarship is a perplexing animal, fluctuating in worth. At a big state school like Alabama, the athletic department is charged $2,700 a year for each football player on scholarship; at Miami of Florida, an expensive private school, the charge is $6,018 (although the true cost to the school is a couple thousand dollars less). Multiply either figure by ninety-five and you get the reason for some of the anguish.

Giving aid to athletes is a bone in the throat of many academicians, cost not withstanding, and as a result almost every year the NCAA convention has to wrestle down those who would require scholarships be given strictly on the basis of "need" — that is to say, given only to those athletes who cannot afford to pay. As a cost-cutting mechanism, the "need" scholarship has merit — and a history of disaster in big-time athletics.

Schools have found the "need" concept so full of pitfalls it is beyond formulae. The demanding criteria make it impossible to police. Questions are invariably left unanswered — such as what to do with the super athlete whose parents are capable of paying but won't, or with parents who lie or simply refuse to open their finances to scrutiny. Converting to "need" almost ruined the Big Ten Conference some years ago. The process so weakened its level of play that the once-proud Big Ten remains a cut below the Big Eight, the Southeastern Conference, and the Pacific Ten — and a thick cut at that.

But an important point is always missed when "need" is defeated as a proposal. "Need" is wrong for Big Football not just because it encourages cheating and deceit. It is wrong because it is hypocritical, at least at the Big Sport level. A delegate arguing in its favor at one NCAA convention said, "The football player should be treated just like other students" and should not be looked upon as a "hired hand." That's the orthodox view, and that's the hypocrisy. In Big Football and Big Basketball, the players are *not* "just like other students." They *are* hired hands, paid in the only way possible, through scholarships and other aid, to spend untold hours beyond the classroom performing valuable services for the universities.

Those services — perfectly legitimate — help generate the income for the university's multimillion-dollar athletic budget. The wrong — and the deceit — lies in the schools' being unwilling to acknowledge that fact. If the athlete is truly going to be a *student*-athlete, with all the trappings, then scholarships should be eliminated entirely, and the athletic program severed from its dependence on the football dollar.

The breast-beating and self-delusions of the loosely knit NCAA membership are, though tiresome, never completely out of vogue on this point. Like a low-grade virus, there persists an element that cannot face up to the reality that major college football is not amateur sport. That there are no surprises when the roll is called for the first day of practice. That these are not pickup but handpicked teams thrilling the alumni and their friends.

But the real argument is not with the failure to define the college game accurately, but with the fallacies in financing it. The "spiraling costs" of football against the return on the investment. The dilemma, for some, of having to face what seems a perpetual inequality of competition. For every Alabama there's a little bit of Vanderbilt. For every booming Big Eight there's a puffing Mid-America Conference.

The question of how big a business college football should be is an issue the game has wrestled with since its inception. Even prosperity is no guarantee against uneasiness. One prominent private school minimizes its considerable football success by sticking the athletic department with such phantom charges as practice field fees and library rentals to tone down the grand figures.

The problem for the NCAA has, in this respect, been twofold: keeping the rules and regulations equitable and workable for the membership as a whole, while allowing a reasonable latitude for those who wish to compete for what might be called the "top prizes" — bowl games, national attention (and TV money), and the simple, hackle-raising gratification of being the all-glorious number-one team. In terms of goals alone the latter are worthwhile, but they have the double edge of being lucrative. It is a game for high rollers.

For those who are in but with their toenails barely over the line, there are always the familiar doubts: How can we afford it? Where is it taking us? Is it really worth the trip? Cursory diagnosis of finances across the whole of college football shows an almost unalterable pattern of the rich getting richer. Tennessee finances a mammoth $8 million sports program, and winds up with an excess of $400,000 because of its football receipts. Vanderbilt, its atonic neighbor, spends little and profits less. Poor attendance and the absence of television exposure limit it to a perpetuating status of also-ran.

Southern Cal, the idol of field and screen, spends $2.9 million to make $3 million. It does not control its budget separate from the school, but it gets back what it needs. It has been in the black twenty straight years. A school with a small stadium (less than, say, 30,000) and a limited budget cannot compete with a Southern Cal. It cannot spend the recruiting money, it cannot draw the crowds, it does not have the supportive alumni. At a time of runaway inflation, it is overwhelmed with the soaring costs of tuition, training-table food, dormitory lodging, insurance, medical care, and equipment.

But in the end, what are costs except a measure against value? College football is financially feasible and salvageable beyond dollars-and-cents reckoning, if there is any reasonable consistency in goals and regulations.

The mistake is to believe that adjustments cannot be made — to believe that if they are *not* made, the game will survive anyway. Believe that and you will wake up with forty schools still playing the game at the top level, and the rest unable to afford it.

When the NCAA decided a few years ago that coaches could exist without twenty-man staffs and one-hundred-and-fifty-man rosters and three jetloads of players and hangers-on going to

next week's game in Corvallis, and determined that it was okay
for players to arrive slightly rumpled looking because they
would no longer be getting their fifteen-dollar-a-month laundry
money, it was thought by some traditionalists that football
would surely sink under the weight of all that austerity. Stronger
words than "sanity," "parity," and "economy" were used to
describe the situation. One coach sued over the new roster
limitations and others called them "cruel." Administrators
argued heatedly and repeatedly over scholarship numbers, the
redivision of the NCAA, the best ways to cut the television pie,
and so forth.

The root of it all, of course, was money — the way it was
spent, the way it was lost, the need to break even. In its original
ideal form, you will recall, college football wasn't intended to
make money. It was intended to contribute to the campus as a
whole, like other worthwhile things. The repertory theater does
not make money. The band, glee club, and student paper do
not make money. Football, despite excesses and occasional
scandal, held a unique position. It was a rallying point and a
means to push the school name, if only onto the Sunday sports
pages.

College football apparently went wrong when it discovered
that it could make a buck, and then made it.

If the only reason a college fields a football team is to make
money, it is making a poor investment. On the whole, and
contrary to its image, college football does not make money. In
fact, the vast majority of football programs at all levels lose
money. Some lose quite a bit. Even in Division I (Big Football)
only 53 percent of eighty-one schools responding to an NCAA
poll in 1978 were in the black — a 5 percent drop in solvency
since 1973.

Of the four hundred and seventy-five member institutions

that played the game at all levels in 1977, only ninety-two, or 19 percent, broke even. The majority of losers, of course, were in divisions II and III. Those schools identify with a time when football was considered important enough in itself, removed from its terrifying fiscal responsibilities.

John McKay tutored me years ago on the hypocrisies colleges traffic in when it comes to financing football. This was before his resistance was finally beaten down by all the money the pros were trucking up to his door to get him to leave USC. We were relaxing, past midnight, in his living room, and although I was alert enough to absorb the clarity of his logic, I was too laden with Mexican food to get outside the circle of his cigar smoke. To profit from the one I had to survive the other. He remarked that football was financially feasible, but that even at the major college level it was not necessary to spend your pockets off to succeed. He said he realized this was heresy, but there was a lot of fat in the game, and a lot of fatheads condemning it.

He said, "Very few people say, 'I'm against intercollegiate athletics.' They say, 'I'm against football.' Why? Publicity. When you're against football you get publicity. They complain about costs. All sports cost money, but football is the only one that has a chance to make enough to pay for itself, and to pay for the others. I said, 'If you had three restaurants and two were losing money, would you harass the one that could keep you in business?' If all we care about is showing a bigger profit, then cut out the sports that have no chance. I personally wouldn't want that because if it's worth having a well-rounded athletic program, it's worth paying for. You don't measure those things in costs. The medical school *costs* money. The business school *costs* money.

"But we have to be sensible about it. There are ways to keep a program in the black. There are ways to cut your losses. Some people try to keep up with the Joneses. We don't. We don't *always* travel first class. We don't *always* stay at the best hotels. We don't spend a lot of money on equipment. We don't need all different color jerseys and three extra pair of pants and twenty-four thousand dummies. We've got enough dummies coaching and playing.

"We don't have thirteen or fourteen coaches like some schools do [this was before the new NCAA limits]. We don't have four or five practice fields. There are coaches who say, 'You gotta have a dormitory like Alabama's to win.' We don't have a dormitory. Our guys stay in apartments. We still win. Players win games, not dormitories. Coaches in some conferences used to say they had to have forty or fifty scholarships, whatever the others got. Since I've been here, the largest number of scholarships we've given in one year is twenty-nine. One year we gave thirteen. Last year nineteen. We have won three National Championships.

"USC has an advantage over an Arkansas or a Nebraska in that it's in a densely populated area. Recruiting costs are a tenth of what some might be. But I don't believe you have to recruit more than sixteen players a year — if you're right on those sixteen. If you have twenty-two, say, and you're right on them you'll have eighty-eight players in the four classes. If you can't win with eighty-eight, you can't win. Numbers is not the answer.

"Coaches are like people. There are good ones, there are very average ones, there are damn poor ones. The very average ones and the damn poor ones have one statement in common: 'Well, if I had *his* players I'd win all my games, too.' That same guy will bring in fifty players a year [no longer legal]. He doesn't say,

'I've got fifty players who aren't any good.' That would be insane. He says, 'You oughta see our freshman team! Wait'll next year!'

"A winning football program generates spirit, everybody running around yelling 'We're number one.' Lose twenty-seven in a row and see how many smiles there are. You have a good program and it's a remarkable stimulus for endowments. Not just for athletics, but for the entire school. USC's fund raisers tell me endowments go up when we win. That it makes it easier back East to walk in and have a potential donor say, 'Hey, I saw the team win on TV Saturday. Great!' He doesn't say he'll donate because the team won, and he might not even be a big football fan, but he's proud to say, 'That's my school.'

"Football is not the only game ever played. A good football team doesn't have a university, a university has a good football team. It can be done anywhere. But it is never going to be justifiable strictly on a money basis, because it is never going to be even for everybody. Places like USC have built-in advantages. Population. Tradition. But even then there are no guarantees. We had tradition, and we had a 1–9 season and didn't go to a Rose Bowl game from 1954 to 1962 [McKay arrived in 1960]. Alabama has great tradition, but it wasn't winning anything until Bear Bryant went back. Bob Devaney took over Nebraska when Nebraska had had twenty years of losing. Now they're big winners. He went to work.

"Is it okay to play at the top level and lose year after year the way Washington State and some of them have had to do? Is it okay to play the game whether you drop a few dollars or not? Hell, yes. Money isn't everything. Winning isn't everything. That's a terrible philosophy to go by. It's enough that you play. You *desire* to win. You *try* to win. But it's enough to play."

Time has passed, and so has McKay (to Tampa Bay), but he has been proved out. Rosters have been cut and coaching numbers have been limited without visible effect on the quality of play. Extravagantly successful programs still have their "amenities," of course. They still have their closed-circuit TV and Henredon furniture in the dorms, with carpet up to the ankles and quadraphonic sound. They still have their fleets of private planes at beck and call, and every new piece of muscle-building paraphernalia and fitness apparatus in the catalogue. Nothing wrong with a little extravagance.

But now is a belt-tightening time for the majority of schools. Even rich old Yale is trimming its huge sports program, and the biggest football schools have had to find ways to be more frugal. One of the leading penny-pinchers in athletics is Georgia's athletic director Joel Eaves. The Bulldogs have never operated in the red since Eaves took over in 1963, though the costs of the program have more than tripled (to about $2.5 million). Eaves is not above posting Day-Glo orange stickers in athletic-department rest rooms to remind people to turn off the lights. Or to advise them to get off the phone more quickly, or to avoid writing unnecessary letters. "We're not too big," says Eaves, "we're just too wasteful."

Ultimately, a school has to make up its mind how important it wants football to be, and if it's ready to pay the price. It has to know its vested interests. How important is it to compete with the best, to vie for bowl games and TV money, even a National Championship? Does it want those things, or does it want to be in the Ivy League? And does it have a stadium that seats thirty-five or forty thousand?

Stadium size has a lot to do with it. A school with a fifteen-thousand-seat stadium can never successfully compete with a school that has one that seats seventy thousand. It can only make real money on the road, playing big-draw schools, because most big-draw schools won't waste their time in a small stadium. It is easily figured: if take-home pay is seven dollars a ticket, teams participating in a seventy-thousand-seat sellout share $490,000. In a fifteen-thousand-seat stadium, they share $105,000.

Of course, stadium size won't matter, either, if the rich continue to make power plays on the poor and forget they are all in this together. Schools who put it on other schools when they're in a slump and aren't drawing are short-sighted. Teams that are down *need* some big home games to pull themselves back up, or to keep from going down for good. It is absurd for a school with a fifteen-thousand-seat stadium to crave a home game with Michigan, but it wouldn't wreck Michigan's budget (crawling in dough) to play before forty thousand fans at another institution once in a while. The superpowers have to exercise some sufferance.

Television has done this, of course, by making money-grubbers of the big teams. As B. has said for years, the pot gets bigger and bigger and the wheel keeps going faster and faster, like a centrifuge, throwing off those who can't hang on. Television rights have tripled. The Nielsen ratings are up. Teams in a nationally televised game will share half a million bucks, and in regional games, more than $400,000. That kind of money can float an entire athletic program.

But what happens? The teams that become TV stars want it all for themselves, like dogs in the manger. The more they get, the better they get and the better they get, the more ABC wants them. Round and round. Since the 1960s, the rich have become outrageously rich, and the poor fight for scraps. It is what B. calls the Vidiot Factor. It could wreck half the teams in Division I if somebody doesn't stop it.

The reliance on television money is habit-forming. It is also counterproductive and degrading. The networks are in a position to dictate, and when they are in that position, says Roger Kahn, the author-historian, they are about as passive as the Gestapo. They dictate to the schools, who are at their mercy. Even the Navy team had to lobby hard a couple of years ago to keep its game with Army on TV, and thus prevent a year-end financial bath.

Regional telecasts have been credited with keeping one floundering program after another from throwing in the towel, and many major conference members — Illinois, Northwestern, Kansas, et al. — admit that TV splits have helped them avoid deficits even though they weren't on the tube themselves. But TV windfalls are often illusory. At most bowl games, for example, the proceeds barely cover expenses. And the trouble with TV money is that schools that get it four or five times begin to rely on it. Like air-conditioning and two cars in the garage and indoor plumbing.

A few years ago business manager John Reed Holley of Ole Miss said that "television has been a lifesaver for us," providing about $200,000 a year from Southeastern Conference slices of the various television pies. "If it weren't for TV, we'd almost always be in the red." But just up Interstate 55 and west a bit from Ole Miss sat Memphis State, doing very nicely without TV. Memphis State's last — and only — televised game had been in 1966. It did not count on another. Its program had been in the black every year since 1958.

San Diego State is another example. At the time, San Diego did not even have a local highlights show, but it had surpluses in its budget that would keep it going "for at least another ten years," according to its athletic director, Dr. Ken Karr. Karr said he held his all-sports budget in line by limiting road trips to one night out, by never leaving California to recruit (fancy that), by discontinuing on-the-spot scouting in favor of film exchanges, and by cutting down on training-table privileges. Can such austerity work? San Diego State was 45–8–2 from 1973 through 1977 under coach Claude Gilbert and won more than one hundred games in fewer than twelve seasons before that.

The frantic search for revenue in college athletics will go on as long as there is an inflationary spiral, and perhaps longer, but it is football that will have to work hardest to keep the wolves at bay. There are some obvious stop-gap measures to be taken. The Big Eight plan for dispersing television and bowl money is a good one, and worthy of universality.

Any time a Big Eight team gets a TV or bowl check, it goes into the league pot, to be shared equally. The exposure, the value of being "on," is reward enough. Certainly Nebraska and Oklahoma, the TV stars of the league, have not suffered from a little noblesse oblige. Other conferences have share-the-wealth plans, too, but there is no continuity. In the Pacific Ten, the money is divided so many ways that by the time a check reaches Oregon it is just big enough to treat the team to Big Macs.

A quick way to increase revenue would be to add a twelfth game. The college season is too short as it is — Bud Wilkinson used to say it was tragic for the colleges to turn December over to the pros just when the appetites of their fans were whetted. The pros are now playing sixteen regular-season games, despite being older, fatter, and less gung-ho. An extra game check would help many college programs over the fiscal hump, and most of them wouldn't even have to extend the season. Open dates are usually available for filling. As for the players, they would rather play than practice any day.

Academicians would, as always, complain if an extra game interfered with semester exams, but studies show that football players do better in class *during* the football season. They are more disciplined then, more likely to be home at night. For that matter, nobody complains about the basketball team playing upwards of thirty games, or the baseball team playing seventy games.

If a school can't find a twelfth team to play, it could easily enough schedule its natural rival for an annual rematch. Everybody has a team they love to hate, profitably. Texas hates Oklahoma. Clemson hates South Carolina. Play that team home-and-home every year, and it's money in the bank.

But in the end, the best, surest, and most sensible way to cut college football costs turns out to be so simple that it boggles the mind: the restoration of football itself. This means one-platoon football, what Abe Martin, the old TCU coach, calls "real" football, and what Iowa coach Bob Commings calls "the safest, best game ever devised." This kind of football allows a player to experience the whole game and not half of it. It is football in its original form. Commings says he has heard all the arguments against a return to one platoon. "None of them," he says, "holds water."

The economics are breathtakingly simple. Two-platoon football is twice as expensive as one-platoon football. Unlimited substitution has come to mean unlimited expense. Even now coaches are not satisfied with the ninety-five-player limit. They want one hundred and five or one hundred and twenty-five players, and that means an extra dozen hotel rooms, airplane seats, and additional expenses, not to mention more coaching jobs. The willingness of hard-pressed college business managers to perpetrate such skylarking is astounding.

But the odds against one-platoon football are long. Abe Martin believes you would have a tough time filling a phone booth with coaches in the country today who would want to see a return to real football, "because they're too used to two-platoon." He says he is not even sure "any of these dang old coaches" would even know how to coach real football. When you tell some of them that Fritz Crisler needed only forty-five players to go to the 1948 Rose Bowl, and that the great Blanchard-Davis teams at Army took thirty-five men on road trips, and that Earl Blaik had only three full-time assistants, they tell you there is a price you pay for quality, that football is more sophisticated now than when Blaik coached, and that unlimited substitution gives more players a chance to play.

In the marketplace of American hokum, that last one certainly attracts the rubes. The modern football player is, indeed, a highly efficient, beautifully packaged playing machine, but he does not play "football." He plays "defensive tackle," or "offensive guard," or "outside linebacker on obvious passing downs." He plays a lot of things, but he does not play football.

A defensive end plays defensive end, period. He learns the basic moves, repeats them over and over, ad infinitum, ad nauseam. He studies volumes of playbooks analyzing every inch of his broom-closet environment, and watches films until he's almost blind. That's all he knows.

Dave Nelson likes to talk about the "educational experience" of football. He says it is a joke when the "experience" is two steps across the line, pivot, watch the pitch, play the block, over and over again. No other sport constricts its participants in such a manner. Players are departmentalized from the time they are eight years old, playing in the little leagues. A left guard at age eight, if his luck holds out, will be a left guard at thirty, never touching the ball, except by accident. He never knows anything else. In light of this specialization, it's no surprise that an NCAA poll taken in 1977 found that players preferred two-platoon football almost two to one. They simply did not know any better.

As for "increased participation," football is the only sport in the world where coaches have been able to peddle that argument, as if the game were played to keep potential delinquents off the streets. There is no doubt that unlimited bodies increase efficiency on the assembly line by allowing for greater specialization and reducing the fatigue factor. Bodies, in fact, is the name of the game.

NCAA figures show that football was played in 1977 by 475 member institutions — with 41,500 participants. Compare that with baseball, which was played at 638 schools by only 19,000 athletes. Baseball has nine men to a side, two men less than football. Baseball coaches must be doing something wrong. If they beefed up their lobby, they could probably add three or four more fielders and maybe have *nine* designated hitters.

Who pushed the idea that more is better? Coaches coaching two-platoon football. Ask any coach who has done it both ways and he will tell you it's easier with more players. You simply hire more assistants, delegate more authority, and elevate yourself to chairman of the board.

But that doesn't make football more fun.

I have heard Bear Bryant complain many times that he disliked the return to two-platoon because it cut into his time with the players. He said when players played both offense and defense "you could take two assistants and coach *ten* teams. I actively coached myself. When LeeRoy Jordan was playing at

Alabama I'd be out there sweating and grunting and butting with 'em, and they believed what we were doing would win. I don't do that anymore, and I miss it."

The result, Bryant says, is that football "isn't the coaches' game it was. There's more of a premium now on getting the top athlete. When we played both ways, we could take a guy like Jimmy Sharpe, one hundred and ninety-four pounds, hone him down, have him so quick that he'd go out and beat a guy who weighed two hundred and forty. Now you've got to have a guy six-five to rush the passer, and a guy six-four to block him. You can't win with the good little guy anymore. No chance. The premium's on ability."

In the one-platoon heyday of his Army teams, Red Blaik contended that a good college team could beat a pro team for much the same reasons: older, bigger men with denser muscles could not keep pace with the younger, leaner, quicker players if they both had to play a full game, offense and defense. Excessive muscle (and even some fat) is not a physiological disadvantage when your talents are needed for only three or four short bursts at a time. No one in his right mind would say a good college team could beat a good pro team today, of course, but the reasoning is still sound. And it does not take an orthopedic surgeon to recognize what the increased emphasis on girth has done to increase the injury problem.

Amazing to any practice field visitor today are the legions of players a head coach must deal with. Dressed in their multihued practice clothes, signifying this specialty or that, players flutter from field to field like trained parrots at a bird farm, their paths crisscrossing in a blur of color. I'd hate to say how many times I've been on a practice field and heard a head coach call down from his tower, "Who made that tackle? Was that you, Smith?" "No, sir, Coach, it's me, Brown."

But do coaches even now say, "Enough"? No, they say, "Let's specialize some more." When they finally eliminated all substitution restrictions in 1973, they had to go right back in 1974 and write another rule because one coach had a guy — the ultimate specialist — who did nothing but run onto the field, give the quarterback the play, and run off.

The pros are the supreme specialists of all this supersophistication. They have two round pegs for every round hole. And they're so deadly-dull efficient they can't score any points. They had to rush through some relief rules for their starving pass receivers in 1977.

As football is now played, the actual time the ball is moving and athletes are running into each other is fourteen minutes a game. When coaches tell their players to "go all out," they don't mean for sixty minutes, they mean for a fourteen-minute game. That's an average of seven minutes for an offensive player, seven for a defensive player, and even less when you interject the goal-line teams, the third-down teams, etc., etc.

Here, then, is the irony. Football practice is hard work. Today's players practice eight, nine months a year, including off-season training. You hardly ever read about "three-lettermen" anymore. Those who could play three sports are too busy devoting all their time to supersophisticated football. Day after day, week after week. And for what? For seven minutes on Saturday afternoon.

The morale problems in two-platoon football have been bugging coaches for years. They have been known to separate entire coaching staffs, wives included. Offensive coaches gripe about the boneheads running the defense — behind their backs, of course. Defensive players complain about the inability of the offense to get out of its own shadow.

Why? Because neither group has to answer for its mistakes. A guy fumbles on his five-yard line, he doesn't dig in to protect the goal, he trots off the field and says, "You take it." In real football, comaraderie is built in and unity is a must. In real football, every position is a "skilled position."

But here is the clincher, the argument that would fly in any budget meeting if they could keep coaches off the runway. Two-platoon football kills competitive balance. It is strictly a rich-get-richer proposition, and always has been.

Unlimited substitution began as three little words that appeared in the 1941 rules, to compensate for World War II manpower shortages. A player leaving the game did not have to wait till the next period but could return *"at any time."* Nobody did much about it for a couple years, then Fritz Crisler platooned his Michigan team against Army and almost pulled a big upset. Pretty soon everybody was doing it, and it got worse and worse until, in 1953, Fritz and a posse of traditionalists voted those three words out again.

And a funny thing happened. In the next ten years, teams like Oregon State, Duke, Rice, Miami, and even Utah State made the Top Ten. So did Abe Martin's "little old country boys" at *TCU*. Auburn won a National Championship, and so did LSU and Syracuse. Consecutively. Even the service academies were ranked.

You have to be blind drunk not to realize what had happened. With two-platoon a coach needs twenty or twenty-five top players to turn a program around. In real football, with the accent on athletes, you can do it with half that. But second-echelon schools are not going to get twenty or twenty-five. They're lucky to get sweepings after the big-budget guys breeze through, because the more you specialize, the more thoroughly you have to recruit.

And, of course, the more you specialize, the less likely you will be to try new things and be inventive. Most coaches are so wrapped up in their Byzantine recruiting practices, watching movies all night, and wiping the noses of one hundred players, that they don't have time to think up sleeper plays and hurry-up huddles and all the things that make football exciting, even at practice.

The argument that helped undermine one-platoon football in the late 1950s was that it did not protect its most valuable and vulnerable athletes, its quarterbacks. Coaches did not want them making tackles. There are, of course, ways to write in escape clauses to get a player or two in and out of the game, but by and large, quarterbacks are not the splinter group they used to be. The colleges have gone to veers and wishbones and other triple options. Quarterbacks are back to being what the old tailbacks used to be — all-round athletes. Runners *and* passers. Rick Leach of Michigan and Thomas Lott of Oklahoma, to name just two, could have played both ways in 1978. Some of the great college quarterbacks of all time played both ways — Johnny Lujack, Arnold Tucker, Sid Luckman, Bennie Friendman. Paul Hornung was a running back in the pros. So was Tom Matte.

The time has come to restore the whole game to the kids who play it. Give them a chance to strike back. Let them know the thrill of scoring as well as stopping the other guy.

If you want to talk about "educational experience," talk about real football.

If you want to promote equality of competition, talk about real football.

If you want to talk about balancing the budget, talk about real football.

But it won't happen because the rules-makers won't buck the pro lobby, which would scream bloody murder if the farm system quit turning out all those lovely round pegs. It won't happen until college football is down to the forty teams that can still afford it.

Joe Paterno said this: "I think our job is protecting the game for the youngsters who play it. It has to be a meaningful experience, something they enjoy and something they get some good out of, or we can never defend it, no matter how much money we make. We can't have a game whose only purpose is to make money." Ironically, it is the coaches themselves who suffer most from the money madness.

The way money flies around a major college football program, through the doors and under the tables and out the windows, is a greater career jeopardizer than any field problem coaches have, and most of them don't know it because they have little to do with — or time to worry about — its flight pattern. The element on every college faculty that is hostile to the football coach resents his empathy with kids and the attention he gets from the community, but mainly it resents his money — the money he gets (his inflated salary), the money he spends.

Except for isolated cases, and during a notably active stretch in the 1960s, this hostility (the "assumption of moral superiority") merely simmers. The smart coach long ago learned to live with it. Bear Bryant learned by making sure he got ironclad contracts, so his superiors "don't lose their guts when the going gets tough." John McKay was a little more diplomatic. "We have to understand the faculty's feelings," he said. "Some of these men have split the atom. All we ever split was the T."

Bear Bryant insisted for years that his salary not exceed that of any Alabama department head, so as not to offend the other faculty members. He wised up to that mistake when he realized he was cutting into his retirement-insurance benefits. Bryant, a conciliatory bear in these later years, invites professors and administration people to team breakfasts, and even lets a few eavesdrop on his pep talks. McKay used to do the same. Bryant and McKay do not have trouble with faculties.

Coaches do not see themselves as rules-benders and manipulators. Most of them see themselves as "the remaining stronghold of the archaic family structure," as one psychiatrist put it, and "the last chance for preservation of dignity on campus," as one coach put it. When coaches' values are tested, however, they often find themselves whistle-to-monocle with critics who know absolutely nothing about what makes them tick.

A few years ago a coach I know had to appear before an athletic committee investigating charges made by black athletes against his program. He said he realized after a few questions that his interrogators "had no idea what we were trying to do, why we said the things we did. They didn't understand the coach–player relationship at all. They give a boy an F and they're done with him. A coach can't do that. He lives with his mistakes. A twenty-four-hour responsibility." Bob Devaney used to say that faculty people telling athletic people how to do their job is like a carpenter telling a barber how to cut hair.

Frank Lauterbur, when he was athletic director and head football coach at Toledo, defined coaches the way coaches would like to be defined: "Coaches are special. Coaches aren't guys with cigars in their mouths, lying and pandering and hating, the way they're pictured in some circles. Robert Ruark was closer to it. He said coaches are kids who never grew up. He might not have meant that as a compliment, but it's true — a coach never gets older than twenty-five.

"Coaches are guys who still get a tingle when The Star-Spangled Banner is played and butterflies before a kickoff.

Coaches never have to be pushed out of bed to go to work in the morning. How do you rate a professor? Tough to do. A coach is rated every Saturday afternoon. Win, lose, tie. He can work as hard as he knows how preparing for a game, and then a kid has a headache or the sun gets in his eyes, and it's a loss.

"Why does he do it? I don't know, except that there is always the excitement — working out game plans, waiting for the films — and the weariness and satisfaction of knowing how hard he and his team have tried to reach a common goal. If the result is defeat, then there's dejection and the coach must take the proper tack, one to ease the pain. But if there is a heaven on earth, it is the locker room after a victory.

"A coach has an enthusiasm for kids, a communion with them. He worries about them, feeds them, sees to their housing, their health. If a kid has a problem, he doesn't go to his professor, or even to his old man, he goes to his coach, because he knows the coach will look after him. When a coach calls an athlete 'son,' he means it."

Left unsaid in that panageric (admittedly somewhat over-drawn, but not by much) is the relationship the coach has with *his* superiors. Basically, the coach's "father" (college president, chancellor, et al.) calls him "son" until the winning stops, then he calls a board meeting. Coaches who do not win and whose programs do not make money — the one naturally following the other — do not get loyalty, and they would be fools to expect it. When the shooting starts, "father" dives under the counter.

Knute Rockne said it fifty years ago. A football coach "must please his athletes, the student body, the faculty, the alumni and the townspeople. If he falls down in any one of these he is doomed. But of the five, the alumni are the hardest to please. They work at some other business throughout the week and on

Saturday go out to see their team in action. They want recreation and enjoyment, and can't have it in defeat. If a bad season comes along, they get the hammers out."

Nobody knows as much about football as a coach — it is a coaches' game. Mostly what alumni and students in the stands and writers and school presidents in the press box have in common is that they are in the dark about most of what happens on the field.

They also share a fundamental need to advise the coach. They all tell him to win. Somehow. If he does not follow this sound advice they combine to move in as quickly as possible to rip out the wires and tear up the terminal box. Coaches at the major college level are often made itinerants by this process. Why they have any loyalties other than to themselves is a wonder. Some, of course, don't.

Firing a coach every time the team doesn't go to the Cotton Bowl is, of course, ludicrous. That it is commonly done is beyond reason. I once had Lee Corso describe for me, in words and actions, how dumb it was from both standpoints, the coach's and the school's.

He was in his stocking feet, pacing back and forth beneath the signs on the paneled walls of his office in Bloomington. One sign, in burned wood, read, "Let me win, but if I cannot win let me be brave in the attempt." The other, in fractured Latin, read: "Illegitimi Non Carborundum" (Don't let the bastards wear you down).

Corso believes that, win or lose, coaching can be fun, a contradiction in terms by most accepted coaching tenets. At Louisville, he rode an elephant to attract attention to his program. The elephant was so big Corso had to hunker down going under viaducts. He got plenty of attention, and scars on his hands and inside his knees from holding on for dear life.

Wherever he coaches Corso leaves no gimmick unturned. He has held Italian nights at the training table, with spaghetti, garlic bread, and spumoni on a checkered tablecloth. He has had pregame warm-ups so flashy that Georgia Tech asked for the routine. "Don't you want any of my plays?" Corso said. When his Indiana team went ahead of Ohio State a couple years ago, he called time out and drew his team together for a sideline picture, with the scoreboard blazing in the background. It was the first time in twenty-five years Indiana had led Ohio State. "I looked it up," said Corso. Ohio State went on to win, 47–7.

"Everything in life is timing," Corso said, pacing in his office. "If coaches are going to win anything, they've got to have the proper time. That's the crux of the problem right now. A coach gets hired with a lot of fanfare and promises, and he starts out . . ."

Corso began to stride, making exaggerated stiff-legged steps — one, two, three —

". . . and doesn't win enough games, and they fire him."

— Stop. Turn, step, step, step.

"They hire a new coach. The new coach starts out, lots of promise, big buildup, and does the same thing."

Corso marched back and forth over the same spot.

"Every time you bounce your coach you start from zero. You can't build a program this way. You can't establish recruiting areas or get continuity going with your staff and players, or anything. Unless you get lucky, you'll be out before you win.

"Some jobs take longer than others, but anybody can tell if a team is improving, and that should be the key. If you've got a lousy coach, you'll know it. It won't matter how many years he has. But if a guy is making progress . . . People don't realize it, but Tom Landry was in his sixth year with Dallas before he even broke even. He had five straight losing seasons, and then he was 7–7 his sixth year. He finally broke even." Corso grinned.

Administrators could, of course, treat coaches like professors. They could give them a reasonable time to show something — say four or five years — and if the criterion was met they could then give them tenure and tell them that, after all, for every winner there has to be a loser (the one immutable factor in games-playing), and not to worry whether the kids go to class or even lose the game on Saturday. Work it exactly the way the professors do. This might happen on the day hell freezes over.

Administrators at major colleges that have football teams do not give coaches tenure, they give them contracts. The contract is open on both ends. It is honored until the coach either doesn't win or until he gets a better offer. Either way, it winds up in the trash can. I suspect more coaches get bought out than sell out, but it is a moot point. Coaches know not to tie their moorings too tight. Coaches realize that for every Chuck Fairbanks, pulling out on Oklahoma for New England, pulling out on New England for Colorado, and for every Lou Saban, pulling out of a series of contracts before winding up (for now) at Army, there are an equal number of Doug Dickeys.

Dickey was an SEC Coach of the Year at Tennessee. When he went to Florida, his alma mater, he had seasons where the team won as many as nine games, and went to bowls. His overall coaching record was twelfth best in the country through 1978. At Florida, he won twenty-one of twenty-four games at home. But he did *not* win the school an SEC championship. This put him in the select company of every coach who preceded him at Florida, but that fact offered nothing to grab hold of when the ship started listing and the gate receipts started dropping.

On November 3, 1978, Dr. Robert Marston, the Florida

president, gave Dickey a vote of confidence, always the kiss of death. Dr. Marston said that in game strategy, team inspiration, discipline, morale, and communications with supporters, Dickey had shown "significant progress." He said he was "pleased" to report this, and to say that he had received "dozens of telegrams and letters" in support of Dickey. Four weeks later, Dickey was fired.

One could say with some assurance that coaches have wound up becoming cheaters for less than that. It is not an excuse if they do, it is just a rationale. But *that* they do is clear enough. It is unfair, however, to blame them for a system so tautly strung and so dependent on a mutual lack of trust and the desperate acceptance of an unreal pressure.

Dan Devine knows about pressure. When he coached at Green Bay, his dog was shot, his daughter spat on. He was virtually railroaded out of the frying pan in Wisconsin — and into the fire at Notre Dame. Coaches have been known to suffer indignities at that holy institution, too. Joe Kuharich had crosses burned on his lawn there in the 1960s. Ara Parseghian spent years living down a 10–10 tie with Michigan State in a year when he won the National Championship.

Devine does not admit he ever cheated, as Bear Bryant fessed up to doing in order to stay alive at Kentucky and Texas A&M, but he says he understands how the process works: "When you're young, you see what a coach does and you say, 'I'll do anything to win.' So you cheat. You teach win-at-any-cost. Then you get older, and your career is in the balance. You say, 'I'll do anything to stay in.' "

There is no telling how many natural enemies a coach has. Today, with the crush for money exacerbated, he seems to gain a newer, tougher foe every day. When the Title IX guidelines were laid down by the Department of Health, Education and

Welfare, a collision course was set between Big Football and women athletes wanting a fair share. I called Margo Polivy, the sprightly, articulate, combative lawyer for the Association of Intercollegiate Women's Athletics (AIWA). I had in mind a couple of minutes' conversation. We talked for more than an hour.

Ms. Polivy did not deliver a lecture on football's evils, she delivered a treatise, in the form of a diatribe. She said the idea of killing football was not repugnant, that football's demise would "improve opportunities for the student body across the board." She said big college football had "no intrinsic value." That within institutions were some programs "*not* in the best interests of education — and football is hardly an educational venture. It's a commercial venture." She said football was "anathema" to the educational system.

And she was just warming up.

There's a double irony here: the hope of college coaches is college administrators, the same ones who abandon them when they need a friend. Whether they like it or not, administrators (the NCAA, at home and abroad) can do it all — make the rules to stop the cheating, stop the cheaters, set reasonable policies, establish reasonable goals, release the valves on some of the pressure. But airy ambiguities do not make sound policies. Mostly when you see college administrators advancing onto the NCAA convention floor they have the look of haberdashers with too many suits on the rack. They have made so many bad policies for coaches to live by that the NCAA staff in Kansas City has to work harder every year just bailing the ship.

But they are up to their worst tricks these days. They have dumped into the coaches' laps their own failure to come to grips with this generation's most serious matriculation problem.

They are admitting morons into colleges, and thus into college athletics. Thugs are passing through the system, by invitation — and when they behave accordingly on campus everybody looks surprised and gets upset.

Arkansas has had rape charges filed against football players two years in a row; three players were charged in both cases. One Arkansas girl said she was raped six times. Eight Kentucky players were suspended after charges of rape and sodomy. Even Notre Dame had a sordid dormitory episode involving women. And those are only the sensational cases. An athletic director who took over a job in an unfamiliar territory told me he was "stupefied" by what he saw passing for ordinary conduct in the dormitories.

One player booted from a southern team for ruining an Atlanta hotel room couldn't understand it when his coach dismissed him. He said, "I thought he'd give me a second chance." He had played a "messy practical joke" on a roommate that the coach said was "beyond rank." The player blamed the coach. He said, "They want you to be animals on the field, then turn it off like a light switch." He said he was one player who "don't take a lot of crap from people."

The fundamental illogic of sending functional illiterates into college classrooms has not yet dawned on educators and administrators. They would rather be liberal than right. They have consistently made it easy for the coach to bring in nonstudents as students as long as they can negotiate one hundred yards in 9.5 seconds. The coach is blamed for this, but it is the administrators' fault. The standards are now at rock bottom: a 2.0 average can get a boy in, and the various testing scores — A.C.T., SAT — are no longer applied. Says Joe Paterno, who used to pride himself in the fact that Penn State graduated 95 percent of its football players, "It's a problem even for us right now, and it's getting worse every day."

The percentage of star halfbacks who would break into a cold sweat at the mere prospect of having to deliver a simple declarative sentence is staggering. Even the Big Ten, which sought for twenty-five years to protect the scholar-athlete image by selecting an All-Academic football team, has about given up the ghost. The Big Ten All-Academic is supposed to be made up of players with at least a B average for the year or for their college careers. In 1978, out of a thousand players on conference rosters, only forty-nine qualified — and eleven of those were from Northwestern, the worst team in the league.

The NCAA, of course, would much rather deal with the more traditional problems. Its Committee on Infractions would rather catch a boy with his hand in the till any day. Cars they understand. Cash money they understand. Fortunately, that kind of cheating is on the way out — too much heat from an expanded, hardworking enforcement agency.

But academic cheating is a cancer that goes right to the heart of the educational process, and to the educators themselves. It starts with the high schools, and is nothing if not an indictment of the current state of public education in this country. High schools do not educate, they graduate. A college recruiter told me it was a swamp. He said there was an all-too-familiar pattern. The requirement for a football scholarship is a C average through high school. A school finds out a college coach is interested in one of its boys. The boy reads at the third-grade level. The boy suddenly becomes an A student.

Though the NCAA cannot trust transcripts anymore, it has to accept them — what choice does it have? But some of them make better fiction than *Gone with the Wind*. The NCAA has a case on file of a New York athlete who showed colleges three different transcripts—three different sets of grades. High schools recognize the miserable job they're doing, so they "help a kid out" by shoving him into college. Let Bear Bryant teach him to read.

The NCAA enforcement wing is powerless because of jurisdiction. The colleges can't police themselves *and* the high schools *and* the junior colleges. The NCAA doesn't even have labels to cover some of the problems, much less statutes. The junior-college program grew like Topsy and was left to its own standards and admission policies —and its own integrity. It thus became a Garden of Eden for system-breakers and scholarship goons. Some junior colleges are no more than barber colleges.

Junior colleges are supposed to help a slow starter on the way, or admit the kid who can't afford a major college. You don't expect Yale, but you do expect some fidelity to scholastic mission and standards. The biggest and best JC system in the country, the one that attracts the keen-eyed football coach if he is looking to round up six or eight prospects in a hurry, is California's. And what is required to enroll in a California junior college? Start with the ability to tie your shoes and you don't have to go much further. A boy doesn't even have to be a high school graduate.

Once in junior college, an athlete is supposed to maintain certain grade points. But the NCAA does not monitor those standards or check a boy's progress. There are no funds for that. It relies on the integrity of the JCs. The NCAA can't even come to grips with its own academic malfeasance. Without uniform standards for progress—which the major colleges don't have—and without first plugging up their own academic ratholes, the majors can't wave a finger. The coaches themselves don't realize what's happening until they wake up one morning and find half their squad in remedial-reading courses. Paterno says it is no exaggeration.

Under the well-intended aegis of "affirmative action," a number of programs have made their way into the academic process, and resulted in wholesale subversions of the rules. There are the so-called "Four Percent" or "Two Percent" rules. At the institutional level, quite separate from NCAA policies or jurisdiction, an individual school can, if it wants, drop the admission barriers for "exceptional and unusual cases," as long as that loosely defined group does not exceed the prescribed percentage of the total enrollment. In California it's 4 percent, and it started there.

The idea — a good one, originally — was to relax the barriers a little for a kid who could draw or play a bassoon but couldn't multiply, or for a kid who had suffered socioeconomic deprivations. The practice, and with it the abuses, is now fairly widespread.

One coach told me, "You'll never get me to admit it, but the problem began when we started ripping down the standards. Now we've got discipline problems, race problems, classroom problems. People like to blame it on the blacks. I've had blacks on my teams for fifteen years. But now, because we have no standards, and because we keep kids in school who don't belong, who *know* they don't belong, they react by making trouble."

Any coach bent on circumvention can find loopholes in the academic requirements. All the athlete has to do in most cases is sit out a year of eligibility while special tutors — some schools call them "brain coaches" — fill his mediocre mind with enough knowledge to get him through with passing grades.

Some of this is justified, of course, and defendable. Earl

Campbell got into Texas without normal qualifications, but worked hard and became a good student, good enough to graduate — and, of course, good enough at football to win the Heisman Trophy. Even the Ivy League admits its share of "exceptional cases" — who happen to be able to run back punts.

The program becomes a joke when you start looking into individual school numbers for that portion of the 2 percent or 4 percent who are scholarship athletes. The NCAA investigated one school in the Southwest and found half the special admissions were scholarship athletes. The NCAA backed off and did nothing. It was a dead end.

What is worse, the NCAA does not have across-the-board standards for what a student is obliged to do *once he gets into school*. Coaches, for some reason, do not scream at this, but it is the greater threat because they have to face those nonscholars across the line for four years. The only standard is one that the individual conferences and/or individual schools set up and describe, in writing, for the NCAA, as "normal progress toward a degree."

"Normal progress" is not the same for everyone. At one eastern school, a boy played four years of football and when his parents discovered he had enough credits to be a sophomore, they were outraged and sued the school. On the West Coast, a boy at California State at Los Angeles played defensive back for four years. He never got a degree (he wasn't even close), and was never offered a pro contract. The boy went home to live with his father. In an argument, the father pulled a gun, and, in the confusion, was killed. When the boy, first charged with murder, and then released, went out to find the cemetery to visit his father's grave, he couldn't get there. He could not read the street signs.

That the NCAA, working in concert with the high schools, could do something about the situation is undeniable. It is not that difficult. If a player gets caught with an altered transcript, he should be banned for life. If the coach had a hand in it, he should be banned, too. If the high school is guilty, put the school on probation.

Some of that TV money the NCAA hoards in Kansas City could easily go toward a study of junior-college requirements and their curricula. Eliminate from qualification the ones that do not measure up. There is nothing wrong with farming out talent to let it mature, but to farm it out to circumvent grade requirements is a sin.

And if colleges must admit a few exceptional cases, make the percentage of athletes exactly the same as the schools' allowable number — in other words, if there is a 2 percent rule, only 2 percent of the 2 percent should be athletes.

If colleges do not stand for something, they will fall for anything. One of my coaching friends tried to feed me some of that new-wave thinking. He is a man I respect, with a great football mind. But he said, "So what if some of our guys couldn't read at a fifth-grade level. We gave 'em a chance and they turned out to be pretty good citizens. Isn't that better than being on welfare? That's what college football is all about."

No, that is not what college football is all about. No matter how convenient it is to forget when the stadium is packed and the drums are pounding, colleges are not built to provide a haven from the cruelties of the world. They are colleges, not the USO. They are supposed to have, and believe in, academic standards. The question is: how willing are they to stand behind those standards?

5.

THE GRASS ROOTS

No sport is more praised than American football. For almost a century it has been fed to America's children and schools as an exemplary builder of body and mind. Father Edmund Joyce of Notre Dame, perhaps more familiar with inspiration than most of us, has defined football as "a game of skill, a game of thrills, a game of inches, a game of courage, a game of spirit, a game of luck, a game of teamwork."

I could not improve on that except to say that it is, or was, probably more fun at the lower levels. By lower levels I mean the football of the sandlots, where positional roles are less definite and player drafts less discriminating (the one-potato, two-potato process), and at the smaller high schools and colleges where there is less form and structure and strategy, but where fifty boys are not confined to the bench on game day.

In short, I'm talking about football unconstricted by the tyrannies of budgets, which does not sink or swim on profit and loss. Football which is pure sport, played and watched for the joy of it on a crisp afternoon in Boise, Idaho, or a sultry night in Shreveport, Louisiana.

It is not easy to have an original thought about football. It has been too close to our consciousness for too long. No back-alley dalliance, the love affair between football and America has been a full-blown romance filled with marvelous public displays, and, in time, a bittersweet accumulation of ups and downs. Mostly ups.

But its endurance was never really questioned until recently, when the flaws in the game began to show through like blotches of rust and dry rot. The violence and injury. The manifestations of avarice and greed. The various courtroom scenes. The startling implications of high school crowds grown so small that a sociable person felt embarrassed being there.

Experts tried to warn me that football could not be categorized for this type of examination. It is so many games in one, from the game in the streets to the one in the giant steel-webbed stadiums, that when you begin to worry about it, you had better check with the night nurse before bringing flowers because you might not have the right patient. But I don't think that is true. If football is to find an enduring form, the whole of it needs to be attended, from the grass roots up. What happens at one level influences the others, although the influence filters down much faster than it does up. Perhaps it should be the other way round. Perhaps not. . . .

When Tommy Mont coached at the University of Maryland he experienced all the thrilling things that attend a college football coach when he is up to the noose line of his neck in the big time. Mont knew important people; he had his picture taken with Queen Elizabeth. He knew large enthusiastic crowds. He knew huge, pressing budgets and cutthroat recruiting, and blue-chip athletes whose talented hands itched to lay hold of professional contracts. He knew glad-handers as well, and eager-beaver alumni and friends who were faithful when he won.

Mont had succeeded the late Jim Tatum, a Maryland legend.

As head coach, Mont proved to be a man of intelligence and wry good humor, virtues that could not save him when his Maryland teams began to lose, which they did, too soon. Barely had he put his ear to the ground to catch the rumblings when he was out on it.

It was my impression that Mont had quit coaching after that, but in fact he had gone — presumably under cover of darkness — to Greencastle, Indiana, to become head coach, and eventually athletic director, at DePauw University, where a man could lose in peace. At DePauw the crowds are small, and television coverage nonexistent. A few lines in the *Indianapolis Star* on Sunday morning is the apogee of exposure for a DePauw team. The white-chip athletes who come to play there do not drive complimentary convertibles, and the alumni are not spoiled by offers to go to the Orange Bowl.

Neither do offers from professional teams turn the heads of DePauw players. Mont had a punter who signed with Denver but did not stick. The punter was distinguished by his sandals and shoulder-length hair (DePauw is a conservative Methodist school, which only recently was willing to concede that a bottle of beer on campus might not evoke God's wrath), and used to debate the length of his punts with team publicist Pat Aikman, trying to get thirty-nine-yarders stretched to forty-one.

Coaching at Maryland did not, as it may have seemed, make an old man of Mont. He is one of those large gray men with droopy eyelids who looks as if he was born old and who can often be seen in the shadows of a scoreboard, looking up despairingly at the figures there.

At DePauw he was granted a golden twilight. If his losing seasons — since 1959 — outnumbered the winners by almost two to one, he was respected for his virtues and was much in demand as an after-dinner speaker. He told his audiences that

DePauw football had everything Notre Dame football had except parking problems. He placed the picture of Queen Elizabeth on his desk and settled down. In time he was even given tenure, which would have been unheard-of at Maryland or any of those schools where football is too important to chance a coach's passivity.

Prim, proper little Greencastle — population 9,000 — is not a town with an unlimited capacity for excitement, but what it gets it appreciates. John Dillinger robbed a bank there forty-odd years ago and townspeople are not over talking about it. A breathtakingly incongruous German World War II buzz bomb is on permanent display in the town square.

Mont, in turn, brought to DePauw football (in lieu of unremitting victories) a certain flair that could be appreciated. In the key game with archrival Wabash in 1960, DePauw scored a last-minute touchdown to cut Wabash's lead to 13–12. Mont had said if it ever came to this — a decision to go for one extra point to tie, or two to win — he would leave it to the fans. True to his word, at that pregnant moment Mont turned to the stands and spread out his hands like a tent preacher. (In the press box, an assistant coach named Ted Katula, thinking Mont was signaling *him* to make the decision, dived for the floor.)

The crowd shouted "Go!"

DePauw went, and won 14–13.

"I could never have done that at Maryland," Mont said.

It was not Mont I had come to Indiana to see, however. Mont was a bonus, like finding a first-edition Melville in the quarter bookrack at the Goodwill store. It was the game — DePauw vs. Wabash — that had drawn me, through the clouds of my own doubts that college football could still get by in the kind of small-town incubators that spawned it so many decades ago.

Wabash had been playing DePauw in the privacy of western

Indiana since 1890, which makes it (orchestra up) "The Oldest Continuous Rivalry West of the Alleghenies." The schools' propagandists cling to this designation as though it were a lifeline, the way other places vaunt their right to be "The Bell Pepper Capital of Kansas" or "The Birthplace of Truman Seymour." There is, nonetheless, a certain cryptic glamour to being the oldest anything, and that is what DePauw–Wabash has enjoyed, "The Oldest Continuous," etc. etc.

Any persevering self-respecting rivalry has to have pains to grow on, of course, and the seeds of a loving enmity were sown early in this one. DePauw claimed a forfeit of the 1891 game because Wabash didn't show. Wabash has no record of it, but has been unable to get it off the books. When DePauw lost in Crawfordsville one year, its student newspaper reported that "the best team cannot win when playing against thirteen men, two of them the officials . . . [who] were personal friends of the Wabash coach." Wabash backed out of another game because of an incident the year before when Wabash fielded a black player. When DePauw records showed a victory over Wabash that year, Wabash officials conducted a "scrupulous investigation" and found that the losing team was actually Wabash High School.

It was not unusual in those days for DePauw and Wabash to engage such teams as Purdue and Notre Dame, but there were even bigger nuts to be cracked. DePauw played the great Illinois team of 1924 and lost 45–0. Red Grange appeared on the field once during the game to pose for a picture. After the game the DePauw coach "was granted a leave of absence."

Wabash managed to drum up a piece of business with superpower Michigan. Outweighed thirty pounds to the man, Wabash succumbed 22–0. It was considered a moral victory.

"Little Giants," someone called them, and the Wabash nickname was born. DePauw's athletic teams are called Tigers. There are no romantic stories about that, but a Wabash professor told me that every time the DePauw mascot — a student dressed in a $300 tiger suit — gets near the Wabash stands he loses his tail. Or worse.

By the 1930s the rivals settled at their moorings like aging ships, taking on only routine passage and finding in each other the best reason for existing. In 1932 the Monon Railroad, which ran through the towns of Greencastle and Crawfordsville, donated a 350-pound bell off one of its locomotives as the winner's prize, and most of the intrigue since then has centered on the stealing of and fighting over the Monon Bell. The series slogged along. It was remarkably even, thirty-six victories for DePauw, thirty-five for Wabash, and seven ties, when I first heard of it.

I made my headquarters the week of the game at the General Lew Wallace Motor Inn in Crawfordsville, motoring in from Indianapolis through a misting rain and a 33-degree temperature. The Indiana sky was corrugated in layers of gray, like an elephant's hide. The sun had made three spot appearances since September, and the bone-chilling dampness had taken root.

Crawfordsville is thirty miles due north of Greencastle on U.S. 231. The tie line is not exactly the labyrinth at Knossos, however, so it is reasonable to say that the towns are compatible. Crawfordsville has a few more people and apparently not as many funeral homes. My first impressions were reassuring. John Wayne was playing at the eighty-eight-year-old Strand Theater. A whistling mailman was making his rounds on foot. The police wore American flags on their sleeves.

One of the latter obligingly led me in his patrol car to the Lew

Wallace, which I had missed on the first pass through. Wallace was the Civil War general who wrote *Ben Hur*. His study is now a museum near Wabash, which he attended in 1840. For six days. Nevertheless he remains the school's most famous matriculator and the only name I recognized on the lists of Wabash alumni.

The General Lew Wallace Motor Inn was formerly a coffin factory. The restaurant there serves an appetizing brand of canned chili that the Wabash coaching staff takes in every now and then. The coaches love it. They think the chili is homemade.

Wabash was a short walk in the rain to the western edge of town, the tiny campus spotted with huge piles of decaying leaves, the only color left on it by the advancing winter. The campus is a throwback. The original building (1832) is still in use, and additions contribute to the vaguely forbidding, bleakly exciting quality of the place. The unmistakable aura of an all-male institution.

I had been told that if you scratch the backgrounds of most Wabash and DePauw students you would find little to distinguish them — middle-class, Protestant, conservative, white. But college students wear their identities like overcoats and tend to adapt to the styles at hand, causing a school's character to harden along certain fashionable lines, and it was here that Wabash and DePauw were said to be antipathetic.

Wabash (from the short DePauw view) is a monastery for the uncouth. Wabash does not have a code of conduct for its men, only that they "behave as gentlemen," which gives them license to develop low brows and manners. You can tell a Wabash student by the way he staggers on weekends. He is the one to be found face down in the wedding cake. He never gets the part straight in his oil-slick hair. Wabash men are called Cavemen (they enjoy the image), and you wouldn't let your sister touch one with a ten-foot prod.

DePauw's image, as pushed at Wabash, is that of a sanctuary for sissies. DePauw men are called "Dannies" and are a hankie-waving bunch. Nevertheless, they are not particularly keen witted. A Dannie carries an umbrella when the sun is out and puts it down when it starts to rain. How does a Dannie get in shape for the big game? The coach dumps him off the bus at Wabash, and he runs like hell for home.

Dannies adhere to a strict school moral code, which is to say they sneak their drinks. When given more freedom than they can handle they are pictured running naked across the pages of *Playboy* magazine. DePauw's student body is 45 percent female. Wabash students therefore consider DePauw a nice place to visit, but they wouldn't want to enroll there.

These differences are mostly symbolic, of course, but it is true that DePauw is a larger, more socially tailored school (2,257 enrollment to 850 for Wabash that year) with a surer financial base, and it *does* have girls. Wabash made a two-year cost study of going coeducational some time ago and decided that girls did not belong in college.

"There it is — you're jealous of DePauw," I said. I was nursing coffee in the offices of the Wabash news bureau with the director of public affairs, Jim Wood, and the sports information director, Gerry Dreyer, trying to find a good reason for being there on such a lousy day. The wooden floors smelled deliciously of age, and on the wall was a laminated plaque announcing the 1907 Michigan game ("Yea! Wabash! Big Mass Meeting of Townspeople . . . The Biggest Athletic Event Ever Pulled Off in the State . . .").

"Of course we are," said a third man, a professor whom Wood had invited in to set me straight on DePauw. His name was Warren Shearer, onetime acting dean of men, a whip-lean man with aggressive eyebrows that leaped when he was hard into a story. Wood goaded him on. Shearer's dramatic voice rose.

"But venturing out for companionship never bothered a Wabash man," he said. By the same token, he said he had noticed over the years a marked deterioration in the vigor of the DePauw people. They had become "more placid," and their professors were hopeless. When emotion ran amok on the field or in the stands at the big game, it was always the Wabash professors who sallied forth to save the peace. "The DePauw professors," he sneered, "just sat in their seats with their arms crossed."

He said it was remarkable how clean Wabash had kept its record, considering. He said there was only one time he recalled ever having to expel any students. Only a handful. For vandalism. "They threw some paint around," he said. "It was not water soluble."

"And the bell?" I asked. "What about . . . ?"

"The Monon Bell! A subject close to my heart."

"Yes, but do college kids really get excited about things like that anymore?"

"Well, I can say to you now that it is in our possession, having won last year's contest with consummate ease [16–7], and it will remain so. It is chained to the balcony rail in the gymnasium for all to see, which is typical of Wabash. DePauw is inclined to hide it, not being sure of its ability to keep it. We have little to worry about. DePauw's actions at best are retaliatory, which brings up a very interesting story."

Shearer then told me how, a few years before when the bell was at DePauw, a Wabash student posing as a Mexican reporter was granted an interview with DePauw president Dr. William Kerstetter, who not only blabbed the bell's hiding place but had the director of athletics take the bogus Mexican around to see it. That night a Wabash raiding party redeemed the bell.

"I think the code name for the operation was 'Frijoles.' It was a dark day for President Kerstetter, who is not known for his ability to take a joke. One of the DePauw deans called me almost hourly. 'You've got to get us that bell back!' he said. I told him he had absolutely no sense of humor.

" 'But it's breaking and entering!' he said. 'A felony!'

" 'But didn't they leave money on the windowsill?' I asked. In fact they had left a dollar fifteen, which was more than enough to cover damages.

"The bell was kept in the woods nearby, where there were regular showings and an occasional dingdong. The dean finally called again. 'I don't want to alarm you,' he said, 'but my students are up in arms. They're coming up to Wabash en masse, four hundred strong, to recover the bell.'

" 'All that will accomplish,' I said, 'is one of the grandest riots ever seen on a college campus. Our students will welcome them with open arms.'

"Ah, it was great while it lasted. But a compromise was made, and an exchange took place at Raccoon Creek, halfway to Greencastle. In secret, they took it to Blackstock Stadium and buried it just beyond the end zone. That's their style. But they had a helluva time. When it was time to uncover it just before the game, the ground was frozen solid."

Professor Shearer was brainwashing me. He knew it and I knew it. What he didn't know was that it was working.

I cannot pinpoint the moment I lost my objectivity and began to care — in Wabash's favor — but I can reconstruct the reasons for it. Something as expressive and unaffected as Wabash vs. DePauw felt at ground level for a spell is quite impossible to resist. If you think you know college football by knowing Texas–Oklahoma or USC–UCLA you are as wrong as you would be if you thought you knew the United States by knowing New York City.

I think the realization struck with a punt that landed on the railroad tracks at practice the next afternoon. The ball slid off an enthusiastic but inexpert Wabash foot, flew up into that grieving Indiana sky and over the fence at an erratic angle and down onto the tracks that split the field into upper and lower levels, and caromed and spun there among the ties, and I heard the train and said to myself, "Well, there goes the budget."

The Wabash coach had told me how the balls popped when the trains passed over them, an ordinance of physics he could do nothing about. But it was the economics that touched me. Football at Wabash is deficit spending, and the pops are never music to the coach's ears. "Every time we open the doors for a game," the coach said, "we lose money." What thrilled me about the remark was that Wabash had no intention of *closing* its doors, as others have, for that reason.

We watched the ball disappear, and I said to the coach, a part Cherokee Indian named Dick Bowman, that this was no place for a penny-pinching outfit to practice. To which he wisely pointed out that the cost of moving the field versus the sacrifice of a few hunks of leather to the railroad was no contest.

Actually, he said, if I really wanted to see the budget at work I should go on a road trip, like the 300-miler to Suwannee when his wife packaged one hundred and twenty homemade pimento

cheese sandwiches only to find out the players preferred
bologna. Leftovers don't lie. Bowman said he broke the trip at
Vanderbilt for a workout on the Tartan field.

"They'd never been on anything like that," he said. The
fields in the Indiana Collegiate Conference, of which Wabash
and DePauw are members, are not always level, nor skillfully
lined, much less synthetic. His boys got out on the Tartan and
"we couldn't *drive* 'em off."

A Wabash player in a dirty white uniform went down and
stood by the track on our side, waiting with his hands on his
hips for the train to pass. In that grim perspective he reminded
me of one of those solitary night people who can be seen
watching stoically in front of the machines at the Laundromat.

The train passed and the ball was still whole on the other
side. "Saved," I said to Bowman. I was actually relieved.
Bowman just smiled and began moving away to get a better
angle on his backfield. He moved with a limp.

"What happened to your leg?"

"Which one? I hurt one knee when I was at Oklahoma trying
to play offensive tackle at two hundred pounds for Bud
Wilkinson. The reason I'm limping now is I got knocked down
at Albion last year and ruined the other. We may not look it,
but we hit pretty hard in this league."

I asked him if it bothered him much, the transition from
Oklahoma to Wabash. He often referred to "the Big Time,"
how this or that player was "almost good enough for the Big
Time," or, "you never see this in the Big Time."

If Bowman weren't an Indian I would have thought he was a
cowboy — lanky and broad shouldered, with a deep-lined face
and a quick, pleasant smile that stretched like a garter.

"I loved Oklahoma," he said, "but I think I loved Bud more.

I think in that atmosphere you are more part of the team than you are a part of the school. I've been back only once in ten years.

"I tell my players, 'You can't eat a football. You can bake it, broil it and stew it, maybe, but you can't eat it. You better get that schooling first.' These boys do." He gestured at the practicing players. "You should see the books they take on trips. Far-out stuff, like Aristotle. They're always underlining."

A boy in street clothes had been standing next to him, waiting to speak.

"You're late, Tommy," Bowman said.

"Had a physics lab, Coach. And I was up to six A.M. on a term paper."

"What on? The term paper, I mean?"

"Witchcraft."

"Gee wiz. See what I mean?" said Bowman, turning to me. The boy walked away. "Tommy's from Waco, Texas. We get 'em from everywhere. Hey, see that one over there? Tulsa, Oklahoma. His father is with an airline. The family can fly for nothing. That's the kind to have."

"How do you get so many?" I said. There were a hundred or more on the split-level field. Some were not the most athletic-looking specimens.

"Walk-ons, many of them. I don't cut anybody. And I write a lot of letters. We can't give a full scholarship, which makes it difficult because some schools in the conference can."

"Do you ever wish for the Big Time? I mean, coaching in it?"

"I made that decision a long time ago. I'm forty-one years old. I couldn't go the other way if I wanted to. It's past me."

Later, over cocktails at Wood's house, a group of them — Bowman, athletic director Max Servies, and a couple others — ganged up on me. I don't know what I said to start it, something about intercollegiate football at a small college being as impractical in today's world as a truck farm, but they swamped me with rhetoric. They said football was not there to make money; where had I been?

"Our budget's less than a hundred thousand dollars," Bowman said. "Gate receipts average about seven thousand dollars a year. We can seat forty-two hundred, and the only time we fill the stadium is for DePauw. No way to balance out."

"Athletics are for the kids, not the other way around," one of them said. "Athletics contribute to the educational experience."

"I like that," I said. "I remember a Dartmouth —"

"Fifteen percent of the student body is out for football," I was interrupted. "Eighty percent participate in some form of athletics."

"Tell *that* to your Notre Dames and your Michigan States."

"And your Alabamas."

"The austerity bothers some of them," Bowman said. "I had one boy sneak out the first night. There's a high attrition rate, too, because of the academics. I'll start eleven freshmen against DePauw, including the quarterback."

"Maybe you oughta pay 'em under the table," I said, dipping into the peanuts.

"Are you kidding? Semipro athletes? That'd be a catastrophe. Where would we get the money? Besides, they're too close as a group within the student body. It'd be bad for morale."

"DePauw has one slight advantage. They can promise their athletes the chance to wait on tables at the sorority houses."

"They used to get an extra day off at Thanksgiving if they beat us."

"There's always a money problem here," Wood said. "You

oughta see President Seymour. He'll tell you. I think he collected a million bucks last year in a door-knocking campaign."

"Old Thad Seymour. And he's an Ivy Leaguer, too."

"It's really not so critical," Bowman said. "The coaches were able to scrape up enough pin money to go out to an authentic Chinese restaurant last year."

The next day I went around to see President Seymour, tracking mud onto the carpet of his office, which reeked of pipe smoke. The laminated handbill announcing the 1907 Wabash–Michigan game was on his wall. Seymour was a large, hearty man with a ruggedly constructed nose that did not precede him so much as it led his interference. He had been the dean of men at Dartmouth, and until he came to Indiana — by train — three years before he "didn't think places like this still existed."

He reveled in it. He had participated in the faculty intramural program and had gotten caught up in Wabash vs. DePauw. He said that at the annual pregame Monon Bell Stag Night in Indianapolis, when rival alumni and officials get together and live it up, he had, in the course of performing magic tricks for the crowd, broken an egg in President Kerstetter's lap. He thought it great fun.

Neither was he above leading the Wabash student body in a cheer or two, he said. His first year, wearing a red and white freshman's beanie, he went onto the field to get one going. The score was 14–7 DePauw. Almost immediately after his cheer Wabash scored. "Unfortunately, we went for two points and missed. If we'd made it, it would have changed my life. I could have sat at my desk and never done another thing."

On my way out I lifted from an anteroom chair a discarded copy of the annual racy newspaper put out by Wabash journalists for the big game. This one was called *The DeBauch* and featured a nude man, partially covered with a DePauw pennant, lounging across the front page. President Kerstetter's head was superimposed on the man's shoulders. The headline said, "DeBauch Pres. Desires Strong Student Body." I stuffed the paper under the seat of my rental car and drove the thirty miles to Greencastle.

It was raining there as well; God was playing no favorites. Pat Aikman filled my arms with indoctrination material and arranged for me to see Tommy Mont. The DePauw newspaper he gave me was crammed with pictures of coeds, indicating to prospective students that the place was *crawling* with good-looking girls in short skirts. There was one pointed reference to the football program: "Victories are not purchased at the expense of scholarship."

Aikman said, indeed, that football was kept in perspective at DePauw, but scholarships were available to football players and they were proud of the accommodation Tommy Mont had made. The squad had a higher grade average than the student body, and 33 percent of the varsity were pre-med or pre-dental students. Tommy Mont's job did not depend on beating Wabash. "But of course, we would like nothing better." Aikman smiled thinly.

We dropped in on Mont. One of his assistant coaches, a pale young man with a red crew cut, looked me up and down and then disappeared. Mont said that one thing he enjoyed about the rivalry was how well everybody got along, especially the two coaching staffs.

Ted Katula said I shouldn't listen to too much of that,

because old Tommy always pulled out the stops for Wabash. He said a few years before Mont changed DePauw's jersey colors at halftime. The ploy enraged Wabash, but it had a salutary effect on the DePauw quarterback who suddenly became Sammy Baugh.

"But the real story was Tommy's halftime talk that day. We were behind ten to nothing and looking hopeless. In the middle of his talk he turned and pointed at me. 'Now you fellas know Ted here. He's been with me ten years. I hate to say it, but he's leaving us. This is his last game at DePauw. Frankly, fellas, I'd consider it an honor if we won it for old Ted.'

"Geez, they almost tore the door down getting back out there. We won thirteen to ten. And as you can see, I had no intention of leaving DePauw."

What, I asked, did Tricky Tommy have cooking this time?

Mont smiled without showing his teeth. "Oh, you never know," he said. "Neither team is exactly overloaded [DePauw's record was 2–6; Wabash's 3–6]. Did they tell you we haven't lost up there in eighteen years?" Later at practice, the red-haired assistant coach came over and told me I was "okay." I said I didn't understand. He said he had checked me out. He'd even called New York. He said they couldn't be too careful this week. "Actually," he said, smiling, "you don't look Mexican."

The telephone at the Lew Wallace jarred me from sleep at 5 A.M. An adolescent voice, brimming with excitement, roared into my subconscious.

"We got the bell."

"Whu?"

"The bell. The Monon Bell. Those stupid Kappa Sigs . . ." He was laughing like a maniac. "Sawed through the chain and carted it the hell out of there."

"Listen, hey. Uh, listen. Who . . . ?"

"Never mind. You probably know about the Sphinx Club getting permission to take the bell down to Greencastle last night . . . ?"

"The who?"

"The Sphinx Club. The Wabash lettermen. They took it on a truck and rang the hell out of it, but those dumb DePauw guys couldn't take it off them. The cops finally chased them out of town. Well, when they got back they just chained it to the door frame in the gym lobby. And the Kappa Sigs were guarding it. *Were*, until a few minutes ago."

"We? Who's we? DePauw . . . ?"

"Naw. I'm a freshman at Wabash."

"You mean you stole your own bell?" I was finally awake.

"Yeah. Wild, huh?" He was still giggling. "You wanta see it?"

"Yeah, but I think I'll wait till dawn. Unless you plan on stealing the Lew Wallace coffee shop."

The four conspirators that made up the raiding party lived in what they called an "off-campus apartment," a ramshackle two-story building whose walls were held together by providence and a thin coat of flaking white paint. The leader of the gang was a slightly built, deliberately scruffy-looking boy named Ken who said his father was a banker in Westchester County, New York.

Ken led me on a triumphant walk down a dark stairwell to a first-floor bathroom which, by appearances, had been out of commission for several decades. There, next to a rusting trash-laden bathtub and a sleeping black cat, was the Monon Bell, painted red (for Wabash) and gold (for DePauw).

"They should never have left it to those Kappa Sigs," Ken said proudly. "We really foxed 'em."

"What you got against the Kappa Sigs?"

"They're a frat. I hate frats."

"Why?"

"*Why?* All that discipline."

I asked him what they were going to do with it. The bell. Already *The Bachelor*, in banner headlines, had blamed DePauw. "Won't a lot of people be up in arms?"

"Dean Moore knows we got it. They'll get it back just before the game."

"Okay, but why did you take it?"

He looked at me condescendingly.

"*Some*body had to," he said. "Those Dannies wouldn't even try."

The missing bell was a conversational leader that night at the Monon Stag in Indianapolis. Jim Wood predicted I would love the stag, everybody getting together and cutting each other up. But it was the low point of my week. The preliminaries were all right — Mont and Bowman were short and sweet; President Seymour produced a red and white "Beat DePauw" sign out of a torn-up napkin — but the toastmaster was excruciating. DePauw had wanted to sub its glee club as the main event, and it would have been a good idea.

On the morning of the game I was up early and over to the student snack shop for breakfast. I ran into two of the players, an end named Hiatt, who had six vials of experimental fruit flies stuffed in his fatigue jacket, and a safetyman named Haklin, the team captain. Hiatt said he had played in the game last year with a separated shoulder, "but there was so much infighting and name-calling going on I didn't realize it."

Haklin was having his team meal, a carton of milk and a blueberry Danish. He said a professor had told him all the games up to DePauw were "scrimmages," and "he's right. Last year when the seniors talked to the team before the game it was like war. They said, 'You better prepare yourselves. And you better win. For your sake, not ours. You'll take a lot of crap if you don't.' "

Haklin looked down at the empty milk carton he was squeezing.

"Next year I'll be in grad school, trying for a Rhodes Scholarship. But I don't know what I'll do without football. I couldn't have made it at a big school, so I came here. I'm sorry it's over."

Upstairs, Dick Bowman looked out at the gray sky over Little Giant Stadium. "Damn rain," he said. "I hope it stays away." He said he had planned no gimmicks for DePauw. A basic Oklahoma defense, the fashionable triple-option offense. "Fundamentals are about all we have time to teach."

He said that he had four bottles of champagne on ice for the victory party. He said that he realized it wasn't enough to get high on.

A Veterans Day Parade in downtown Crawfordsville was the only competing event at game time. Despite the threatening weather, the Wabash crowd arrived early and filled its side. The DePauws were late in coming and did not fill theirs. "They don't wanta see any more than they have to," a young humorist standing next to me on the sidelines said.

The Monon Bell came clanging into the stadium on the back of President Seymour's swaying 1938 Packard, eliciting a ponderous cheer. The DePauw band was thumping overhead as Tommy Mont faced his black-and-gold-clad warriors in the dressing room and offered them clemency for a "bad season." He called on them to play "the doggonedest football game you ever played." They whooped and crowded the exit to the field.

It might not have been that — the doggonedest football game ever played — but it was a fine one, lacking neither skill nor drama. I stood with Mont's coaching staff in the first half in a vortex of partisanship. A stocky, mud-caked player came off shaking his head in wonder. "It's euphoria, man," he shouted, wide-eyed. "I think I'm moving like hell, but I ain't moving worth a shit."

On an out-of-bounds play, a pileup occurred at my feet. Mud flew, and bodies, and a near-hysterical voice at my elbow screamed, "Crack his head off!"

Wabash, meanwhile, had unleashed a treacherous attack of orthodoxy that overshadowed Mont's more imaginative football. Coach Bowman's freshman quarterback, Cogdill, got over a case of the flutters (a fumble, an intercepted pass) and put his team in for two touchdowns in the first quarter.

Then DePauw came alive. A 92-yard touchdown march made it 14–6 just before the half. The extra point was botched. "*Dang*," Mont said, turning sharply on his heel. "We've been doing this thirteen weeks, now we're dumb." But as we moved off the field he winked at me and said, "Helluva college game, isn't it?" It was, too.

I offer, in somewhat expurgated form, as a classic of its kind, Coach Bowman's halftime talk to his Wabash players: "Gentlemen," he said, "you have thirty minutes to play. For some of you, it's the last thirty minutes. DePauw hates your guts. You hate their guts. You got thirty minutes to put together all that hate and all the courage you can and kick their tails. Now relax and have a good time."

On the Wabash side I had difficulty deciding which action to follow. The Sphinx Club, those redoubtable rowdies, made a human pyramid that collapsed wildly in the grass. They also offered their own refinements in cheer lyrics:

"Rah rah ree, Kick 'em in the knee!

"Rah rah rass, Kick 'em in the wee-knee!"

Thad Seymour, a hawk-nosed specter in red and white, came out of his president's box to lead his annual cheer. "Gimme a W!" he shouted, waving his arms.

"*Duba*-ya!"

"Gimme an A!"

"A . . ."

Wabash scored again on the first series after the kickoff, lightening some of the suspense. But a Tiger named Simpson scored his second touchdown on a 71-yard run, and a two-point play cut the difference to 20–14 in the fourth quarter.

Tempers shortened as the end drew near. Hiatt grabbed a rival after a pileup, and a player close by me yelled, "That's what we need, a good fight." But the fight did not materialize. The game ended with Wabash in control at midfield.

I don't know what I expected to happen then, but nothing riotous did. Champagne flowed (briefly) in the Wabash dressing room. Dick Bowman gave me a bear hug. I went over to the DePauw dressing room to extend condolences to Tommy Mont. He was sitting on a bench, settled there as heavily as nut pudding on an unaccustomed stomach, and didn't seem eager to talk.

One of his assistants was outside and I made a few gestures of commiseration. He had the look of a man who had seen a cow break loose and kill the butcher. The series was tied, he said.

"Geezus, after all these years we gotta start over."

One of those chestless collegiate types who have acquired enough insouciance to cover up their insecurities was next to me as I walked away. I had seen him before, but couldn't place him.

He said, "Well, what do you expect from a school like this."

"What do you mean?" I ask.

"Didn't Mr. Aikman tell you? Didn't he tell you about when they tried to get football started here about six thousand years ago? How the team was so bad they tried to sell their only football?"

I said, no, I hadn't heard that one.

But I didn't doubt it.

To this day, of a Sunday morning in the fall I find myself scouring the sports pages for the scores of Wabash and DePauw, counting myself lucky to find at least that. Late in the season, when I know they are going to appear on the same line, my anticipation quickens — this happens every time — and though my partisanship has waned (both deserve the best), I note with a twinge of pride that Wabash continues to dominate.

For some time, the tie that bound was Thad Seymour, posting long graceful letters about the latest intrigue in the rivalry. I think old Thad missed me. In any case, he finally moved to Florida, to become president of Rollins College, and the letters stopped. President Kerstetter had retired from DePauw as well, a loss for adolescent cartoonists and pranksters.

But Max Servies was still around as Wabash's athletic director when I called for an update. He said Dick Bowman had, alas, gone on to the Big Time, as an assistant coach at West Point, but wound up selling sporting goods in New Jersey. He said Bowman "kept in touch." Tommy Mont had quit coaching but was still DePauw's athletic director, looking as old as ever.

Wabash had been winning consistently, making the Division III playoffs. I asked Servies what kind of budget he now worked with. He said football costs, roughly, were up to thirty thousand dollars a year, with a four- to five-thousand-dollar outlay for recruiting (mostly letters and phone calls). There were still no athletic scholarships, per se; the basis for scholarship help at Wabash is "need," and 75 percent of the student body gets some kind of help. Wabash football had its best year in 1978, averaging three thousand fans at home and taking in eighteen thousand dollars. With salaries, the net was a loss of around ninety-two thousand dollars.

"But that's not why we have football," said Servies.

"I know," I said.

Wabash had won three in a row in the rivalry with DePauw, he said, but in 1978 a miracle happened. DePauw students — reconstituted Dannies — had invaded Crawfordsville and swiped the Monon Bell.

The following night, five hundred Wabash students descended on Greencastle, variously (but not seriously) armed. There was a massive confrontation that cooler heads, and cops, quickly and successfully arbitrated. No one was hurt. There was only one arrest — the goalie of the DePauw women's field hockey team, who was dressed in her uniform for a costume party and was carrying a mean-looking hockey stick.

The exact center of Montana is a spot on a kitchen sink in a house in Lewistown. The land was made for ranchers and farmers; Lewistown needs them more than they need Lewistown. In the late fall, when the earth is opened in long deep slashes to receive the seed, the smell of the land reaches into the city. The Lewis and Clark trail once passed near here, and so did Blackfoot, Crow, and Shoshone. Now the Crow are on a reservation near the Little Big Horn and pan-faced Blackfoot girls with bouffant hairdos lean against the tavern walls of Great Falls. The Indian Problem is for other towns and the foreign government at Washington.

A town's character, like a man's, is shaped early, often by the stress under which it is born. Lewistown was born poor. It sprouted in 1881 out of an old trading post named Reed's Fort, its nativity unblessed and unheralded, only recorded, like a booking in a seaport log. Shaped by hard truth, the people of Lewistown take life without varnish. Lewistown historians sternly point out that C. M. Russell, the famed cowboy artist, made the town sheriff's blotter twice, once for gambling and once for assault. A Lewistown man who knew him told me that whenever he saw Charley Russell he was full of lice.

The antelope and elk were already coming out of the foothills when I got to Lewistown. Pushed along by the advancing frostline, they could be seen grazing speculatively beside the snow fences and the great bunkers of packaged hay — ever closer to the guns of the townspeople. No self-respecting Lewistown male goes the season without getting his buck, and he prepares for that moment — restoring equipment, hoarding shells — as diligently as he prepares for the drastic Montana winter.

Main Street, Lewistown, is a log chute swooping down into town from a blinking light on U.S. 87. In its infancy the city was laid out on a bias to accommodate existing fence lines. Not even the natives are sure which way is north. Downtown, bankers and storekeeps and bowlegged ranchers in Stetson hats greet on first-name basis. Copenhagen Snuff is a big seller at The City, a combination drugstore, gun shop, pool hall, and gin-rummy parlor. On the magazine racks respectable Lewistown housewives can catch up on cosmopolitan advisories just by scanning the covers: "Bedroom Hopscotching Among Adults"; "Nudity Can Save Your Marriage."

In the afternoon the kids come into The City to shoot pool, and the old men, divided from the young by the gun rack, play gin rummy with loud voices. The kindly justice of the peace who owned the place when I was there was known as the hanging judge by the kids. He sentenced them to haircuts.

At the first tempering of dawn I was deep into a platter of pancakes at the Gem Cafe when four men came in and with a good-natured clattering of chairs took the table next to mine. One was a black, the proprietor of an auto-repair shop. Two wore cowboy boots and were geared for the range. The fourth, leading the conversation, was a man in a pharmacist's jacket, though his conversational style was more like a dentist's drill.

The pharmacist had gone down that weekend to see Montana State University play football. He said he liked to make a regular thing of catching a college game every five or six years, "just so I can really tie one on. Get sloshed and have a time." The trouble was, he said, he didn't get much out of those games because he couldn't keep track of the ball.

"On TV they show you right where it is all the time. In person, I can't follow the ball. I mean in those college games. I don't have that trouble here with Don's team. They fumble the ball enough so you can keep an eye on it."

From that ringing endorsement, I could not wait to get around to see the Lewiston High football players at practice that afternoon. They were a handful — twenty-five or thirty — and they were working out at a field that was tiered on one side, like an amphitheater. The team's distinctive wardrobe included a wide variety of jersey colors and irregular pants. Every now and then a player would reach down and toss a rock off the field.

The coach's name was Don Perkins, a shiny-eyed man moving into middle age with a gray-on-black crew cut and a flashy, worthwhile nose. The high nasal quality of the Midwest was in his voice. What I was staring at, he said, was a drive-in football stadium, perhaps the only one of its kind. There were enough spaces on the three levels to park one hundred and fifty cars and, theoretically, keep a thousand people from freezing to death on a Montana Friday night.

The coach said he carried about twenty-five men on the varsity, but that was academic because he never cut anybody. His star halfback was a boy named Schultz who was in the upper 10 percent of his class and planned to run off to California to be an engineer at the first opportunity. The other players called Schultz "Rosey Hands" because they said his hands were always pink from dropping passes.

Perkins came from Minnesota fifteen years before to be the Lewistown coach and said that by now he was comfortable in it. Yes, even happy. He figured out one year that his annual coach's stipend ($800 over his salary as a biology teacher) broke down to 32 cents an hour. After that he never wanted to figure it out again. In 1964 his team did something outrageous. It went undefeated. "People didn't know how to act," he said. "Everybody wanted to give us a banquet. I finally had to tell them to stop giving us banquets."

On the far corner of the field was some flat, unpretentious construction that appeared to be progressing very slowly. Perkins said it was a new warmup house he had asked the school to spring for. Evidently 1964 was too long ago to be remembered. A civil suit was holding up completion of the warmup house.

Perkins would get the warmup house eventually. He also had an order in for ten new helmets for the jayvee team. He thought he'd get those, too. No, he didn't think they'd be getting a new stadium any time soon. He said he really couldn't complain, because the school itself was fifty years old.

As a man who earned only 32 cents an hour, Don Perkins would seem to be a novel specimen, even in a less inflationary time. His drive-in football stadium might be novel but he wasn't. As a group, high school coaches are all waiting to get their rewards in heaven, because as long as they are high school coaches they are going to be underpaid on earth. But there are exceptions . . .

Interstate 75, a thundering tape measure marking the miles from Sault Ste. Marie to St. Petersburg, skirts Valdosta, Georgia, to the west, expediting the escape route to the sands of Florida and taking the play away from old U.S. 41, a more serene, edifying conveyor. A voice named Benton was making the car radio tremble: ". . . ray-nee night in Jaw-juh . . . ray-nee *niiiiiiight* in Jaw-juh . . . it seems like it's raynin' all over the world . . ."

Ahead of me the folds in the earth rose gently. Tobacco country, and soybeans and cotton and pines that yield the gum turpentine. Spanish moss hung from the trees like bridal trains, recalling the wedding of the people to an older, mellower time.

"Welcome to Valdosta. Church of Christ one-half block."

The churches, gleaming white, seemed to be everywhere, two to a block. The police cars were white, the streets clean, the society stratified: 10 percent controlling about 90 percent of the wealth. Langdale, Strickland, and Goodloe were names to know, or to be reckoned with.

In the center of town stood a marble statue, erected in 1911, of a soldier in anachronistic fighting gear. The inscription said it was dedicated to "Our Confederate dead. CSA." White people, hanging to the thread, do not want to give up their roots either. In 1969, when some black people raised the roof over the playing of "Dixie" at high school sporting events, the whites blamed "outside agitators."

Despite ax-handle rhetoric from the state capital, the integration of Valdosta High School had gone smoothly. The school was one of the first to be integrated in the state and it was a balanced, meaningful integration. The Valdosta High School football team, the best team in Georgia year after year, was coached then by a man named Wright Bazemore. Bazemore did not have stars. He only had boys he considered his children. Fifteen percent of his children were black.

I missed the hunting trip I had hoped to make with Wright Bazemore. I got there too late on a Saturday afternoon and he had already gone and returned.

"Get your birds?" I asked.

"Got me a few."

"What's a few — the limit?"

"Yes." He smiled.

"Well, maybe we can try tomorrow."

"I'm a Christian," he said.

"Yes?"

"I don't hunt on Sunday. I go to church on Sunday."

To fill you in on all of Wright Bazemore's qualifications might be a fairly suffocating thing, but for those who cannot resist box scores, a medium-length rundown is offered. He is retired now, but at that point he was fifty-three years old, a moderate to small man with gray hair and batwing ears, and a rather nice smile under licorice eyebrows. A shy man, he usually let his wife, Bettie, do most of the talking when other people were around. He was born sixty miles up the road in Fitzgerald, where he once scored ten touchdowns in two high school football games. He went on to play at Mercer when Mercer was taking lessons from teams like Army and Navy and Georgia Tech.

Wright had been coaching the Valdosta High football team for twenty-nine years. He did not have to die to get into the Georgia Hall of Fame, because his teams had won 266 out of 313 games and fourteen state championships. He rode in on a

wave of adoration. Four trophy cases crowded the school halls
and were crammed with little gold men kicking footballs, old
retired jerseys, and half-deflated footballs that had scores like
48–0 and 54–6 painted on them. (Winning isn't everything.
Total annihilation can be fun, too.)

Since I had missed the hunting, Wright said there was no
need for me to miss supper, too, and took me to his house for
hamburgers with the family. Bettie, an informative woman,
talked about the country's debt to the Negro and how it was
being paid in Valdosta, but admitted to an honest concern
about having to drive her daughter across town next year to what
had been an all-Negro school. I had seen the uneasiness
everywhere. Busing is fine until the horn toots for thee.

The subject of her concern was a slim, very dark-eyed girl
who was on the verge of becoming beautiful. Every time the
telephone rang the girl was the first one to it. The family was
having trouble keeping boys off her trail. The boy at the table,
her brother, had a strong jaw and a curl on his forehead — "a
straight-A student," Mrs. Bazemore said — and only recently
was a regular linebacker on Wright Bazemore's varsity.

After dinner Wright drove me around to meet Dynamite
Goodloe, a town hero. I had heard about Dynamite Goodloe
but I didn't know he was one of *the* Goodloes. Dynamite was
relaxed in a chair in his sprawling ranch-style house, wearing a
monogrammed T-shirt and dungarees and chewing on a pipe.
Even in repose he was a striking figure, almost a perfect square,
maybe five-six or -seven, 240 pounds. Despite his physique, he
had been an outstanding athlete: football at Georgia Tech and
an enviable record in amateur golf. When Wright first started
coaching at Valdosta High, Dynamite used to come around and
scrimmage with the team. Without pads.

Coffee was served, and Dynamite began talking about "this

man" Wright Bazemore and what he had done. And Wright just sat there quietly and listened. As I understand it, it had worked this way:

Wright Bazemore's effect on Valdosta was not to make football the logical focal point of a town's pride, but to make football the town's purpose. Kids in cradles were rocked toward the day they would be in on the program. The program, which Wright had set up as city schools' athletic director, consisted on junior high school teams that were fully equipped and played ten-game schedules. These fed the ninety-five-member high school varsity. (I could not help but think of Perkins's meager twenty-five in Lewistown.) For the varsity there were no rags, only riches. A Touchdown Club was organized, at ten dollars a member, and the club donated thirty-five hundred dollars a year so that Wright could take one hundred and ten players to a deluxe two-week football camp in the summer. The club provided plate money so that each player could have chops and steaks when other kids in school were eating tunafish.

Wright's abilities were compared with those of Bobby Dodd and Bear Bryant; the mayor had called him Valdosta's "number-one citizen." Dynamite Goodloe said he was the number-one deterrent to juvenile delinquency. Wright did not allow his players to drink or smoke. One who did smoke was kicked off the team and a few days later came to Bazemore in tears. His father would not let him eat with the rest of the family, he said, and had banished him to his room every night after supper. "Coach," said the boy, "I'll kill myself if you don't take me back."

Every game was a sellout in a stadium that had twelve thousand seats. The only way to wrest a season ticket from a regular was to get it willed to you. Parents who had moved away brought their kids back to town when they were of age for football. And athletes who had moved away hid their cigarettes and came around to see Wright Bazemore before visiting Mama and Papa. A New York company chartered a plane to bring alumni home to see the games on Friday night. A boy in the Air Force had his mother send tape recordings of game broadcasts.

Bazemore's personal needs, meanwhile, were being taken care of by a flexible school and salary policy, and he obliged by not turning his head to college offers. He was rewarded for his fidelity in still other ways: a new Buick, and a camper, and a trailer, and a color television set, and a boat. And there was always somebody who would fix his TV for free, or bring around some avocados.

"This is a very good place to coach," said Wright Bazemore.

"Because of him, Valdosta is a better place to live," said Dynamite Goodloe.

"Here, we believe in football," said Wright Bazemore.

And then, just as we were about to call it a night, Mrs. Bazemore said something that I have not yet forgotten. Nor have I decided what conclusions to draw, if any. My feelings then and now are ambivalent. I was sitting there in the glow of Wright Bazemore's great success, convinced that at last I had found the high school coach who was not only worth his salt but was getting it, too, when Mrs. Bazemore said what a blow it had been to be tied in the championship game that year.

The team had won twelve straight, and then was tied 26–26, by Athens, Georgia, and, she said, "all Wright could do afterward was go around saying to people, 'I'm sorry, I'm sorry, I'm sorry,' as if he'd lost. As if he'd failed. Just 'I'm sorry, I'm sorry.' I felt so bad for him."

I have saved for last a look at little-league football, the tenderest root, the "future" of the game. I suppose it would have been more reassuring never to have looked at it at all. Or to have gotten no closer than the last row of the last set of bleachers on a misty Saturday afternoon, and then to have entered and exited as quickly as possible.

In the beginning, kids play football because they enjoy it. Adults want kids to play little-league football for a lot of reasons. When the little-league season is in full swing, we are reassured by its advocates and commercial sponsors that it is good stuff, keeping kids off the streets and out of the clutches of juvenile authorities. Also teaching them discipline, teamwork, respect for authority (i.e., coaches), zone defenses, veer and winged-T offenses, and the value of making more effective use of their little bodies — forearms, heads, elbows, and other weapons.

Little-league football, being more costly to operate, did not catch on as quickly as Little League baseball (the latter is capitalized, courtesy of the Congress of the U.S.), but once it did it spread like tidewater across the country. Apparently there was no stopping it. From the lofty hamlets of Colorado to the red-neck towns of Mississippi, in spacious Montana and spaced-out Manhattan, eight- and ten-year-olds, wearing globular helmets that sometimes spin on their heads at impact, go to war against other eight- and ten-year-olds, often bewildered but always stylish in eight pounds of vinyl, polyurethane, and viscose tailoring, at $100 per costume. Miniature cheerleaders bounce up and down like fish on a line, cheering indiscriminately (it is difficult at that age to tell offense from defense). Sometimes bands play.

Little-league moms and pops, bursting with pride that their youngsters have been detoured from lives of crime, crowd the sidelines to encourage them, the veins sticking out on their necks. Grown-up officials in striped shirts blow their whistles in a cacophony of authority and tower over the action like Gulliver over the Lilliputians. Coaches scream and yell at the pint-sized warriors and sometimes tell the officials a thing or two as well, in the best tradition of American athletic encouragement. "I've been asked if I sometimes think I'm Vince Lombardi," said one kids-league coach in Boston. "I say that sometimes I think I'm Lombardi and other times I think I'm Knute Rockne."

Little-league football runs along very well-organized lines, like Little League baseball, but it comes in a greater variety of packaging. Most popular is the Pop Warner League, credited with launching the whole business in 1929 when Joseph Tomlin, a Philadelphia stockbroker, formed the league and named it after the old Carlisle coach, Glenn Scobie ("Pop") Warner. Warner must have made a big impression on Tomlin because he also named his son after him (Glenn, not Pop).

The Pop Warners have lost a little of their luster and a few of their members in recent years because, for one thing, some nitpickers in California couldn't get answers to the question of where their registration money was going. They requested a financial statement and were refused. Nevertheless, the Pop Warners still account for 6,200 teams (about 210,000 young people) in forty-three states and Mexico and make up the only national group. Other local and regional leagues such as Football United International, American Youth Football, and Khoury League sprung up like pizza parlors across the country and were structured along similar lines, usually requiring a franchise for the league, and proof of birth and registration fees of ten to thirty dollars for players. Those whose parents do not pony up get their unconditional release.

League makeup varies. If a parent has the nerve, he can shove Junior into the Dallas recreation department's football program at five, providing Junior is potty-trained, but usually a boy must reach the ripe old age of seven before he is strapped and cushioned and sent to battle. Leagues are divided by age (seven- and eight-year-olds, nine- and ten-year-olds, on to fifteen) or by grades in school; and by weight (40- to 70-pound "tiny tots," 50- to 80-pound "junior peewees," on up to 150-pound "giant bantams" — nomenclature differs regionally).

The kids must wear suspension helmets, face guards, mouthpieces, hip and kidney pads, cleats (or sneakers), and thigh and knee guards. For the most part they play their games on regulation fields, with paid adult officials. Injuries are said to be minimal; some coaches would have you think they are nonexistent. The figures were indeed impressive when I looked into it in the mid-1970s — one broken bone in seventeen years of play in Pop Warner ball in Boston, etc., etc. Certainly, trussed up the way they are, and incapable at seven or so of delivering many foot-pounds of force per square inch, the kids are relatively safe. The only danger would seem to be muscle and eye strain from lugging home and studying the thick pro-type playbooks some pro-minded coaches dispense.

There is a long list of "name" coaches who have been in the program. Former LSU halfback and ex-pro Ray Coates and Dr. Les Horvath, the Heisman Trophy winner from Ohio State, coached kids. So did Charlie Doud, star tackle at UCLA, and Leon Clarke, an ex-USC and Rams end. Many other coaches have played at the college, or at least the high school level, or have learned a lot watching weekend games on television. The latter pick it up as they go along, together with fanatical enthusiasm for kids' football. That Boston coach (Lombardi-Rockne) was quoted by the *Boston Globe* as saying the three things in his life he was proudest of were his family, the Marine Corps, and his association with Pop Warner football. Others take their glory where they find it. One San Francisco coach's claim to fame was that, some years ago, while holding tryouts on a patch of grass near Kezar Stadium, he selected a dozen players and told O. J. Simpson to go home.

The animal clubs — Elks, Lions, and so forth — put money into the act, as do dry-cleaning establishments, mortuaries, taco emporia and pest-control firms. Around Boston, Pop Warner had franchises in forty communities, each operating on an annual budget of about $17,000. There were 2,448 players on 115 teams in the Minneapolis Park Board lineup. In the Detroit area 200 teams played in three counties. In Southern California exact figures were not kept, but estimates ranged from 800 to 1,000 teams, or about 30,000 players.

Outside Kansas City, Johnson County, Kansas, had a forty-acre complex on which eleven games could be played simultaneously, two under lights at night. As many as 10,000 fans would turn out for the Saturday program, to say nothing of 1,500 girl cheerleaders. Houston had eleven separate booster clubs soliciting donations, publishing game programs, and conducting dances and raffles to maintain two stadiums. Individual clubs sold advertising space on the fences, and seven adults were assigned to take up collections and maintain order at each game.

In Illinois, kids-league banquets were said to be more elaborate than those of many high school or college teams. Trophies and gifts were passed out like supermarket flyers. The boys' pictures appeared on the place mats. "It's too much," said the athletic director at a high school in Elgin, who also said he sometimes wonders what it's all about.

There have, of course, been many salubrious side effects of the kids-league phenomenon, according to its advocates. The *New York Times* reported some years ago that delinquency was truly on the wane in Westchester County because of the lessons being learned on the playing fields of Scarsdale. Dean Rusk was seen there, coaching his son in the kicking of a football. Entire communities mobilized around their little Packers or Redskins. In Levittown, on Long Island, community spirit seized and uplifted (by prop jet) twenty-five parents who escorted their twelve-year-old heroes to a Daytona Beach "bowl" game. Travel money was gleaned from door-to-door candy sales and by putting the touch on local merchants.

Several years ago a Pop Warner team from Marin County, California, was flown, with parents, to the Honolulu Bowl, at a cost of $10,000. The money was raised by public subscription, much to the consternation of some stick-in-the-muds who reasoned that the money could have financed three more teams, or 105 boys, in regional competition. The junketeers didn't help matters by allocating $500 to a parents-only cocktail party.

Detractors of midget football have never been quite vocal enough, but there are still some around. They include Joe Paterno, who says we just "oughta let kids be kids," and Fran Tarkenton, the record-breaking quarterback, who said psychologists had told him to steer clear. Tarkenton vowed never to let his son play little-league football "unless the organization changed drastically." Perry Smith of the St. Louis Cardinals told his son to "play tennis, bowl, play basketball, do anything, but stay away from football." Jackie Smith of the Cardinals said he had seen the little leagues operate. "There's a lot of sitting around while the coach yells and screams, and then everybody runs a lap and goes home." He encouraged his son to take up the guitar.

George Welsh, the Navy coach and ex-All-America quarterback, said right out one day that he was "absolutely opposed" to it. Welsh thinks organized football is too tough a game, physically, mentally, and emotionally, for eight- and nine-year-old children, and that they become mired in it too early. "A kid becomes a tackle at eight and he stays a tackle the rest of his life," Welsh says. "How could that be much fun? At his age he should be learning all the skills. He should learn to throw and catch and run with the ball."

Pickup games would be better, Welsh and Tarkenton believe, because football presents unique problems in this respect. A Little League baseball player, no matter what his position, gets to throw, catch, hit, and run bases. All basketball players get to dribble, pass, and shoot the ball. Football — formal, eleven-men-to-a-side, blood-and-guts football — could be played with a pecan waffle as far as offensive tackles or guards are concerned. They wouldn't have to know the difference. Tarkenton says such structured situations deprive kids of "a chance to devise their own strategy, be innovative, be creative. Kids should not be foils of adults."

This truth is not lost on the kids, though some do prefer to hide in a position that will not draw much attention (or criticism). And perhaps there are others who view it as did a twelve-year-old in St. Paul, who was put at offensive guard a couple of seasons ago and came home in tears. "They got me playing the position that pays the least," he wailed.

Larry Csonka got my attention on the subject when he told me of the time he went out to watch a boys' team practice in Fort Lauderdale. He was appalled. Csonka is not a man who recoils from spilled blood, his or anybody else's, but he was horrified by little-league football. "The coaches didn't know much about what they were doing," he said. "They just yelled a lot. They acted like they imagined Lombardi or Shula would act. Why, they had those eight-year-olds running *gassers* [postpractice wind sprints], for crying out loud."

Csonka said he would not let his two sons play in the kids leagues. "Take a little kid, put him under the pressure of a big championship game before his parents and his entire world, and it can be very bad for him," he said. "Especially if he loses. The whole country loves football, and so do I. But parents don't stop to consider all the things that can go wrong for a young fellow pushed into that kind of pressure. For one thing, he can come home with a handful of teeth. Worse, he can come home soured on athletics for life."

The problem of the jaded peewee athlete is no laughing matter to Jim Nelson, who had been coaching for almost thirty years at a small Missouri college when the little-league syndrome got to him.

Nelson said he yearned for the good old days, "not because we did everything right, but because we had fun. Nobody watched us play, and the fact that we played anyway proves we had fun. Now you see kids who've played little league five or six years. By the time they get to high school they've already been to bowl games and all-star games and had all that attention. What's left? It's too bad, because they need football more at the high school level. Not many sixth-graders are exposed to liquor and cars and drugs. High school kids are. They need an interest like football."

The burned-out football player is not unusual, of course, but when Minnesota Viking center Scott Anderson quit training camp one summer he pointed out that he'd been playing organized football since he was eight and had had a bellyfull. It doesn't have to take that long. Gerald Astor, writing in the *New York Times Magazine*, told of a Ridgefield, Connecticut, ten-year-old with "star potential" who quit because he tired of practicing "every day after school" and of "never having time for myself." And of a thirteen-year-old who was alienated from his peers by a coach in Westchester who objected to the boy's dad dragging him home to supper at 6:51, since it was forty-five minutes before quiting time. "The coach thinks football is the only thing in the world," said the boy. He retired at thirteen.

A more widely shared complaint against kids' football, one that applies to any regimented kids' sport, is that it brings the virtues of adulthood down hard upon all those little heads. Too many parents and coaches are bequeathing to children the same dogged intensities that make them the cocktail-party bores they are today. Too many parents clog the sidelines for no better reason than to hurl profanity at coaches, players, and officials. A California psychiatrist once took a tape recorder to a little-league football game and set it up near the stands. "You've never heard such vile, vicious language," he said. "With clenched fists and livid faces those parents goaded their children with nasty needling [and] yelled at the referee as if he were a criminal!"

Such gung-ho parents flock to the kids' leagues. Or become coaches. In Scarsdale, Gerald Astor wrote, one coach addressed an errant young warrior as "you stupid bastard." Others simply call their irresolute players "stupid," "slowpoke," "dumbass," or, when things are really bad, "crybaby."

One coach, explaining why he called a lesser player "Mother," said it was because the boy's parents seemed to "hover" over him. The coach said the boy "really shouldn't be out here. Somebody years ago told him to be nice. He doesn't hit anyone." Another coach's way to teach the forty-pounders on his team how to tackle was to steamroll through them in his street clothes. "He thought he was tough," said a team member. "So one day we surrounded him and jumped him and stomped him good. He thought it was funny but we were serious."

It is no wonder some parents hover. Even the less-outgoing adults sometimes feel coerced into joining the fun, to protect their interests. Says a little-league mom in south Florida, "If you want your kid to play, and not get yelled at too much, you volunteer. Your husband becomes an assistant coach. You become a sideline regular. You run car pools and work refreshment stands. You never get supper on before eight P.M., and you develop sciatica sitting on foldup parade stools." Another mother, taking a more direct route, wound up in divorce court after her friendly persuasion made too noticeable an impact on the head coach. The coach said he knew he was hooked when he made her boy — who "ran like a cow" — a starting halfback.

Within what has been described as this "rat's nest of psychological horrors," it is not unusual for a child to have his parent and/or coach falsify his birth certificate to get him into a favored division, one in which he might excel. Or submit to starvation diets to make a weight. One coach in Florida says that he sees these kids "flying around so high on diet pills they can barely tell you their names."

A parent can ruin his son early, according to one Kansas City child psychiatrist, "by making him feel like a scrunge for not playing football" when the son might be more inclined toward the violin. But the coach deserves as much credit; and coach and father may be one and the same. Chuck Ortmann, the former Michigan All-America who quit as chairman of a league in Glen Ellyn, Illinois, in which strife and debate over recruiting violations had long been rampant (a fist to the lip of a league official ended one discussion), was amazed by the win-at-any-cost mentalities he encountered. "They tell their players, 'Go out there and break that guy's arm.' They won't even let all their kids play. Forty on a team, but only eleven or fourteen play much."

One poignant protest from a little-league mom appeared in a letter to the *Miami Herald*. Her son's coach screamed at referees, screamed into the faces of the boys, and, worst of all, allowed only twelve of his eighteen players to play. She wrote, "The other boys sat on the bench for the second week in a row, not being allowed in for even one play. These are 11-year-olds who give up every night of the week to practice, come home late, tired, dirty, hungry, but with the thought it will be worth it when they play on Saturday. Ha." In Minneapolis, adults running one "midget" division silenced this kind of insubordination by waiving the must-play rule for twelve- and thirteen-year-olds. By that age, said a suburban little-league official, the inferior players "know it's not their sport."

Doctor Thomas Tutko, a professor of psychology at San Jose State who collaborated with Bill Bruns on a book called *Winning Is Everything and Other American Myths*, says that the "growing and disturbing preoccupation in this country with professional sports" has been a major contributor to the mania of win-at-all-costs — and "it is steadily engulfing children's sports. We organize them, give them uniforms, hand out trophies, send them to bowl games and encourage them to compete at earlier ages."

Doctor Tutko asks: "How many million do we have to sacrifice so that 10 players might entertain us in pro games? How many good athletes are scarred by injury or burned out psychologically by the time they find they are unable to meet the insatiable needs of their parents, their coach, their fans or their own personal obsession?"

In Chatsworth, Georgia, it wasn't exactly a peewee league but more like an older cousin that got caught up in the obsession. According to a report in the *Wall Street Journal*, Murray County Junior High's eighth-grade Warriors had a marvelous 1978 season. They walloped all eight of their opponents, including nearby Ringgold Junior High (48–6). "We got mauled," said Ringgold principal Melvin Edwards, "but we're not going to play them again. We can't compete against that bunch of monsters."

The *Journal* found out what he meant by "monsters." Murray parents were intentionally holding players back academically. An extra year in the eighth grade made their boys bigger and stronger, and, according to the rationale, increased their chances for a college scholarship. (A boy cannot be held back once he is in high school.)

Twelve of the Warriors were on the eighth-grade team for the second time. Even more, said the Murray school superintendent, would be held back the following year. "We believe sports are an important part of a boy's education here," said the superintendent. He said the playing field "was like life. You learn to kill or be killed out there. You know what I mean?"

The *Journal* found the practice, a kind of modified redshirting, common in small towns of Georgia, Texas, and Pennsylvania. The paper was told that college coaches approved, even recommending it as a leg up. Well, not *all* college coaches. Indiana coach Lee Corso called the practice "ridiculous," and said there were other ways to help a kid grow — proper diet, weight training, etc. Objecting administrators had another complaint. Holding kids back costs a lot of money.

With the largest of pressures riding on the outcome of the littlest of games, it was not surprising a few years back to see serious violence creep into kids' football. In Kissimmee, Florida, a mob of adults attacked four coaches of a winning team of twelve-year-olds with clubs and pipes, sending one coach to the hospital. A cry from the crowd, "He's dead!" apparently satisfied the mob and it withdrew just before the police arrived. The coach was not dead, only unconscious for four hours. One little-league pop in Miami got into a fistfight with a coach who wasn't playing his son at his idea of the right position. A coach in Palm Beach strode to the center of the field after a particularly heartbreaking loss and extended his hand to the star player of the rival team, then punched him in the stomach, knocking him down. When he realized what he had done, the coach did not wait to be suspended. He quit.

Such incidents have caused massive end sweeps into the nearest circuit court, where big-league litigation is the next thing the little fellows are taught. The Optimist Athletic Conference has twice been to court in Miami, once when an entire 250-player group was expelled and again when a coach was suspended for threatening a commissioner. The teams won reinstatement; the coach did not.

In 1963 the *New York Times* used the word "grotesque" to describe a kids' bowl game it covered on Long Island, and *Life* magazine pointed out that the American Academy of Pediatrics was opposed to little guys banging each other about because of the vulnerability of their epiphyses (the soft bone tips where growth originates). Deformities were said to be around the corner.

Life contended that the greater danger was psychological. "In sandlot ball you can always pick up and go home," it quoted a

Big Ten physician as saying, "but in this game you must remain in competition. You must make your blocks and tackles. This can make a boy wary of competitive sports — either because of sheer boredom or because he's afraid."

Making football boring, I think, is the greatest of the little-league sins. The campaign against boredom is one that coaches must wage relentlessly. When the trains pass, the kids stop and watch; when the planes go over, they stare. "Let a fire truck go by and it's Looney Tunes," says Dickie Maegle, a star halfback at Rice in the 1950s who coached little leaguers in Houston. "Suddenly they're out of it. I've seen 'em so excited at kickoff, with the crowds yelling and bands playing, that the kicker completely missed the ball. I've seen 'em running for a touchdown when their pants fell to their knees. I've seen crepe paper draped down from the cross bar and when the kids tried to run through, they fell down."

Maegle is one of those muddled thinkers who do not object to this kind of foolishness. He thinks kids ought to be allowed to act like kids. So does Galen Fiss, an ex-Browns linebacker. One day in Kansas City one of Fiss's linemen came out of the huddle hopping and skipping to the scrimmage line. "For an instant, our coaches were horrified," said Fiss. "That's not the way you're supposed to approach the line. Then we realized, he's a ten-year-old kid! That's his way of having fun."

Bob Cupp is a dear friend of mine. Nearing forty, he is a father of three and describes himself as having a Charlie Brown head under a Buster Brown haircut. He lives in Tequesta, Florida, a punt and a pass up the waterway from Palm Beach. An all-sports star in high school, Cupp went to the University of Miami on a baseball scholarship, played quarterback on his service football team (coaching high school football on the side), became a professional golfer and then a golf-course designer. He is still a golf-course designer, for Jack Nicklaus, out of Nicklaus's Golden Bear offices in North Palm Beach. Cupp is also a professional illustrator, and he sings professionally as well as in the church choir.

Bob Cupp is one of those curious people who loves small children, even his own. His only other weakness is that he enjoys coaching children, even other people's. He somehow finds time for this year-round: kids' football, basketball, and baseball. Cupp smiles and laughs a lot, as though he might know something about life that no one else knows.

When he had been coaching little-league football for six years — his son Bobby, then eleven, was described in a local paper as a "grizzled veteran," which the Cupps thought was pretty hilarious — Cupp developed some revolutionary ideas about what ought to be done with kids' football, some of which he put to the test.

Cupp thinks that most coaches are not necessary, that referees are not necessary, and that parents are not necessary, except in a strict biological sense.

He also thinks every kid should get to touch the ball every game — throw it, catch it, run with it. That being a favorite view of mine, we had discussed it many times during his coaching cycles, sometimes debating far into the night in a mutual effort to find ways. Invariably my views were less pragmatic than his. Cupp had learned to accept, or at least anticipate, the game as it is in the small time.

"We had a coach in one league who had access to diet pills," he said. "The kids could get them for nothing. You never saw such a hyper bunch. But one of 'em was a lost cause. He came to the weigh-in in his daddy's heavy rubber suit, his face red with sweat. He looked like a cherry sticking out of a duffel bag. When he took off his sweat suit, his poor fat little body was pink as a salmon, but he missed by four pounds.

"Parents will allow their kids to go through any torture to play. This fall the boy who'd been kingpin of the eighty-pound league for two years tried to make the weight again. He dieted and dieted and still weighed eighty-six. The coaches told him he was good enough to move up to the next division. His parents said no. The boy didn't think he was good enough. He quit. He couldn't face not being the star anymore.

"Coaches are as guilty as parents. One I know decided to give his team a little boost by injecting a stimulant — Benzedrine, Dexedrine, something — into the oranges he always fed them before a game. He used a hypodermic and kept upping the dosage. After the third or fourth game the players started complaining of headaches and throwing up. The coach later admitted to me what he'd done, but at the time everybody blamed the oranges.

"Most of the coaches I have seen, more than half, I'd guess, haven't even had high school experience. They teach a lot of things wrong, even fundamentals like stances and handoffs and blocks. They see something on TV, and even though they don't understand it they try to put it in. I had a guy try to use an end-in-motion on us. I pointed it out to the referee, and he laughed and threw his flag. The coach came running over. 'What the hell,' he said. 'The Cowboys do it, why can't we?' The ref explained that it wasn't the end the Cowboys had in motion, it was the flankerback.

"The sad thing is, the really qualified guy isn't always the best for kids. Can't always relate. We had one last year who had all the credentials and loved the game, but he was a wild man. He reduced his team to tears daily. I've seen him, and others, too, manhandle kids, pick them up and throw them around. He'd yell things at 'em like 'You're gonna block if I have to kick your ass all afternoon!' The kids were eight-year-olds. They'd just turn to jelly, walk off the field crying. Another coach criticized him one time for not playing some of his lesser kids. He said, 'Why should I play kids who look up at the sky and chew grass while everybody else is sucking up their guts in practice?' The other coach said, 'Maybe if the kids played more they wouldn't look at the sky so much.'

"We had a rule that the son of a father or legal guardian who is coaching has to play for his father or guardian. I looked up one day and a coach was trying to add somebody's grandmother to his coaching staff — a black woman with gray hair who happened to have three of the best players in the area living in her home. Two were brothers and one a cousin, all of them little O. J.s, just the right age. A gold mine. Grandma was their legal guardian. When the coach announced at the league meeting his plan to add her to his staff, the place went up in smoke. You never heard such carrying on. He finally withdrew his motion.

"This one really ticked me off. One of our less-charitable coaches had a kid who was kinda lousy and the coach didn't want to play him. We have this must-play rule where every player is supposed to play a series every quarter. I let mine play longer so the poorer players can improve, but some don't think along those lines. Anyway, this guy worked out a scheme whereby he'd send the poor player, Number Fifty, say, in with, say, Number Sixty. The woman who checks the substitutes — we call her the watchdog — checks off Fifty and Sixty, coming in. Then as soon as Fifty gets to the huddle he turns around and runs back off with the player Sixty was sent in for.

"The watchdog wasn't asked to check who went out, only who went in. Number Fifty never played. And nobody caught on till the fourth or fifth game, after his team had won four straight. The watchdog who spotted it couldn't believe her eyes. She asked the boy if he'd played at all. 'No,' he said, 'I just run in and out.'

"The league called a special meeting to decide whether to forfeit the team's games or suspend the coach, or both. The league president made a good case for throwing the coach out. Then the team's sponsor got up. He waved his checkbook over his head and announced that if the decision went against his team in any way, his sponsorship would be withdrawn. He was serious, too. The league needed sponsors. The question never came to a vote."

Another challenge, Cupp said, were those pretty young mamas who want Junior to play quarterback or some other glamour position. "They're not always subtle about it — they can come on pretty strong. When I see it coming I always start talking about my wife and kids, but I've known it to get pretty rough for some guys. Mama comes around in a tight pair of pants and a halter and wants to engage in a philosophical discussion about football. At her place.

"Fathers try to influence you, too, but they have to do it the hard way. Some of them lug big coolers of beer around and stash them behind the stands on a hot day so the coach can sneak back for a short one now and then. A couple beers and the coach is calling for his kid, to put him in."

Cupp did not escape the behavioral pattern of kids'-league coaches in one respect — no one seems to be free of bad temper. He let his whole team have it after a loss because he thought they'd given up, the one thing he told them he wouldn't tolerate. "I chewed 'em out pretty good. When I got home afterward my son handed me his jersey and said he was now an ex-linebacker. He said he couldn't play for a crazy man. I got the message.

"In another game, on the very first play, a coach sprang a sneak play on us and scored. One of those sideline passes without a huddle. The receiver was all by himself. A sandlot play, but legal, and great. I should have just laughed. Instead, I blew my top. Ran out on the field, complaining and yelling at the ref. A regular buffoon. My ego had been hurt, see. I'd been had. And I wound up getting my kids so riled up they just poured it on and won thirty-nine to six. The other coach hasn't spoken to me since, and I don't blame him."

Cupp believes that "coaches and their personalities, the way they relate or don't relate" is the crux of what is wrong with little-league football. "Coaches don't get along, don't even try. It rubs off. The drive to win is so great the kids don't learn anything. The Lombardi philosophy is ridiculous at this level. Losing isn't death, winning isn't everything. The idea is to have fun. Period. If a kid isn't, if he's not enjoying it and quits, the coach should ask himself, 'Would he have quit if I'd done a better job?' "

Eventually, Cupp got around to the problem of making the game more fun for everybody. He first proposed a selection process to make the teams more even.

"The idea was foreign to everybody, but my boys had won everything the year before, so the other coaches listened. We had a get-acquainted clinic, and all the coaches rated all the kids on a scale of one to ten. Then we sat down with the commissioner, right out on the field, and drew for teams. And something happened to those coaches. We got along great the whole year. The league was tight, and I think we all had fun. I know my kids did. You'd see 'em during a game running back to the huddle and sliding in on their knee pads. It didn't look like the Dolphins, but it was fun.

"Our practices were chaos. Half the time I'd just tell 'em to go over there and play pickup. They should be playing more and practicing less, anyway — playing three or four games a week instead of seven or eight a season. Practicing one-on-one, hitting dummies — that's a drag. A kid wants to play. Lord knows, he's going to find less time for it later on."

Cupp believes that if everyone involved would step back and take a look at what is going on, most of these problems would be solved. Parents, he says, should stay home. At least in the lower levels of kids' football. "A preadolescent has a great need to please his parents, and his failures shouldn't be scrutinized. Just being watched puts pressure on a kid. Maybe by the time he reaches the ninth grade he can bear it. Maybe."

Fathers, suggests father/coach Cupp, should not coach. Not if their sons are in the league. "Fewer coaches would be better all around. At the youngest level one good coach could easily handle four teams. Two coaches at the most, providing encouragement, teaching a few techniques, refereeing the fights. Even officiating. Coaches could be impartial referees if the parents weren't breathing down their necks. And kids should get the idea that games can be played on the square without having to pay a policeman. A lot of our officials are just in it for the money, anyway.

"After kids advance to the older leagues, they still don't need more than two coaches per team. Qualified guys, though, who've played the game, who know at least enough not to teach them things that could hurt. The idea is to let a kid learn more on his own. Developing talent is really a kid's responsibility, not an adult's. A kid learns by playing, by imitating. The last thing they need is an unqualified coach messing them up."

The most radical of Cupp's proposals was our mutual favorite, and the one that he knew when he proposed it would not get him elected little-league coach of the year. He worked out a plan whereby every player got a shot at glory by playing a position in which he actually handled the ball. Cupp said coaches laughed when he suggested the idea. Later, "when we were running them out of the ball park," they quit laughing.

"I used to see stagnation set in when kids were relegated to a position like guard or tackle for the whole year. It was like a sentence. Before long, many of the linemen wouldn't even show up for practice. They were usually the smallest guys, anyway — that's the way it works in the little leagues — and what did they need with extra punishment? They were getting enough on Saturday. I couldn't blame 'em. They were typecast. One coach used to bring a roll of masking tape to practice and slap 'Guard' or 'Tackle' on the players' helmets, like a brand.

"Let's face it. Running the ball, throwing it, catching a pass, making touchdowns — those are the things kids think of as football. Sustained drives and quality blocking they may think about later, when they're in high school, but for now they don't and shouldn't have to. We're not a feeder system for the high school coaches."

A questionnaire gave league kids a choice of playing for a losing team or sitting on the bench for a winner, and they voted almost unanimously to play. "They'd rather play than sit any day," said Cupp. "Busting into the line with the ball can be an unforgettable experience for a fat little kid who will never get the chance again. Next year he may be a guard for good."

He worked out his rotation system this way: with fifteen players, he drew up three different offensive teams. Each player, every game, had to play three positions: a ball-handling position such as halfback, quarterback, or fullback; a receiver; and an interior lineman. The more talented players got to play two ball-handling positions, but every kid got a shot at at least one.

"Funny things happened. The parents objected, some of them. Some of the kids objected, too. One kid refused to play anything but center. He said he didn't want to goof up. But after a while even the prima donnas came to realize there was more to football than being the star and everybody else blocking.

"One coach, a good friend of mine, said that what I was doing was impossible. 'You're nuts,' he said. He beat us pretty good the first time we tried it. Then, when we got rolling, we beat him twenty to nothing. He said, 'Maybe you got something.'

"The thing is, it was fun for the kids, and fun for me. I can't tell you the kick I get seeing a kid discover the joys of football. When I was coaching the real little guys, the peewees, I'd see one show up on the first day, thigh pads hanging over his knees, knee pads around his shins, shoulder pads on backward with the underarm straps under his crotch. He didn't know a linebacker from a carburetor. He wasn't interested in 'sticking' anybody. He didn't even know what that was.

"And then when he ran his first sweep it was a problem just holding on to the ball. But he excited you with the possibilities. You watched him run, all wide-eyed and open-mouthed, with a smile on his face. It's a joy.

"The trick," says Bob Cupp, "is to keep him smiling."